PROVEN WORD BOOKS

- Have *proven* themselves where it counts—among the thousands of readers who have made them best-sellers, who have found these books meaningful in the arena of real life

- Were best-sellers in hardcover and are now made available at more affordable prices in deluxe paperback bindings

- Offer new, built-in study guides with questions to encourage private pondering and group discussion

- Meet the widespread needs of people everywhere who are searching for answers to the pressures and problems of living in the modern world

PROVEN WORD

LLOYD J. OGILVIE

Other books by Lloyd John Ogilvie:

Acts, Volume 5, Communicator's Commentary
Congratulations, God Believes in You!
The Bush Is Still Burning
When God First Thought of You
Drumbeat of Love
Life Without Limits
Let God Love You
The Autobiography of God
Loved and Forgiven
Lord of the Ups and Downs
If I Should Wake Before I Die
A Life Full of Surprises
You've Got Charisma
Cup of Wonder
God's Best for My Life
The Radiance of Inner Splendor
Gift of Friendship
Gift of Love
Gift of Caring
Gift of Sharing

ASK HIM Anything

LLOYD J. OGILVIE

PROVEN WORD

WORD BOOKS
PUBLISHER
WACO, TEXAS

A DIVISION OF
WORD, INCORPORATED

ASK HIM ANYTHING
Copyright © 1981, 1984 by Word, Incorporated

Unless otherwise noted, all Scripture quotations from the Old Testament are from *The New American Standard Bible* copyright © The Lockman Foundation 1960, 1962, 1968, 1971, 1972, 1973, 1975. And all Scripture quotations from the New Testament are from *The New King James Bible* copyright © 1979 by Thomas Nelson Inc., Publishers. Used by permission. The New Testament quotation marked NAS is from *The New American Standard Bible*.

Quotations marked KJV are from the King James Version of the Bible. Quotations marked TLB are from *The Living Bible, Paraphrased* (Wheaton: Tyndale House Publishers, 1971). Quotations marked RSV are from the Revised Standard Version of the Bible, copyrighted 1946, 1952, © 1971, 1973 by the Division of Christian Education of the National Council of the Churches of Christ in the U.S.A., and are used by permission. Quotations marked PHILLIPS are from *The New Testament in Modern English*, copyright © 1958, 1959, 1960 by I. B. Phillips, used by permission of The Macmillan Company.

Library of Congress catalog card number: 81–51224
ISBN 0-8499-2982-2
Printed in the United States of America
First Proven Word Printing—July, 1984

To Beth Rettig
A special person to my wife and me;
Once like a daughter; now a cherished friend.

Contents

Preface

IT'S TIME TO LISTEN. To people and to God. There is nothing more foolish than an answer to an unasked question or a response to an unexpressed need. And there is nothing more impelling than God's answers in the Bible to people's most urgent questions and to their deepest needs. Real communication is seventy-five percent listening and twenty-five percent response. This book represents the result of listening with the ears of the mind and the heart to the questions people are asking in America today.

The aching problem, both inside and outside the church, is agnosticism. Many people "just don't know" what they think or believe in response to the awesome questions of life. Most of them are afraid to ask and even more frightened that they may be asked and be unable to answer. At the same time, they are troubled by easy answers and pat phrases that do not stand up to authentic spiritual and intellectual honesty. "Click words," esoteric jargon, and flip theories do not satisfy when life falls apart or tragedy strikes. There are far too few opportunities for Christians and honest inquirers to ask the questions that have been lurking beneath the surface and to get straight-arrow answers. This book is my attempt to provide a context for asking and answering these questions.

In preparation, I asked my congregation of the First Presbyterian Church of Hollywood and the viewers of our nationally syndicated television program, *Let God Love You,* to submit the deepest questions they are facing in daily living. People at conferences where I spoke were also surveyed for their questions. The wording of the request was significant: "What's the one question you've always wanted to ask? Or what's the urgent question you'd like to be able to answer for the people in your life?"

The result of my survey was a diagnostic feel of the pulsebeat of the American mind and heart. All of the questions were asked with searching integrity. The answers incorporated in the chapters of this book are meant to honor that with empathy, intellectual responsibility, and biblical authority.

With a large suitcase packed with the thousands of questions from all over the nation, I headed off for a prolonged study leave in Edinburgh, Scotland. There, in solitude and amid the magnificent resources of the library at New College, I read each question prayerfully, and with sensitivity to the real persons who had exposed their inner needs in their questions.

The first step in preparation for writing my responses was to sort and sift the questions and then to cull them into basic themes. Because no one book could deal with all the questions submitted, my concern was to select those which were most urgent and frequently asked. In each category I selected the wording of the person whose question best represented the theme; these questions became the title of each chapter. Then I grouped the chapters into natural sections: questions about God; questions about the Christian adventure; questions about relationships; and questions about daily living. It is very significant that church people and nonreligious Americans are asking similar questions. The challenge before me was to write in a way which would be enabling to Christians but would also provide a straightforward apologetic for Christians to share with questioning friends.

The second step was to listen to God for his answers in the Scriptures. I am convinced that answers to our deepest questions are in the Bible. My calling is as an expositor of God's Word. Therefore, I tried to find passages which spoke most saliently to the questions in each chapter. In every case, my search was rewarded by one particular passage which became the fulcrum on which the chapter could turn. My concern has been, in each chapter, to digest one passage, and to illuminate it with biblical and contemporary illustrations. My hope is that each chapter, though rooted in one passage, will give a comprehensive sweep of the biblical answer to the question being addressed.

The overall text for this book could well be, "Now when the queen of Sheba heard of the fame of Solomon, she came to Jerusalem to test Solomon with difficult questions." (2 Chron. 9:1). I am gratified that a "greater than Solomon"—Jesus Christ, the Word of God—can answer whatever we need to ask. He has spoken and speaks in answer to our hard questions. My effort has been to stand by listening to what he has to say, and to be as faithful as I could be in prayer, scholarship, and writing to articulate in a contemporary way what he communicated to me.

Therefore, this book is not meant to be just my answers, but the Lord's sensitive, loving response to real people with urgent questions—questions we must take as seriously as he does. So many of these questions came out of suffering, anxiety, and frustration, as well as out of intellectual inquisitiveness.

The questions were searching and painful
  Ruthless and bitter and hard,
The answer is very costly,
  And it has the scent of nard.
The season of questions is over,

The winter of asking is done.
Now is the hour for the answer,
The spring of the world has begun.

Writing this book has been one of the most exciting
challenges of my life. It has been a moving spiritual experience to communicate hope for the problems and
needs the questions represented. I felt like I was carrying
on a dynamic three-way conversation between people, the
Lord, and me. I am thankful for the high honor of being
part of a great family of friends throughout this nation
who give me the privilege of listening to them and the
Lord, and then of speaking and writing in response to
both.

I am gratified by the friendship in Christ expressed by
my administrative assistant, Jerlyn Gonzalez. Her encouragement and faithfulness in typing the manuscript for
publication has made completing it an adventure.

Now, my prayer is that you, the reader, will find answers
to your deepest questions. The Lord is able to help us. We
can ask him anything!

LLOYD JOHN OGILVIE

1

What Is God Like?

IT WAS A STARTLING conversation with an old friend. He looked me in the eye and said, "Lloyd, I've been a closet agnostic for some time now. I used to be so sure of what I believed, but now I have to admit I've known *about* God, but never really known God. I've got so many unanswered questions. I guess my mind has finally caught up with my heart!"

I should not have been surprised. Now, as I look back over the years, I can see that there were clear danger signals. The man's simplistic and traditional religion had never grappled with life's deepest questions—the tough intellectual questions that defy easy answers. He had evaded them, thinking that to question was to deny faith. Then personal difficulties, problems with other people, and anguish over the immense tragedies of the world had hit him with hurricane force and sent him into a tailspin of doubt and discouragement. He had lived in two worlds: one of vague, cultural religion, and the other of profound, unresolved questions. When his worlds collided, he realized God was not very real to him.

Agnosticism is the silent agony of our age. It's not questions about God's existence that trouble most people, but questions about what he is like and how they can know him. The unanswered questions about God, about his nature, will, and ways have surfaced as an honest but very unsatisfying, "I just don't know!" And this uncertainty troubles people both inside and outside the church.

It's when our lives sour or the suffering of the world stabs us awake that we realize we do not really know the God in whom others profess to believe. The animated question marks of our existence stir the brewing agnosticism in our minds. We are like Kipling's "Elephant Child":

> She sends 'em abroad on her own affairs
>   From the second she opens her eyes.
> One million hows, two million wheres
>   And seven million whys.

All our hows and wheres and whys eventually lead back to questions about God—about some aspect of his nature and relationship to his creation. That's the conviction which gripped me as I was studying to respond to the thousands of questions submitted by my congregation and television viewers. Then, after weeks of reading, praying, and aching over each question, it came to me. As I watched the sun rise one morning, I realized with sudden clarity that *every* question I had been struggling with was rooted in a need to know God, how he acts, and what he has said about himself. Whether the question was about the *where* of God in our needs, the *why* of suffering, or the *how* of the origin or extent of evil, the answer was hidden in God himself.

The questions about unanswered prayer, why bad things happen to good people, the dark night of the soul's doubt, how to find guidance and to live abundantly were all, in one sense, *agnostic* questions about God. Every question, from how to pray to how to stop worrying and start living, was a rearticulation of the deeper question: "What is God like—and how can I know him?" That's why we must begin our search for answers to life's most urgent questions by getting to know God.

Actually, I am convinced God is the author of, as well as the answer to, our aching questions. It is because he is at work in us that we even dare to question! Honest intellectual questioning is a sign of growth, not denial. God wants us to get in touch with the questions which have kept us from growing spiritually. Our questions reflect our inbred, divine desire to grow. God knows that if we dare to think, eventually our questions will lead us to him, and into the profound relationship with him for which we were created.

Essentially, I believe life's biggest questions are the result of the fact that our God has been too small, our vision of him too limited. Therefore, the only antidote to our quandary of questions is to learn to fully acknowledge God's greatness. That was Paternus's advice to his son: "First of all, my child, think magnificently of God. Magnify His providence; adore His power; pray to Him frequently and incessantly. Bear Him always in your mind; teach your thoughts to reverence Him in every place, for there is no place where He is not. Therefore, my child, fear and worship, and love God; first and last, think magnificently of God."

Failing to "think magnificently" was Israel's problem during the excruciating experience of the Babylonian exile following the destruction of Jerusalem in 586 B.C. The Holy City had been razed and the Hebrew people were led out of their cherished Palestine into the idol-worshiping land of pagan Babylonia. They were forced to realize how agnostic they had been about their God. Anguishing questions surged to the surface. How could God allow this to happen? Were they not his chosen, cherished people? Why did the innocent have to suffer along with the guilty? Did God know or care about their plight and the unquenchable longing for their homeland? Did his sovereignty extend beyond Palestine to heathen places such as Babylonia? Their world had been blown to pieces, and their questions were pulling them apart.

Israel's limited concept of God as only the Lord of Palestine was the root cause of their anxiety and fear—all their wrenching questions. And God's own answer in Isaiah 40, particularly verses 25–31, was his answer to pull them together. It gives us the basis of thinking magnificently about God. The exciting thing about this passage is that it proclaims God's greatness and his grace, his might, and his mercy; his almightiness and his availability, his power and his presence. It begins with his sovereignty and ends with the strength we experience when we truly know him.

Thinking magnificently about God begins with his holiness. In response to our questions about what he is like, he counters with a mind-expanding question: "'To whom then will you liken Me that I should be his equal?' says the Holy One." Both the question and the name of the questioner confront us with the holiness of God. Holiness means separate, distinct, and beyond the categories of human definition. Whatever words we use to define his nature fall short of his greatness. He is not the object of our search, but the Subject of his own revelation. All we can know of the Holy Other is what he tells us about himself. The only words we can use are the words he has chosen to use about himself. We can know God only as he elects us to know him.

With God there is always mystery. And remember that an aspect of the word mystery in Greek means, "To shut one's mouth." Awe and wonder, coupled with praise and adoration, is the appropriate response to the holiness of God. He is the unmoved mover, the uncreated creator of the universe. In him all things congeal and are held together. As a great scientist put it, "If God stopped breathing, the universe would disintegrate."

When we think magnificently of the holiness of God, we realize there is a veil between us and him that only he can

open. The choice is always his. We search for him because
he has chosen and called us. Seeking to know him is like
looking through an opaque, clouded window. It is only by
his choice and by his revelation that we are able to know
him. We can never say that we decided to look for God,
found him, and know him completely. What we *can* say
with praise is that he elected us and made us for himself,
that our longing to know him is his gift.

The awareness of God's greatness and holiness is what
the Hebrew people languishing in Babylonia needed to
recapture. God was not one among many gods. He is the
Holy One—greater than any image formed by human
hand or any words articulated by human tongue. And
that's where we must begin. God is greater than we are—
greater than the false gods of our culture, greater than the
theological formulations we have written about him or the
religious customs we have developed to worship him.

That leads to a renewed sense of wonder, and the second attribute of God which enables us to think magnificently of him. Listen to the prophet's challenge to the
homesick Hebrews. In Babylonia, their God was now in
competition with Marduk, the Babylonian god of creation
and the lesser gods of Babylonian religion. Each of these
many deities was believed to dwell among the stars, and
the stars were named after them.

Into this polytheistic confusion, the prophet gives the
trumpet blast of praise to the Holy One who alone is
creator of the universe, the one who fixed the stars in their
places. "Lift up your eyes on high and see who has created
these stars, the One who leads forth their host by number,
He calls them by name; because of the greatness of His
might and the strength of His power. Not one of them is
missing." It was as if he was saying, "Look up! Lift your
drooping hearts and think magnificently of God as the
creator of the universe. If he knows all the stars by name,
and is greater than all the Babylonian gods, he knows each
of you. God will take care of you!"

The greatness of God is revealed in his creation. The vastness of his universe engenders a sense of wonder. Think of it! If we were to drive a car day and night at top speed without stopping it would take us nine years to reach the moon, three hundred years to reach the sun, eighty-three hundred years to reach the planet Neptune, seventy-five million years to reach Alpha Centauri, and seven hundred million years to reach the Pole Star.

This is the reason the Psalmist, even with his limited cosmology, could say, "When I consider Thy heavens, the work of Thy fingers, the moon and the stars which Thou hast ordained; what is man, that Thou dost take thought of him? And the son of man, that Thou dost care for him? Yet Thou hast made him a little lower than God, and dost crown him with glory and majesty!" (Ps. 8:3-5). Who wouldn't be astonished by that?

When we are startled by the wonder of the created universe, in which God has boldly written his signature, we are amazed that he knows each of us and has a plan for our lives. That led the Psalmist to say in a later Psalm, "Thou hast made me to drink of the wine of astonishment" (Ps. 60:3). We are astonished by his creation, but even more by our own creation. W. H. Davies was right: "What is life if, full of care, we have no time to stand and stare?" I've found that standing and staring at creation and then contemplating my own unique and special individuality by God's design, helps me think magnificently of God, and helps put my world in perspective.

H. A. L. Fisher, in his book, *An Unfinished Autobiography*, recounts a conversation with Rodin, the famous sculptor, who summed up the barrenness of the arts at that time by saying, "My companions have lost the art of admiration." That is the tragic plight of many of us; we no longer are amazed by our creation. The poet John Davidson expressed our condition when he wrote, "The fires are out; I must hammer the cold iron." Yet the fires of wonder can rekindle our enthusiasm, if we stop to stare in amazement at God's creation. Yeats said in his autobiography, "Can one reach God by toil? He gives himself to the pure in heart. He asks nothing but our attention." Has your Creator caught your attention?

But press on! Next think magnificently of the omniscience of God. He is all-knowing. It is awesome to think of his holiness, and astounding to contemplate his creation, but it is both alarming and assuring to reflect on his omniscience. To a bereft and depleted people who thought they were forgotten by their God, Isaiah 40:27–28 questions: "Why do you say, O Jacob, and assert, O Israel, my way is hidden from the Lord. And the justice due me escapes the notice of my God? Do you not know? Have you not heard? The everlasting God, the Lord, the creator of the ends of the earth does not become weary or tired. His understanding is inscrutable."

God knows all about us. He knows our deepest inner hopes and dreams, our fears and frustrations, our desires and disappointments. He knows us absolutely and utterly. He sees into us with x-ray vision.

The prophet draws on the magnificence of God's omniscience as a great source of comfort for his people. They could trust their God for vindication and ultimately for victory. God was in control. He would have the final word. That's what we all need to know when life falls apart or when we feel the injustice of life.

And yet, knowledge of God's omniscience is of little comfort without an assurance of his omnipotence. It's one thing to know that God is aware of our needs, but another to be confident he has the power to act in our behalf. But note the names Isaiah uses in this passage for the God of Israel. He is "the Lord"—*Yahweh* in Hebrew, from the essential verb meaning "to be." He is the God who makes things happen, who wields sovereign authority. His power is revealed in creation and history. He is everlasting, without beginning and end, the One in whom all power resides, and he is greater than the gods of the Babylonians as well as their kings and rulers.

In verse 28, the names "everlasting God" and "creator" are kept together around the fulcrum name *Yahweh* ("the Lord"), because they express the fact that he is God over time and space, and yet has been constantly involved in caring for his people. He is worthy of his people waiting for him to act with power for their deliverance. God, who is everlasting, has been infinitely patient with his people; now they are called to wait patiently for him to act. The omnipotent, powerful Yahweh never grows weary.

That assurance leads to one of the most encouraging of the attributes of God. Think magnificently of the fact that God who has all power entrusts strength to us when we are weary. The people who were completely exhausted and without strength were given a great promise: "He gives strength to the weary, and to him who lacks might, he increases power" (v. 29). This passage focuses on the weakness of Israel and on the strength of their God. It emphasizes that human strength is always inadequate and limited, that even young men grow weary and tired and stumble. But then it continues with its magnificent words of assurance: "Those who wait for the Lord will gain new strength; they will mount up with wings like eagles, they will run and not get tired, they will walk and not become weary" (v. 31). Note the qualities of immanence and availability which are added to omnipotence. God knows, he acts with power, and entrusts that power to his people.

We will spend an entire, subsequent chapter on the image of the eagle as a metaphor for God's nature and for our potential. Now, however, I want to emphasize one point about an eagle's flight that is crucial to this passage. The eagle soars when it is caught up in the stream of the wind. It does not soar on its own strength. The bird's innate capacity to fly is multiplied by the power of the wind, which lifts and impels it. So it is with us when we wait for

God. God's Spirit has the power to infuse the tissues of our impotent minds, our depleted emotions, our wayward wills, our weary bodies. God's omnipotent power is gloriously revealed in the energizing, vitalizing, and uplifting of our human nature; we were created to be inadequate until filled with his magnificence.

From the Isaiah 40 passage, what answers to the question, "What is God like?" can we glean? We get a vivid picture of the magnificence of God. He is holy, hidden— but revealed to us because he has chosen to make himself known. He is the creator, the Lord of the universe. He is all-knowing and all-powerful, and he gives supporting strength to us when our own strength fails.

All these words—holy, creative, omniscient, omnipotent— can be used to explain what God is like. But ultimately all our language of description falls short of the mark. We stutter with secondary observation until we listen intently to and behold attentively his own Word about himself.

What is God like? Look and listen to Jesus Christ— Immanuel, "God with us." John helps us articulate our wonder: "And the Word became flesh and dwelt among us, and we beheld his glory, the glory as of the only begotten of the Father, full of grace and truth.... And of his fullness we have received, and grace for grace" (John 1:14, 16). The Word of God—Logos—through whom everything was made, the omniscience and omnipotence of the Lord, his wisdom and light, his love and forgiveness—all these took human form for us to behold. Now we see God as he wishes to be known. The more we know of Christ, the more we know of God. All we've said in answer to the basic question, "What is God like?" from the Isaiah 40 passage is manifested clearly in the Savior.

Paul's rhetoric gives our words wings. "He is the image of the invisible God, the firstborn over all creation. For by Him all things were created that are in heaven and that are on earth, visible and invisible, whether thrones or dominions or principalities or powers. All things were created by

Him and for Him. And He is before all things, and in Him all things hold together.... in Him all fullness should dwell" (Col. 1:15–17, 19). When we think magnificently of God, our thoughts begin in Christ, God's light in the world, and they return unendingly to him.

God is the supreme Light, the source of all light, for he is the Creator of the universe, the sun and moon and stars and all the light in the universe, especially the light of human understanding. Modern science has helped us to realize that we only see light when it is reflected off an object. Light moves so fast that our eyes cannot keep pace with it. This is also why we cannot see God. Our minds cannot keep pace with him. But out of sheer love, he has incarnated his light into human form so that we could see him in his fullness. He encounters us as a person and speaks to us face to face. Christ, the light of the world, is the eternal light of God slowed down for human comprehension and observation. From the fullness of God, we have received a revelation with nothing left out! Christ is the "freeze-frame" of God's magnificence for us to behold with awe and wonder.

Then we can say with the apostle John, "That which was from the beginning, which we have heard, which we have seen with our eyes, which we have looked upon, and our hands have handled, concerning the Word of life—for the life was manifested, and we have seen, and bear witness, and declare to you that eternal life which was with the Father and was manifested to us" (1 John 1:1–2). There you have it—the light of God's love, forgiveness, reconciliation and power—in the incarnate revelation of what he is like. Now the question in Isaiah 40:18 can be answered at last: "To whom then will you liken God? Or what likeness will you compare with Him?" The answer is Jesus Christ, "the power of God and the wisdom of God" (1 Cor. 1:24).

There's a wonderful story told about Carl Sandberg that suggests what should be our response to God's revealed magnificence in Christ. Sandberg became so immersed in his study of Lincoln that he thought of little else. The people in the town where he studied and wrote decided to test his concentration on Abe with a practical joke. They noted that the historian went to breakfast at the same time and place each day. So they dressed up the tallest man in the town as Abraham Lincoln and had him walk down the street just in time to meet Sandberg as he walked to the restaurant. Everyone watched and listened as the two met. Without blinking an eye or slowing his pace, Sandberg tipped his hat and said, "Good morning, Mr. President," then went on to his breakfast. He was so engulfed in his Lincolnology that he was not surprised to see Lincoln on his own street!

The same thing happens to us in a much more significant way when we focus our thinking on the magnificence of God in Christ; we are not surprised when we meet him face to face! He is not distant or aloof. In fact, he is the initiator of all our thought about him. He has had each of us on his mind since the foundation of the world. All the questions we can ask will find more than a conceptual answer. We will find him because he has already found us. But truth *about* God will never satisfy us. It only becomes real as we live it by giving all of ourselves to however much, by his gift, we know him personally. How would you live the rest of your life if you really believed all that we've said about God thus far? When we think magnificently about God, we will build our lives on his greatness:

> As the marsh hen secretly builds on the watery sod,
> Behold I will build me a nest on the greatness of God....
> By so many roots as the marsh-grass sends in the sod,
> I will heartily lay me ahold on the greatness of God.[1]

2

Is God Really in Control?

I CAN TELL THE STORY now. Both men are dead. The father died of a broken heart; the son of a dissipated life.

Memory of the first time I saw the son lingers to this day. He was the softest-looking forty-year-old boy I had ever met. His face was smooth, without the character wrinkles brought on by laughter or hardship. His voice had the oily tone that comes from the lubrication of an easy life. He was all front door, which you opened only to find yourself in a garbage-strewn backyard. His self-centeredness left little room for compassion or sensitivity; he was bordered north, south, east, and west by the perpendicular pronoun. No one—man nor woman—had ever said no to this man. And as a result he had become an opulent opportunist who used people to satisfy his unbridled desires and then cast them aside in disdain.

The father asked me to see the son; he really hoped I could help the selfish man-boy grow up. But the son tried to manipulate me as he had everyone else. When I resisted becoming a pawn to further checkmate his father, he refused to see me any further. Each appointment was cancelled with well-articulated equivocation.

In the few visits we did have, I discovered some things that helped me understand the son's character. His father had never disciplined him in love. He had never given him a sharp edge with which to cut out his values; instead, he had done everything for him. There had been no freedom to fail or to learn from his mistakes. The father had planned his son's life for him from the beginning, purchasing entry for him into the finest prep schools and colleges. (The son had drifted from one to the other, leaving whenever any demand was put on his underdeveloped intellectual and volitional muscles.)

Life had been ladled out to the son with a solid gold spoon; his father had given him everything except a taste of reality. He had softened every crisis, cushioned every failure, assumed responsibility for every moral or financial disaster. The one thing he did not give him was a chance to become a person. In trying to spare his son the rigors he had endured in scratching his way to wealth and power, the father had denied him the opportunity to develop any strength of character or self-control. And by the time he realized what he had done, it was too late both for him and for his son.

I have recounted this sad tale of dominance and debilitating control, and the uncontrollable results it produced, because it sharply focuses by contrast the fatherly control of God's loving providence.

Is God in control? So many have asked. Yes! But with infinite wisdom. We are ushered into the very heart of God to find the answers to our questions about the nature and extent of his control. There we behold and experience both sides of a paradox which yields to a greater truth. God is the absolute sovereign of the universe, but he has given us freedom. He created us to love him, but there could be no mature love between us and him without our freedom of choice.

There are three presuppositions which must guide our answer to all the questions about God's involvement in our troubled world and our often-calamitous existence. First, God is supremely in control when he limits his control.

Second, he is sensitively in control as he grants us the gift of free will, knowing what we may do with it. Third, he is sublimely in control as he intervenes and brings good out of evil that happens to and around us.

Fortified with these three gigantic truths about the nature of God, we can confront the disquiet within us about the checkered record of history and about our own topsy-turvy lives with their concerns, crises, and complications.

"If God is almighty, why doesn't he do better?" some have asked. That brash question might be stated more delicately by others of us: "Lord, why don't you make life a little bit better?" But the question is the same. We struggle to balance three other true, but time-tarnished, assumptions: that God is omnipotent, having all power; omniscient, having all knowledge; and gracious, having all love. We are often tempted to sacrifice one or more of these three rocks of our intellectual and spiritual foundation in seeking to explain what we go through and what happens in the world around us. If God is all-loving, all-powerful, and all-knowing, why doesn't he do what we want when we think we need it? Unable to endure what was meant to be creative insecurity leading to faithful trust, we say with sophomoric persistance, "Either God is all powerful and not all knowing, or he is all knowing and not all powerful."

But what happened to the "all loving" leg of the tripod? That's the secret: absolute love guides the Lord's exercise of his omniscience and omnipotence in the affairs of his people. What he does with what he knows is always conditioned by what decisions will enable us to become mature, healthy persons. Greatness of character and personality is not produced by a smooth, easy life. It is in the difficulties as much as in the delights of life that we are forced to grow. The sure conviction of my life after over thirty years of experiencing God's providence is this: he never allows more than we can stand. He uses all that happens to us to bring us into deeper trust and dependence on him, and his interventions are perfectly timed to help us without negating our freedom.

We've been reluctant to grapple with the implications of the paradox of God's control and our freedom. We've clutched one side or another of the paradox. There's been a softness in our thinking. We put God on trial for the things he's allowed, wondering why he's not done better, only to find that we are the ones on trial ... and he's the judge. We throw the ball to him demanding explanations about how he's running the universe, only to find he throws it back to us. God is the pitcher, not the catcher, of our hard questions about the condition of humanity. But we find it difficult to catch; our fists are clenched with arrogant consternation over the state of the world. And if we do dare to catch, what God pitches stings our gloves!

The truth we must catch, however much it hurts, is that God had to give us freedom, knowing what we might do with it. There is no alternative; we had to be either puppets or persons. Because of his love for us, God wants us to be persons; what the misguided father of the soft man-boy did to his son, he refuses to do to us. And so we must dare to be what he created us to be, with all the dangers of misusing our freedom.

The great assurance is that he does not leave us alone with that freedom. He loves us so much that he uses the circumstances he allows to happen to help us grow. He will not deny us the depth of maturity which comes in the things which force us to cry out, "God, help me!" Be sure of this: nothing will ever happen that will not ultimately be used to help us claim our destiny as co-creators with God in shaping a person to live with him abundantly, now and eternally. Then, in partnership with him, we can work with relentless zeal to communicate his love to others. We can become indefatigable in the use of our freedom to live under his rule, proclaiming the kingdom of God in all our realms of responsibility.

The eloquent truth of God's unique and wise kind of control is the essence of the biblical message. Two passages from the Old Testament are especially helpful in understanding the control God has in the world. The first is part of an awesome series of questions and promises God makes to his people in a passage from Isaiah which follows the one we considered in the previous chapter. The second is the poignant story of what happened to Joseph's relationship with God through what God allowed to happen to him.

Isaiah 45:9–11 has been a powerful intellectual and spiritual benchmark for me at times when I am tempted to question God's management of my life, the people I love, or the perplexing circumstances of life. In periods of illness in my family, I have been shocked into deeper trust. Difficulties and disappointments have forced me to quiet humility, asking what I can learn. Most of all, it has put into perspective God's control, and cures the arrogance which would dare to tell him how to do his job better. Listen to what the Lord has to ask and then to what he promises.

"Woe to the one who quarrels with his maker—
An earthenware vessel among the vessels of the earth!
Will the clay say to the potter, 'What are you doing?'
Or the thing you are making say, 'He has no hands'?
Woe to him who says to a father, 'What are you begetting?'
Or to a woman, 'To what are you giving birth?' "
Thus says the Lord, the Holy One of Israel, and his Maker:
"Ask Me about the things to come concerning My sons,
and you shall commit to Me the work of My hands."

Notice the two very different ways of asking questions about God's control. One is a demand for accountability and explanation, the other is to humbly ask in response to his invitation. One is given woe, the other results in wonder. The Lord refuses to justify his strategy as creator, potter of the clay, the father begetting, the woman giving birth. Those words tell me that God is involved in a creative process with my life. When things do not go as I've planned or I cannot see the meaning of some misery, I have no authority to imperiously demand from God a clearly detailed strategy of what he is doing through what is happening to me. What I am permitted to do is ask him about the things to come and commit myself to the molding, shaping work of his hands. I am to ask him for wisdom and discernment to understand and accept the way in which he is working out his plan. He's never finished with us. Our great need is to put a particular perplexity into the perspective of his providence.

What an awesome thing for God to say to us! What a magnificent gift he's given us for prayer. A gracious command to focus on the things to come. The Lord is constantly planning and preparing for the next step in his strategy for us. This frees us to move beyond asking, "Lord, why have you allowed this?!" to, "Lord, what can I discover in this for what you are preparing for me to be and do?" Then we can hear and accept the promise, "For I know the plans I have for you, says the Lord. They are plans for good and not for evil, to give you a future and a hope" (Jer. 29:11, TLB).

Now let's see how this was worked out in the life of Joseph, the youngest son of Jacob in the land of Canaan. Genesis 37–50, paints the portrait of a man who discovered that God is most in control when circumstances seem to deny it. The basic presuppositions and assumptions with which we began are all blended into this stunning portrait. There are the bright splashes of color mingled with the gray of difficulty, the dark browns of temporary disappointment, and the mauves of patient waiting for God's justice to triumph. Here is a man who experienced the truth that God is in control even when he seemingly limits that control; God is still in control when he allows us the freedom of choice, and his control is revealed in on-time, and in-time interventions to accomplish his greater purpose. Joseph found that God is indeed all-knowing, all-powerful, and all-loving. The story is punctuated by the assurance, "And the Lord was with Joseph." That led to the great affirmation of his life, "Men meant it for evil, but God meant it for good." A brief synopsis of his life reminds us of how Joseph arrived at this liberating conviction.

We first meet Joseph, the favorite son of Jacob, as a boy of seventeen. He was a dreamer, and his dreams told him that he was a man of destiny. He dreamed that he and his brothers were binding sheaves in the field and his sheaf arose and stood upright and that his brother's sheaves gathered around his and bowed down. That wasn't exactly the kind of dream that would pacify natural sibling rivalry. But that was not all Joseph dreamed: "Behold, I have dreamed another dream; and behold, the sun, the moon, and the eleven stars were bowing down to me" (RSV). That was too much for his brothers. It was one thing to endure the frustration of their father's sentimental devotion and favoritism to Joseph, but this blatant arrogance aroused all of the jealousy and anger that had been building up for years.

One day Joseph's father sent him to deliver food to his brothers who at the time were working in the valley of Dothan. When they saw him coming in the distance, they plotted to get rid of the dreamer. They would kill him! Only his brother Reuben's caution saved Joseph: "Shed no blood; cast him into this pit, but lay no hand on him." When Joseph arrived on the scene, his brothers were waiting in ambush. They tore off his colorful coat, a prized gift from his father Jacob, and threw the kicking and screaming boy into a wide-bottomed, narrow-necked, bottle-shaped well.

Several days later some Ishmaelites stopped by on their way to Egypt, and Joseph was sold to them as a slave for twenty sheckels of silver. And to compound the felony, his brothers splashed goat's blood all over Joseph's coat and took it home to their father as proof that their brother had met with foul play and was dead. An evil deed. Why did God allow it? He could have stopped it. But if he had, the unfolding of his plan for the future good he intended would not have been accomplished.

When the Ishmaelites got to Egypt, they sold Joseph to Potiphar, the captain of the Pharaoh's bodyguard. And it wasn't long before Joseph's unusual leadership qualities attracted Potiphar's attention, and he placed him in a responsible position over his entire household. "And the Lord was with Joseph, so he became a successful man."

After a time Potiphar's wife became attracted to the handsome young man who was around the house all the time. And one day her sexual fantasies drove her to demand that Joseph go to bed with her. Joseph's refusal because of his allegiance to God and his loyalty to Potiphar, resulted in the full vengeance of the rejected woman's ire. When her husband returned home, she accused Joseph of trying to attack her, and Potiphar threw him into jail.

But once again the Lord intervened and used the worst for his best. The Genesis story identifies the Prime Mover behind the seemingly negative circumstances. The repeated phrase, "But the Lord was with Joseph . . ." identifies the secret of the serendipities that happened to and around him. We read that Joseph was given "favor in the sight of the chief jailor," and it wasn't long before Joseph was placed in charge of the whole jail! What an amazing turn of events!

As the story continues, we learn that two of the prisoners in the jail were the Pharoah's chief butler and his chief baker. They had offended the Pharoah and were placed in confinement. One night both of these men had dreams which they were unable to understand. When Joseph heard about their dilemma, he offered to help. So the butler described his dream, and Joseph was able to give him the interpretation—he would be released from prison and restored to his previous position. The chief baker, however, was not so fortunate. The interpretation of his dream indicated that he would be condemned to death. Everything turned out just the way Joseph predicted, and the chief butler returned to his place of power in Pharoah's palace.

Two years after that incident the chief butler heard that the Pharoah was very puzzled over two dreams he'd had and none of his advisors could interpret them for him. The butler suggested that Joseph might be able to help out. As he stood before Pharoah, the interpretation became clear—the next seven years were to be times of great prosperity. But immediately following that would come seven hard years of famine.

Joseph was careful to give God the credit for his insight. And when he had finished the interpretation, he went on to give Pharoah a plan that would insure Egypt's survival during the years of hardship and famine. The Pharoah was so impressed by Joseph that he released him from prison and put him in charge of a task force assigned to insure economic stability for the next fourteen years.

God was with Joseph! Note how God used the pain of tragedy and difficulty to hammer out the man he wanted him to be. An arrogant youth was shaped into a man of destiny who became the Lord's instrument of blessing in saving not only the Egyptians but his own family as well.

During the seven years of prosperity and plenty, Joseph filled all the granaries of Egypt to overflowing. Then when the seven lean years came, Egypt was prepared. But then comes an intriguing twist to the story. Joseph's homeland of Canaan was not as farsighted. And when his father Jacob learned there was plenty of grain in Egypt, he sent his sons to obtain the necessary food that would save their lives.

The unfolding drama of Joseph's two encounters with his brothers is one of the most impelling in Scripture. Obviously, his brothers did not recognize this mighty leader in Egypt, and the account of how Joseph dealt with them is fascinating and filled with pathos. Finally, though, he could restrain himself no longer, "I am Joseph! Is my father still alive?" Imagine the complex of emotions he felt—hurt, anguish, homesickness, loneliness. But more than that, through God's grace in his life, he was able to offer forgiveness and acceptance: "And now do not be grieved or angry with yourselves, because you sold me here; for God sent me before you to preserve life. For the famine has been in the land these two years, and there are still five years in which there will be neither plowing nor harvesting. And God sent me before you to preserve for you a remnant in the earth, and to keep you alive by a great deliverance" (Gen. 45:5–7).

Eventually Jacob and all his sons were settled permanently in Egypt. After Jacob died, Joseph's brothers came to him asking forgiveness for what they had done to him. His response was filled with the wisdom and greatness that his own suffering and hardship had produced. What he said gives us the key to understanding God's providence in our own lives. "Do not be afraid," Joseph said, "for am I in God's place? And as for you, you meant evil against me, but God meant it for good in order to bring about this present result, to preserve many people alive" (Gen. 50:19–20). Those words plunge us into the deep waters of God's sovereignty, our free will, man's fallen inhumanity to himself and others, and yet God's power to use it all to eventually accomplish his ultimate purposes.

Joseph refused to take God's place. He would not play God over his brothers or judge what they had done to him. All that he had been through had broken his pride and enabled him to praise God. He trusted God unreservedly and was able to give him glory.

God knows today what he's doing with you and me. If we can say with Joseph in life's calamities, "Men meant it for evil, but God meant it for good," then we have discovered the secret of living with freedom and joy.

Joseph's confession of faith foreshadows the cross. At no point in history could it be said with greater force that men meant it for evil, but in that cosmic event God meant it for ultimate good. The resurrection is his final word to us that nothing which happens to or around us can defeat us. In each situation surrendered to our Lord, there will be his interventions and a resurrection. Out of the worst, God promises his best.

Yes, God is in control. Unlike the father of the son I described at the beginning of this chapter, God allows the rigors of reality. He is all-loving, all-knowing, and all-powerful. God is in control as he limits his control to give us freedom, and he intervenes to express his control in ways that move us on toward greatness. His purpose is to make us like Jesus. That's all any of us needs to know. We can sing the words of the old song, "Though wrong seems oft so strong, God is the ruler yet!"

> Behind our life the Weaver stands,
> And works His wondrous will
> We leave it all to His wise hands
> And trust His perfect skill.
> Should mystery enshroud His plan
> And our short sight be dimmed
> We will not try the whole to scan,
> But leave each thread to Him.

Before going on to the next chapter, I want you to put this book down for a moment. All that we've said in this chapter is to help us get our life off our hands and into the hands of God. Here's a way to begin. Position your open hands before you. In one hand place the triumphant truth that God is in control. In the other place your life—focused in specific relationships and needs. Now bring your hands together, symbolic of the fact that the two can never be separated. Folded in oneness, lift them up to the Lord saying, "You are in control, I will trust you completely."

3

Where Is God When I Suffer?

DARKNESS DRAWS THE curtain down on the day and it becomes night. And as the sweet stillness of the night invites
us to rest, we say to ourselves, "Everything will have to wait
until tomorrow. There's nothing that can be done tonight.
Ah, 'sleep that knits up the ravell'd sleave of care!'"

But then, after a few hours of sleep, long before our
bodies or psyches are rested, our minds stir us awake. It's
still night and the black darkness enshrouds us. And that's
when we realize that there *is* something we can do before
tomorrow: we can worry and wrestle. Suddenly we are
attacked by the pestilence which stalks its prey in the
dark hours of the night. All of our questions about the why
of suffering, about our concerns with the people we love,
or about the pain which throttles our troubled world leap
from the prisons of our daytime repression and suppression
and dance about fiendishly in our minds. We are alone
and vulnerable. We feel the full impact of the reality of
anxiety and suffering and long for dawn to bless us with
the distracting diversion of another day. But in the anxious hours of waiting, the darkness around us is matched
by the darkness of the night in our own souls.

And yet, many of us have discovered that the dark night
of suffering is not limited to sleepless hours. It can come in

the brightness of high noon or in any unguarded moment when our own or others' suffering gets at us. The demanding question slips from our hearts, "Why, God, why!" And with that it's night again regardless of the time of day.

Each of us is a diminutive world with its days and nights. We all know times of suffering when our personal planet of existence is seemingly hidden from the warmth and brightness of any blessing. What is it for you? Your own physical pain or disability? The emotional tension of unresolved memories or fear of the future? Strained or fractured relationships? Disappointment over life, yourself or someone else? Loneliness that's deeper than the absence of people? Grief over the loss of a loved one no amount of time seems to heal? Turbulent worry over what's happening to a loved one or friend whose pain has invaded your heart? Or is it the incredible suffering in the world around you?

We all have one of three things in common: we have known the night of suffering, are in the night right now, or are deeply troubled about someone who is. And we have something else in common—the question as to why God allows it. In the dark night of suffering, we readily chime in with Job's counselor, Elihu, as he rolls back the curtain on the nakedness of human anguish, "Where is God my maker who gives songs in the night?"

Only one who has endured the long night and has heard the Lord's song in the midst of suffering has any right to answer. But the answer does come to us from Psalm 42, a succor to sufferers through the ages. And there, along with Luther, Kierkegaard, Bonhoeffer, and nameless millions of God's people, we discover a way to deal with suffering by listening for the Lord's song of hope in the night of pain, persecution, grief, or discouragement. Out of the depths, the psalmist shouts the assurance, "The Lord will command His lovingkindness in the daytime; and His song will be with me in the night" (Ps. 42:8).

This is no easy, glib, pious platitude. The writer was in

the nighttime of his life when he wrote those words. Along with other captives he was led away from his beloved Jerusalem on the way to an excruciating exile. During the endless days of forced march, he had been taunted by his captors and ravaged by pain of body and soul. It was somewhere on the slopes of the mountains of Hermon, where the springs of the River Jordan rush down into the valley in roaring cataracts, that he and his fellow captives were allowed a brief respite. We see him sitting there with a longing, wistful gaze yearning back to Jerusalem and his cherished homeland. His soul was eclipsed from all that had provided joy and delight in his life. All he could do in the darkness was utter a sad soliloquy of his suffering which finally turns into a dynamic dialogue of authentic prayer. As we listen in, we discover how to face the questions which lead to the ultimate question of the night, find the purpose of the night, and finally hear the song of hope in the night.

The questions of the night all blend into one. Where is God when I suffer? Why does God allow suffering? Does he send it as a punishment? If so, what did I do to deserve this? Does God send trials, sickness, and problems into my life to discipline me? Must I accept this as the will of God? How can God be both omnipotent and loving? If he were, would he allow this suffering to occur? Either God does not care, or he is powerless to prevent it. We try to say the familiar words, "Almighty God, our loving heavenly Father," and suddenly realize that the ascription is really the cause of the disquiet brewing in us. Almighty? Loving? How could he be if he allows this pain of body, emotion, or mind?

Suddenly, though, in our imaginations we are inside the psalmist's skin. The taunting questions of his enemies have seeped through the fabric of his faith. His pain multiplied by disappointment finally equals despair. Their question now became his: where is your God?

Indeed, where is my God? It's the question of prolonged

sickness, of unexplainable calamity, of life's bitter reversals. The inevitability of the questions of the night. We try
with Kafka to "see through the thickness of things" and
feel what Camus called "the hopeless encounter between
human questioning and the silence of the universe." T. S.
Eliot in his *Murder in the Cathedral* said that "Humankind
cannot bear very much reality." But when the night of suffering comes with its stark reality, there is no alternative. And
then we are faced with the ultimate temptation—to make
God our adversary and not our advocate. We say with the
psalmist, "Why has thou forgotten me?" That's the dark
night of the soul.

I remember talking with a young man who was battling
the virulence of cancer. He looked me in the eye and said,
"Help me! I have done very well with this so far, but the
questions of my friends and family are getting to me. It's
not what they say, it's what's in their eyes. Their questions
about why God would allow this may be unspoken, but
they are expressed in the way they look and in their body
language. I've held out against the questions as long as I
can, but now I wake up in the night and wrestle with them.
I can't take the pain without God's help but the questions
stand in the way. I've made God an enemy when I need
him the most!"

What would you have said in response? No platitude
spoken with a stained glass voice would do. It was a time
for clear thinking. The false presuppositions that haunted
the young sufferer had to be cleared away. God does not
send suffering. He doesn't have to. There's enough of it to
go around in our weary world. But why is the world like
this? We are tempted to blame God and demand an explanation. Then we realize that we owe him an explanation.
The awesome expression of his love was to give mankind
freedom. The perfect creation was allowed to be tarnished
by what we did with that freedom. There are few things
from which we suffer which are not traceable to the head-

waters of that gift of freedom. The more we discover of the source of germs and physical malfunctioning, the more we realize that our distortion of nature has its root in our rebellious misuse of what God gave us.

But what about calamities—floods and hurricanes and earthquakes? Does God control what happens when these strike the innocent? If he doesn't, who does? But that presses deeper questions. Would we have done it differently? Would we have created a catastrophy-free world? Is our happiness the sole criterion of creation? Is it even the chief criterion? Is the best of all possible worlds one in which human pleasure and painlessness exist? We must say "No!" for a trouble-free existence would rob us of discovering the heart of God. Eventually, we must accept the notion that a free world in which suffering and pain are allowed is the best possible world in which to discover the joy of fellowship with God, now and forever.

What is at issue is the quality of person God created mankind to be. Human freedom is essential for the accomplishment of this—and so is the suffering we endure. Without the power of choice, even wrong choices, we become the marionettes we talked about in the previous chapter. To take away human freedom, and a world in which suffering is a possibility, would cause a worse kind of chaos in which we could never know the development of the fibre of a soul fit for eternity. Is there anything the omnipotent God can't do? Yes! Make great personalities without giving them and their world freedom.

We may say with Omar Khayyam's simplistic arrogance, "To grasp this Sorry Scheme of Things entire, . . . shatter it to bits—and then Re-mould it nearer to the Heart's Desire!"

But what would be your heart's desire? To live in fellowship with a person who would know your deepest nature, experience dependence on you, know your love, and be prepared to live with you forever? Well then, how would you do it differently?

Do you see what the questions of the night have done for us? We are pressed to the precipice of thanking God for the gift of our creation, our freedom in it, and even the suffering that comes as a result. But now deep calls to deep. We are on the raw edge with the psalmist. And now our question yields to the essence of praise—we are not the moving target of the Almighty's wrath, but we are the object of his love. Can we praise him for his strategy in creation? Will we surrender to him the anger behind "What is the meaning of this?" for the more probing question, "What is your meaning for me in this?"

That leads us to the purpose of the night. I've often wondered whether the psalmist didn't wrestle with despair before he wrote down that magnificent prayer in Psalm 42. The topic sentence of the prayer is really the triumphant conclusion. "As a deer pants for the water brooks, so my soul pants for Thee, O God. My soul thirsts for God, for the living God." That's the distilled desire which flows from surrendered despair. Whatever God allows in our lives is to bring us to that basic prayer.

The special gift of suffering is that it exposes all secondary satisfactions. We live in a world that has made a false god out of quantity rather than quality. It measures greatness by how long we live and not how well we live, in the number of breaths we breathe instead of the breath-taking experiences we enjoy. The passion for trouble-free health has robbed us of a passion for God when it is interrupted. Our false idea of happiness anesthetizes us from finding joy. We cannot tolerate any infractions of our prescribed agendas where everyone lives to be a hundred, is happily married, has perfect children, makes a good living, and retires to trouble-free leisure where the only problem is how to battle boredom. We find ourselves unable to tolerate the imperfect, the incomplete, the inconsistent.

But those secondary expectations are not God's pattern for us. It is only as we come to know "life's smoothness turned rough," that we find a deeper reason for our existence. And that follows the heart-cry, "My soul pants for Thee O God, my soul thrists for God, the living God."

Suffering had given the psalmist a precious gift: an intimacy with God greater than the happiness of joining the procession to the Temple, better than the festival celebration in historic ritual of the acts of God in the past. When despair finally brought him to the wrenching prayer of trust, his previous experiences of the God of the past were replaced by the penetrating experience of God in the present. The purpose of the night was to move from the soliloquy of self-centered pity to the dialogue of God-centered praise. God did not waste the tragedy. He used it to give more than answers; he became the Answer.

The writer pressed beneath the surface in Psalms 42:11 to ask the crucial question, "Why *are* you in despair, O my soul? And why have you become disturbed within me?" It is our response to suffering that exposes the depth of our relationship with the Lord. And it is after we put him on trial, only to find we couldn't have made a better world, that we suddenly realize that it is we who are on trial. Then the inner attitudes and values of our hearts are exposed. As the psalmist found that he loved Jerusalem and his religion more than God, so too, we are forced to admit that we have made God a support system for our cult of success, health, and a trouble-free life.

Be sure of this, God will never give us anything which will ultimately separate us from him. And he never permits more suffering than will allow him and the sufferer to know one another better. It is when we dare to ask why we are in despair and disturbed in our souls, that we are able to face our raw need for God. He will not intervene too quickly and keep us from the discovery of the meaning of our suffering. He loves us too much for that!

The psalmist's drowning descent of ruthless honesty with his own soul through the early verses of Psalm 42 finally reached the firm footing of the Rock of Ages. Now he was ready to pray. God had allowed him to talk until he knew what he had to say. "O my God, my soul is in despair within me; therefore I remember Thee . . ." What he admitted to himself inwardly he now confessed openly to God. Then he goes on to attest that rather than just waiting to go back to a geographically confined experience of being in Jerusalem, he had found God in the night of his exile from the familiar. Thank God for the painful stuff that turns life's smoothness rough! Trouble gives us tread as we run to God. And the very circumstances of our night of suffering become sacraments to remind us. Now the psalmist writes that he remembered God in the place of his difficulty in the land of Jordan. The peaks of Hermon lifted his soul to the greatness of God. The tumbling waterfall became the intimation of his power. The foaming breakers and the waves became an assurance of Yahweh's never-ending love (Ps. 42:6,7).

I know how he felt and what he heard. When I was studying this psalm in preparation for writing this chapter, I was in the western highlands of Scotland. There I spent hours pouring over the questions about suffering and the pain and anguish they represented. And I poured over this forty-second psalm, identifying with the pathos of the writer. His night of the soul along with the hundreds of questions ushered me into a night of the why of human suffering.

Late in the evening one day, as the shadows of night were falling, I took a five mile hike along a lonesome road which borders a small loch. I saw no one for hours. It was raining and the wind was howling fiercely. The wind frothed up waves on the loch and whistled through the scraggy heather. The complex questions tumbled about in my mind. I tasted the bitter gorge of discouragement. And then I did something I have never done before. I asked for a sign. "Lord give me some assurance that you know and care and will use the suffering my people are enduring. Is my answer on the right track?" Suddenly, the wind subsided and the loch was calm for a brief moment. And then, just as the thought formed that the assurance of the Lord's presence is peace and calm, the wind burst through the valley with hurricane force.

Was that a sign from the Lord? It was for me! What the parable of the wind told me was that God is Lord of the calm and of the turbulence. He is no less in one than the other. Then I could pray, "Father, you are Lord of Hollywood and a Highland loch. The calm of peace and the tumult of the wind are yours. Thank you for this sacrament of your sovereignty." That night the Lord had introduced me again to the deeper person in me that longs for him more than anything or anyone else.

I have come to see now that the questions of the night reveal the purpose of the night so that we can hear the Lord's song in the midst of suffering. The psalmist heard it and so can we: "And His song will be with me in the night." Be sure of that! What is the strange but strengthening song? It is God himself breaking through the pain, loneliness, and fear of our despair. Hope is the Lord's song. Brunner was right, "What oxygen is to the lungs, so hope is to the soul."

The Lord's song was heard and then sung by Abraham on Mount Moriah—Jehovah-jereh, "the Lord will provide." It was the song which flooded Moses' soul at Marah—Jehovah-rapha, "the Lord healeth." Gideon heard the song when he surrendered his impotence to the Omnipotent and heard, "Peace to you, do not fear," and his song was Jehovah-shalom, "The Lord our peace." It was Jehovah-ra-ah to a lonely shepherd named David, and he sang, "The Lord is my shepherd." Jehovah-tsidkenu, "the Lord our righteousness," became Jeremiah's song, and Jehovah-shammah, "The Lord ever present," was for Ezekiel. The Lord's song in the night is the whisper of his name and the assurance of his faithfulness.

But all of the lyrics of God's song for the night of our suffering are swallowed up in one great name that swells the chorus: Immanuel; God with us! God came, comes, and is coming. It is Jesus who saves us from our sins; Christ, was the anointed, suffering Messiah. It wasn't just the best of all good men suffering on Calvary's cross for the people he loved; it was God himself, the "fullness of the Godhead bodily" taking our place for all time. Calvary will not let us forget this profound truth: he suffered for us so that when we suffer we might know his limitless love. And in the night, when we pray for the dawn of relief, we know the song of Immanuel—"Let not your heart be troubled . . . in this world you will have tribulation. Be of good cheer, I have overcome the world." Remember, our song is not only "When I Survey the Wondrous Cross," but "Christ the Lord Is Risen!" The empty tomb becomes our assurance that no suffering can have the final word.

Paul heard the Lord's song in the night of his tormented soul, "Saul, Saul, why?" Later he sang a song for any night, "For me to live is Christ!" And he gave the world a final doxology to sing in the midnight hour: "For I am persuaded that neither death nor life, nor angels nor principalities nor powers, nor things present nor things to come, nor height nor depth, nor any other created thing, shall be able to separate us from the love of God which is in Christ Jesus our Lord" (Rom. 8:38–39).

Sing that song in your night! It spells out the cosmic dimensions of Christ's victory over Satan, pain, death, all dimensions of time—past, present, and future. It speaks of impossible circumstances and troublesome people, our sin and failure, and our depleted dreams. But nothing can drown out the Lord's song of victory. With that greater song of hope, on this side of Calvary and an empty tomb, we can say to our timorous souls the psalmist's words with Immanuel's joy, "Hope in God, for I shall yet praise Him, the help of my countenance, and my God"!

Listen! It's the Lord's song for your night. You've dared to ask the hard questions, earned the credentials to hear by surrendering your suffering, and now the song of Jesus is your song, "I will never leave you or forsake you! I am with you always!"

Slip your hand into his and notice with assurance that it is a nail-pierced hand of suffering. Jesus knows our need in the night. And then his voice blends with ours in a night song to our souls:

> Be still, my soul: the Lord is on thy side;
> Bear patiently the cross of grief or pain.
> Leave to thy God to order and provide;
> In ev'ry change He faithful will remain.
> Be still, my soul: thy best, thy heavenly Friend
> Thro' thorny ways leads to a joyful end.[1]

4

How Can I Know
God's Perfect Will?

I SMILE INSIDE EVERY time I think of it. The experience taught me a good lesson about opening sermons with a rhetorical question. I was a guest speaker at a college and began my address with the question, "What is your greatest need and your greatest fear?" I had already decided what the response should be and had planned an incisive answer to my own question. My mistake was to pause too long after asking the question.

Suddenly, a young man in the second row stood up and blurted out an unexpected answer to my question! He was a new Christian and unfamiliar with the sermonic craft of setting up a question the preacher intends to answer himself. He really thought I wanted an answer then and there, before the whole student body in the chapel.

"Sir," he said honestly and insistently, "my greatest need is to know God's perfect will for my life and my greatest fear is that I will miss it, or if I know, that I will resist doing it."

My authenticity and integrity were on the line. Had I really wanted an answer or not? I was faced with an immediate choice. I could honestly tell the young man and the entire audience that I had planned to answer my own question with another subject that I had predetermined was their greatest need and fear, or I could scrap what I had prepared and respond to the urgent, serious question which had been posed. I was stopped in my tracks.

I'm not going to ask you what you think I should have done! But what I did do was ask the audience of bright, vital minds if the young man had really articulated their answer, hoping they would say, "No," so I could get on with what I had prepared. Once again, I should not have asked. They all nodded agreement and a professor voiced an enthusiastic, "Hear, hear!"

I felt like the London preacher who overheard two cockneys discussing his sermon topic, "Is There A God?" posted on the bulletin board outside his church. "I say," one remarked sardonically, "wouldn't there be a caution if 'e said there ain't!"

Having learned my lesson about rhetorical questions with spontaneous audiences, I set aside my prepared talk and attempted an answer to what turned out to be the deepest question among both students and faculty. My answer, frankly, was more than an off-the-cuff ad-lib. I have wrestled with the question myself and with thoughtful inquirers for years.

Therefore, I was not surprised when one of the largest group of questions submitted by people across the nation had to do with knowing and doing the will of God. What did surprise me was the use of the adjective "perfect." Hundreds of people asked, "How can I know God's perfect will for my life?" Several asked, "What is the difference between God's perfect and his permissive will?" All of the questions expressed the college student's sincerity and urgency. We all fear missing the reason we were born or the danger of wrong choices that will make our life less than maximum.

The Apostle Paul gives us an answer which challenges us to thoughtful exposition. The Christians at Rome were asking probing questions about the will of God. After summarizing the essence of the gospel of God's love and forgiveness through Jesus Christ, Paul uses a transitional "therefore" which almost demands an exclamation point. "I beseech you *therefore*, brethren, by the mercies of God, that you present your bodies a living sacrifice, holy, acceptable to God, which is your reasonable service. And do not be conformed to this world, but be transformed by the renewing of your mind, that you may prove what is that good and acceptable and perfect will of God" (Rom. 12:1-2).

The word perfect leaps off the page. The Greek word Paul used is *teleion,* from *telos,* meaning, end, purpose, goal. The word good, *agathon,* meaning good in quality and acceptable, *evareston,* implying intention, annotate and heighten the impact of the word perfect. The perfect will of God is that we fulfill the purpose we were created for: to know God, receive his love, and enjoy fellowship with him forever. Jesus put it succinctly in the Sermon on the Mount: "Therefore you shall be perfect, just as your Father in heaven is perfect." The astounding promise is made concluding God's explanation of extraordinary love. We can accomplish our purpose as God accomplishes his. God's perfect will for our lives is that we love him, ourselves, others as he has loved us, and live in his world as he intended.

But any use of the word perfect implies that there must be something less than perfect. That plunges us into the deep waters of what we have done with God's original promise. He created us with intellect, emotion, and will. A response to his love includes all three. We can know him with the understanding of our intellect, receive and respond to his love emotionally, and will to do his will obediently. All three are awesome endowments. But the will holds the thermostatic control over the flow of our intellectual and emotional response. God entrusted us with freedom to will, choose, to fulfill our purpose to glorify him and enjoy him forever.

What went wrong then? That's the sad tale of history.

God's perfect will for us has been blemished by our misuse of the volitional freedom he has given us. That misuse ushered in the dispensation of his permissive will. What mankind did with the awesome gift of freedom of will had to be dealt with in some creative way.

God's perfect will is what he intended; his permissive will is what he allows. Instead of obliterating mankind for the refusal to live in intimate harmony and trust, God continued to work with his world, allowing freedom, but persistently seeking to accomplish his perfect will among those who would respond and will to do his will.

The Old Testament is the account of how God's chosen people struggled with their freedom. The hall of fame of Israel's history lists those who sought to know God's perfect will in the midst of the tragic distortion of his permissive will. David expresses the longing of Abraham, Joseph, Moses, Gideon, and the prophets. "Teach me to do Thy will, for Thou art my God; let Thy good Spirit lead me . . ." At each of the bleakest periods of Israel's history God raised up a leader who longed more for what God intended than for what he would allow.

A startling example of the perfect and permissive will of God is found in the Exodus. God's perfect will was to create a totally dependent people to be his people. He worked with their wrong choices, rebellion, and murmuring. He did spectacular works to convince them of his triumphant adequacy to be their God and guide. All he asked of Moses and the people was to follow the cloud by day and the pillar of fire by night. Psalm 106:12–15 records the misuse of free will. "Then believed they his words; they sang his praise. They soon forgot his works; they waited not for his counsel: but lusted exceedingly in the wilderness, and tempted God in the desert. And he gave them their request; but sent leanness into their soul" (KJV). That's the way it is: God's best offered; man's rebellion; the leanness of less than God intended.

Another classic illustration of God's permissive will is

found later when Israel wanted to be like other nations and have a king. This was neither ideal nor perfect. They were to be a special treasure of the Lord, dependent on him as their king and obedient to his guidance through his appointed leaders.

As we read the story in 1 Samuel 8, we can feel the struggle from inside Samuel's skin. The response to Samuel's prayers had clearly indicated that Israel was not to be like other nations, but was to be a uniquely blessed people, totally dependent on their God. But the repeated insistence of the people sent Samuel back to God.

Finally, God yielded and Saul was anointed king. But God made it clear that this was not his perfect will. And yet, God persisted, seeking to bring good out of the willful insistence of the people to run their own lives. Saul was a disaster; he characterized the rebellion of the whole people. But God did not give up. He had David waiting in the wings of the stage of history. David was described as the apple of God's eye, a man after God's heart. God's love never gave up!

But even in this God-sensitive leader who affirmed the realization of the Lord's perfect will in saying "The Lord is my shepherd . . . he leads me," the permissive will had to be expressed. God's perfect plan for David did not include Bathsheba, the murder of her husband, Uriah, and the dynasty of degradation that resulted. And yet, God was waiting, willing to bring good out of evil when David prayed, "Against Thee only have I sinned." God is always ready to go back to square zero with us and begin again.

The ministry of the prophets was one of call and recall back to God's perfect will. "Seek ye the Lord, while He may be found!" was their cry; and their urgent plea was to do justice, have mercy, and walk humbly with God. And the Old Testament closes with the alarming account of what happens when we misuse God's permissive will to resist his perfect will.

And yet, not even that diminished God's persistent pursuit of a people to do his perfect will. At the lowest ebb of history he came himself in Jesus Christ, the Mediator. In human form he exposed his perfect will and displayed for us to see what total obedience was meant to be. The Mediator's persistent prayer was, "Not my will, but Thine be done." Jesus taught his disciples to pray, "Thy will be done on earth as it is in heaven." And then out of sheer grace, he went to the cross to suffer for the sins of the world, amassed in the misuse of God's permissive will.

So that we might never be in doubt about what is God's perfect will, the Messiah both stated and exemplified its essence. Two salient statements become our foundation of building a life on God's perfect will. "For I came down from heaven, not to do My own will, but the will of Him who sent Me . . . And this is the will of Him who sent Me, that everyone who sees the Son and believes in Him may have everlasting life; and I will raise him up at the last day" (John 6:38,40). Add to that the Master's clear description of eternal life and you are on the holy ground of God's perfect will.

Jesus' prayer on the night he was betrayed, just before the crucifixion, allows us to look into the heart of God's purpose. "And this is eternal life, that they may know You, the only true God, and Jesus Christ whom You have sent" (John 17:3). After praying that, Jesus went to the cross to make his prayer a reality. Calvary is the ultimate exposure of the permissive will of God and the accomplishment of his perfect will. What God allowed in the anguish of Golgotha was for what he intended: a new creation of people who would have as their passion to know and do his will.

The Resurrection was God's sublime transformation of evil into good. Pentecost was square zero again for humanity. God poured out his Spirit. The disciples had had their wilful independence melted by Calvary's love, and their assurance of God's victorious intervening providence at an empty tomb. Now they were ready to experience the essence of God's perfect will in the intimacy he had intended since man's equivocation in the garden of Eden. The account in the Book of Acts of the infant church, the new creation, is a benchmark in history of what God can do with a totally obedient, receptive, and willing people.

But what does all this mean to us 2000 years later, when we struggle to live life, make our choices and decisions, and discover and do God's will? Everything! We have a liberating legacy. We know what God's perfect will is, what can happen when that is our only goal, and have a basis on which to make our daily decisions.

What is God's perfect will for my life? To know him as he has revealed himself in Jesus Christ! He is with us in the power of the Holy Spirit. The perfect will of God is Christ: meeting him, knowing him, being filled with his Spirit, and allowing our character to be transformed to be like him. Now we can savor what Paul meant. We can present our total life (that's the implication of "body") as a living sacrifice. It is our reasoned choice controlling the surrender of our wills. We can be extricated from the world's floundering in God's permissive will of what he allows. And our minds can be engendered with clear guidance of the implications of God's perfect will of what he intends for each day's choices and decisions.

There's a humorous but pointed story about Robert Redford, the famous Hollywood actor, and director. One day he was walking through a hotel lobby. A woman saw him and followed him to the elevator. "Are you the real Robert Redford?" she questioned with star-struck excitement. As the doors of the elevator closed, he replied, "Only when I'm alone!"

It's who we are when we are alone with ourselves that reveals whether we are in the delight of God's perfect will or living with the second best of his permissive will.

Our concern about God's will usually arises at a time of crisis or choices. Whom we shall marry, what job we should take, how we should decide at a crossroads impasse. Times like these force us to get back to basics. Often God will withhold clarity about secondary choices until we meet Paul's delineation of knowing God's will:

1. The surrender of our total life to God.
2. The experience of his indwelling Spirit.
3. The commitment of our wills to do God's will.

Look at it this way. The illustration of human relationships is never totally adequate, but they give us a clue. I think I know my wife very well. Out of the intimacy of thirty years, I know without asking her purposes and preferences. If I want to make a choice pleasing to her, I think I know what she would want. I don't need to talk with her about what she wants in most of life. Where there is a question, our close relationship provides conversation in which, based on what I already know, she can give me new input.

Christ wants us to know him so well, living in the quality of eternal life so profoundly, that he becomes the Lord of the nerve center of our wills. That relationship begins when we respond to his invitation, "Come, follow Me!" It is deepened when we abide in him and he in us. "If you abide in Me, and My words abide in you, you shall ask what you desire, and it shall be done for you" (John 15:7). When we abide in him and he in us we are guided in what to ask—and what not to ask. His message gives us sufficient data for most of life's decisions. And for those decisions that deal with life's specific choices, waiting and listening provides both the intellectual clarity of what is best, and the emotional peace which assures us that a particular direction is right for us.

Now, that raises a question. Why do so many Christians who believe in Christ as their Savior have so much difficulty discerning the Lord's will? Is it possible to be a Christian and be out of the will of God? Yes! We can accept Christ's salvation and still run our own lives. Once again the Lord's permissive will must be involved. He must work to bring good out of our wrong choices. We are thankful that he does, but its not the best he intended.

The consistent, habitual surrender of our wills is the secret to finding the Lord's will for us. Jesus gave us this formula when he responded to the Pharisees who wanted to be sure he was who he said he was: "If anyone wants to do His will, he shall know concerning the doctrine, whether it is from God or whether I speak of Myself" (John 7:17). The key is in the words, "If anyone wants to do His will." We are promised that if we accept the Lord's love and really want to do his will, we will know the specifics of his perfect will for our lives.

Someone reading this may respond, "Isn't that a bit simplistic? What about the tricks our minds play on us? Isn't it possible to want something, pray, and convince ourselves that what we want is what God wants?" Of course. History and our own personal experience are filled with tragic examples of that kind of transferance. Unbelievably destructive things have been done when people thought they had divine approval on some expression of self-will. That's why abiding in Christ is so crucial. He can and will use all means to guide, correct, and redirect us if we are willing.

When some of the recruits for the Crusades were enlisted, baptism was required for the warriors in the cause. Some of them, however, kept their sword hand out of the water, reserving for their own will how they would wield their weapon.

For some of us, the will was left out of the water of our commitment to Christ. Or perhaps it was our presuppositions or our prejudices or our determined course for life, career, or future.

We are like the young man who was confused about the direction of his life. He went into a church sanctuary alone to find God's perfect will for his life. He knelt down, took a piece of paper, wrote down all the promises that he was going to do for God, and signed it. He sat back then and waited for God to tell him his perfect will, but no response came. Then after hours of waiting, the Lord spoke in his inner heart. "You are going about it all wrong. I don't want a consecration like that. Tear up what you've written." The young man reluctantly followed instructions. Then the voice of the Lord whispered, "Son, I want you to take a blank piece of paper, sign your name at the bottom, and let me fill it in." Years later, after years of missionary service, the man confessed, "It was just a secret between God and me, as I signed the page. And God has been filling it in for the past twenty-six years."[1]

This moving account makes us wonder what we have written on our page, expecting God to bless it. We will not know the joy of God's unfolding, perfect will until we sign the blank sheet, leaving the results up to him. The signature is itself God's perfect will that we should depend totally on him.

Once we have expressed our ultimate purpose of knowing and following Christ, he never leaves us in a quandary. Living out the perfect will of God is not like flying on automatic pilot where you turn on the flight pattern and forget about it. Rather, it is a sensitive relationship in which the Lord uses everything in us to communicate the implications of specific guidance. He helps us to think with him, feel what is maximum, and will what he wants.

There are four aids to discerning God's will which we can use to sharpen our perception. The Bible is basic. It is the magnificent account of how the Lord guides. It give us the irreducible maximum of the Ten Commandments and the message of the Master. He will not guide us to contradict what he has said. Daily reading of the Scriptures has a releasing residual effect. Day by day, the verities of the Lord's plan, purpose, and providence are kneaded into our thought patterns through thoughtful study of Scripture. So much that would be open to question for others, is already there in our minds to provide clear thinking about God's will.

Consistent prayer, coupled with the Bible reading, enables us to spread out before the Lord the choices and decisions before us. We can give him lead time to work in our minds, emotions, and wills if we commit forthcoming decisions to him and allow him to give us the wisdom we will need to make the best choice. But most importantly, as we commune with God in the dialogue of prayer, we will find that our values, goals, desires, and hopes will be inadvertently reshaped around his. Many of the things others fret over, will be immediately clear to us. Others will be clarified by prolonged "abiding" until we are sure. The only bad decisions I have made were those I made precipitously without prayer. Any decision which is weighty is worthy of waiting!

Recently, I was asked to become a member of a board of reference for a very controversial program. At first, it seemed to be right, and I responded affirmatively without praying about it. Later that day I felt uneasy. In my prayer time I confessed my hasty decision and asked the Lord to either confirm it with a sense of peace or use whatever means at his disposal to show me I'd made a wrong choice. The days that followed provided no peace. While reading the Bible, I came across a basic principle that showed me that however right the cause seemed, I would be contradicting an essential biblical truth of how to deal with controversy. I wrote a letter and reversed my hasty decision.

Another way the Lord guides us is with trusted friends. These must be people who have no ax to grind or preset agendas for us to be fulfilled. I find it's best to select people who have nothing either to gain or lose by the decision or choice we are facing. For example, years ago when I had to make a decision on a call to move to a different church, I went to each of the twelve lay Elders of the session of the church I was serving. Eleven of them definitely felt it was not God's will for me to go. One said he believed it was the call of God. It just so happened that the eleven were very positive about my leadership and the one was negative! We laugh at that, but it points up the need to go to people who are not intertwined in the outcome of the guidance. The Lord will use them to give insight and make suggestions. And yet, the final decision will be alone with him.

There is a further aspect of knowing and doing God's will that we must grapple with. What if we make what seems to turn out to have been a wrong choice? Relax! The Lord is able to use even our wrong choices. We do not need to question in the dark what seemed to be right in the light. Our lives are interwoven with others and the greater movement of God's purpose. Just because a seemingly guided decision causes conflict or turmoil does not mean it is wrong. And all of our decisions won't necessarily get us a cheering section among our family or friends. Tranquility within us, not around us, is the assurance of God's approbation.

Having said that, we all can look back on what time has proven to be a bad decision that had more rebellion than relinquishment in it. We acted out of selfishness, pride, or prejudice. God could not bless; his permissive will allowed it. But that did not end the matter. We must live with the mess we've made. And yet, the moment we confess it and ask for God's help, he weaves it into his ultimate plan for us. God uses what he has allowed to work for what he intended.

Now we must press on to consider the things which happen to us because of others who are stretching out the long rope of God's permissive will. What do we say about the tragedy or misery caused by those who are not in God's perfect will? And what about the circumstances we did nothing to cause?

Leslie Weatherhead worked out a helpful delineation. He talks about God's intentional, circumstantial, and ultimate will. For those who have experienced the assurance of being in God's perfect will, all three are crucial. We can trust what God intends, believe that he will use whatever happens, and know that his ultimate will cannot be dissuaded. What a profound assurance!

From within the context of God's perfect will we can dare to live with confidence. He will never guide anything which will destroy that relationship for which we were born, now and for eternity. In that context we can ask about the alternate possibilities:

1. Is it an expression of our relationship with the Lord?
2. Will it bring us into deeper union with him?
3. Does it express to others what God has been to us?
4. Will it extend the kingdom of God in and around us?
5. Is it in keeping with the long range goals which have been discovered in prolonged meditation?
6. Do we want to do it with a "converted wanter?"
7. Is it consistent with the Ten Commandments and message of the Master?
8. Try it on in our imagination. Follow through to what our life would be if we did it.
9. Have we relinquished it in total surrender to our Lord?
10. Do we have inner peace?

The final point I want to make is that the quest for the will of the Lord is a sure sign that we belong to him. He has called us and made us his own. Our longing to know his will is because he is about to press us out into a new stage of his strategy. He never creates a desire for something he's not more ready to give than we are to ask.

We began this chapter telling about the danger of rhetorical questions. But now I want to ask one which I want you to answer for yourself. The Master wants your response. Have you accomplished the reason for which you were born? If not, why not? If not now, when?

We often use the expression "It's all down hill from here." In a way, that's the motto of a person who has experienced the purpose of being in God's perfect will. All

our choices and decisions are easy after the ultimate choice
to be his person. And now not even our wrong choices can
separate us from him.

> I've found a friend, Oh, such a friend!
> He loved me ere I knew Him;
> He drew me with the cords of love,
> And thus He bound me to Him.
> And 'round my heart still closely twine
> Those ties which naught can sever,
> For I am His, and He is mine
> Forever and forever.

5

How Can God Know
and Care about Me?

THE WOMAN SEATED NEXT to me on a cross-country flight was avidly devouring the most recent horoscope magazine. I noticed that she smiled with relished satisfaction and giggled to herself with glee as she digested what was apparently good news in the section for Virgos. Then she leaned back in her seat obviously picturing in her imagination what the constellation of the stars assured her would be good fortune for the next thirty days. Since I was born in September, we struck up a conversation over what she was smiling about with such delight.

"Do you really believe your destiny is predetermined by the stars?" I asked. She nodded enthusiastically and replied, "With everything so uncertain these days, it's a real comfort to know what I can expect." She went on to tell me that it was so very helpful to know the propitious things to anticipate and the problems to avoid.

"What if I were to say that I could tell you what could be the final destiny of your life and then interpret the meaning of everything that happens to you in the light of that. Would you be interested?" I offered intently. She turned in her seat with a mixture of wonder and caution on her face. "That's quite an offer. Who are you, anyway? Some kind of fortune teller?" she asked with interest. When I told her I was a Presbyterian clergyman, her retort was incongruously humorous. "Then I suppose you believe in that ghastly doctrine of predestination!"

Amazing. Here was a person studying the stars to find out what was going to happen and gainsaying her misguided prejudice about a belief that God has a plan for bringing good out of all that happens. Her idea of predestination was little less than fatalism and yet she faithfully followed her fetish over what she read from the stars. But she was obviously intrigued by my offer to prophesy her destiny and interpret the meaning of the events of her life. What resulted was an intense conversation about God, his plan for our lives, and our destiny which is predetermined if we will dare to accept it.

The woman's questions about predestination were not unlike hundreds which were submitted when I asked people across the nation to write me their most urgent questions. "We don't still believe in predestination, do we?" many asked. "How can we reconcile predestination and free will?" some queried. "What about double predestination—could a God of love create some to be blessed and some to be damned?" others demanded. "How is predestination different than fatalism?" still others wanted to know. The most incisive group simply asked, "How can I be sure I am chosen among the elect?"

As I contemplated an answer to these questions, I was also working on another group which asked the age-old riddle, "How can God know or care about me with all the billions of people on earth?" It suddenly struck me that both groups had the same concern. We all want to know if God knows or cares. Does he have an individualized plan for us? The answer to the first group of questions about predestination really is the only satisfying answer to the second group. In this chapter, I want to attempt an answer to both.

Before any intellectually sound, biblically rooted understanding of predestination can be allowed to grow, we must first cultivate our minds with some clear thinking, pull out the weeds of truculent perceptions of predestination, and fertilize with what the Bible really says. The same offer I made to the "horoscoptically" confused woman on the plane is what I want to offer you. I can tell you with assurance what your destiny can be and interpret what's happening and will happen to you throughout your lifetime. Interested? Read on!

My offer is essentially the same as Paul made to the Christians at Rome. They, too, wanted assurance that God knew and cared about them in their struggles, frustrations, and difficulties. In response, the Apostle lyrically penned one of the most magnificent descriptions in Scripture of the essence of predestination. Romans 8:28–30 vividly and awesomely describes God's purpose, plan, and promise for each of us. "And we know that all things work together for good to those who love God, to those who are the called according to His purpose. For whom He foreknew, He also predestined to be conformed to the image of His Son, that He might be the firstborn among many brethren. Moreover whom He predestined, these He also called; whom He called these He also justified; and whom He justified, these He also glorified."

This passage gives us the five golden links of the chain which hold us with final assurance. Predestination is one of these, but its linkage to the rest demands an exposition in context. I want to explain what I think this powerful passage means to us and then the weeds of misconceptions about predestination will wilt in the presence of its "weed and feed" potency in the soil of our minds.

The other day a lawyer called me asking if I knew the whereabouts of a man whom I had known in a church I had served in the East. I had not seen him for years and had lost track of him completely. "You're not the only one," said the lawyer. "I've been searching for him for weeks. I'm the lawyer for his late father's estate, and I want to tell him about his inheritance. He's now a very wealthy man, and I must find him to read the will. If you can locate him, tell him to call me immediately. I've got good news for him."

When I finally found the man, he was living alone, eking out a meager existence. Astonished by the news of his inheritance, he explained that there had been a broken relationship with his father which he admitted was his own fault. He had returned for the funeral and then slipped back into his recluse anonymity, not knowing how much his father cared for him and had left him.

I think of that experience every time I contemplate the meaning of predestination. It's like a last will and testament from our Heavenly Father. Explaining its true meaning is like a lawyer sharing the good news of an unexpected inheritance to people living as paupers because they did not know what had been left to them. Listen! Your name and mine are among the blessed beneficiaries.

Predestination is no doctrine of fatalism. It does not teach that our lives are controlled by some nameless fate. Nor is it the belief that God has chosen some to be saved and others to be lost. And it's not the exclusive conviction of Calvinists or Presbyterians. Rather, it is the announcement of the sovereignty of God. It positively states that our salvation is God's gift. It is not by chance that we long to find him, that we learn of his love, that faith springs up in our hearts, and that we claim our inheritance. We have not earned it, deserved it, or become qualified for it. By grace alone, we belong to God. It is in that assurance that we listen to the reading of the will. And the central focus of it all is that God has elected to be our God. He has a purpose for each of us. That's the preamble to any consideration of what Paul means in our exciting text.

Savor the nourishment of Paul's assurance of our purpose. We are to be conformed to the image of Christ. The Greek word for conformed is *summorphous,* meaning to bring to the same form or to form like. We are in the process of being formed into the image, *eikōn,* exact manifestation, of Christ. God not only knows and cares about us, but his purpose is to make us like Christ. That's the fulcrum truth around which this whole passage revolves. Each of the golden links of foreordination, predestination, calling, justification, and glorification become the fetter of freedom which bonds us to this liberating purpose for our lives.

Irenaeus said, "Jesus Christ, in his infinite love, became what we are, in order that he might make us who he wholly is." And Athanasius said, "He became what we are that he might make us what he is."

Ponder that with me! Allow your mind to picture the person you were meant to be—filled with Christ, reformed around the character of Christ, guided by the mind of Christ, illuminating the radiance of Christ, and exuding the power of Christ. Do you believe it? The promise is, "We shall be like Him, for we shall see Him as He is" (1 John 3:2). Like Jesus Christ, imagine that! Is it a foolish dream? Can we dare to believe that nothing less is God's plan and purpose... not just someday, but now? The Christian life is the evolving process whereby we grow to be more and more like Christ daily. This is the distilled essence of what the New Testament means by predestination. By the sovereign choice of God we have been singled out to be conformed—mind, soul, and body—into the exact likeness of Christ. Predestination is the exercise of the will of God by which his purpose before determined by him is brought to pass.

Now we can understand the progression of Paul's thought in these three salient verses. Verse 28 is a frequently quoted, but little understood, favorite verse of many. "And we know that all things work together for good to those who love God, to those who are the called according to His purpose." The rendering in the old King James and now in the New King James misses the mark of the original Greek in the strongest of the ancient manuscripts. Even Dwight L. Moody took to task the King James translation of this verse. He said it was more Stoic pantheism than radical monotheism in which God is in charge of all things. God is the subject of "work together" in the original manuscript. Both Westcot and Hort's as well as Nestle's Greek New Testaments use *God* in brackets to recognize this. Thus the verse should read, "And we know that God keeps on working everything together for good for those who love God, who are called according to his purpose." The word for know is *oìdamen,* to know with certainty, with no reservations. What we know becomes all the more exciting when "everything" or "all things" is understood in its original meaning of "every single part of the whole." Now we can affirm the sweeping truth with this annotated insight. "For we know with absolute certainty that God keeps on working every single part of the whole together for good for those who love God, to those called according to his purpose."

What this means for us is that everything, every single part of the whole of our experience is used by God to accomplish his purpose of conforming us to the image of Jesus Christ. G. Campbell Morgan said it directly, "The good toward which all things work together is that we are conformed to the image of Christ."

When we know where we are going, getting there becomes part of the adventure. God will not allow anything to happen to us which cannot be used in molding our character into Christlikeness. When I contemplate that truth, pressures, problems, and difficult people fade into perspective. I can take anything if I know it will accomplish this incredibly wondrous purpose.

Now we are ready to consider the steps by which the likeness to Christ is accomplished. God's foreknowledge is first. "For whom He foreknew." Foreknowledge, *proginōskō,* is to know beforehand. This affirms that God knows us before we know him, seeks us before we seek him, selects us to be his people before we decide to believe. Stated simply, it means that God himself chooses to be our God.

Because God is sublimely omniscient, he knows the future as well as the past. He had us in mind before the foundation of the world.

This puts everything into the perspective of praise, not pride. We did not find God, he sought us out. An authentic experience of God's invasion in our lives always admits that he was the initiator. God's foreknowledge is his love. He created each of us out of love, for love, and blesses us because of love. Everything else flows from the headwaters of that initial truth. And why? Simply because God is love and wants us to experience the fullness of being like Christ. Let the startling truth sink in: God knew about you before he put the stars in their place and came in Christ for you so that you could be all that he had in mind.

The second golden link in Paul's progression of thought is predestination. Now we can consider what it means in all its vital power. "Those whom He foreknew He predestined." The verb means to set a boundary or a limit beforehand. The Greek verb is *proōrisen,* a combination of *pro,* "beforehand," and *horizo. Horizo* is the word from which horizon comes. It means the boundary or limit of our vision. When applied to God, "forehorizoned" means the self-imposed limit or extent of his vision for the world. God has no other plan for creation other than what he has revealed in Jesus Christ. And that's more than we can fathom.

What we do know is that he has elected us to be conformed into the image of his Son. This is expressed in Paul's doxological statement in Ephesians 1:3–6. "Blessed be the God and Father of our Lord Jesus Christ, who has blessed us with every spiritual blessing in the heavenly places in Christ, just as He has chosen us in Him before the foundation of the world, that we should be holy and without blame before Him *in love,* having predestined us to adoption as sons [and daughters] by Jesus Christ to Himself, according to the good pleasure of His will, to the praise of the glory of His grace, by which He has made us accepted in the Beloved." You and I are the focus of the horizon for God. Before the foundation of the world God elected to save the world through his Son and established the plan of salvation through his message, life, death, and resurrection. He "horizoned" you and me to be part of his redeemed people.

Does God know and care?! Indeed. "In love" is the lever which springs open the whole meaning of predestination. And "in Christ" is the boundary of God's horizon. He has known us, hedged us about, yearned over us, impinged on our consciousness, elected us to hear and respond to the gospel of his love in Christ.

What God has decided about us is communicated in the next golden link. "Moreover whom He predestined, those He also called" (Rom. 8:30). God communicated his election to us so that we could know how special we are to him. Again no achievement or accomplishment on our part motivated the call. Ask Peter and Andrew, or tax collector Levi or Nicodemus, or persecutor Saul, or defecting Mark, or any of the heroes of the faith through the ages, and their response would be, "I am lost in wonder and praise—he called me when I was least worthy. But call he did, and I know that even my will to respond was a gift!"

That puts us into the thick of things. God calls, but we must respond. Our belief in God's foreknowledge, which leads to our election and issues in a call, does not deny that we have free will. We can say "No!" and join the chorus of those who have refused the offer of God's love through history. We can adopt the rich young ruler as our patron and turn away because our perception of the cost blocks our deeper longing to follow our call. God's election is limited only by our unwillingness to share his love and by the arrogant self-sufficiency of those who harden their hearts when the call is sounded.

I have ached over too many people who have said "No," to deny the power of free will. I remember a man who was dying. Though he had been raised in the church, he had rebelled against Christianity because of religious people (lame excuse!). I talked to him about the fact that he was missing God's love while nursing those hurts from loveless Christians. The power of his strong will kept him locked in the prison of his own making. I pleaded with him that day as life oozed from his body. "Thanks, but no thanks!" were his dying words. Was that because he was not among the elect? No, it was because he elected not to accept God's election.

Predestination does not deny free will. It affirms it. God calls; we must answer. We must want what God wants to give us. He is ready to work with a mustard seed of willingness. As someone put it, "The elect are whomsoever will and the non-elect are whomsoever won't."

When we do respond to God's call and accept the gift of his love, we are ready to experience the next golden link toward the accomplishment of our purpose. "Whom He called, He also justified." The word means righteous or righteousness. God came in Jesus Christ to make us right with himself. Our sin had excavated a yawning gap which we could not bridge by effort or self-righteousness. God placed the cross over that canyon of hopeless self-centeredness and came to us with undeserved, forgiving love. Man's resistence to predestined election had to be dealt with so God's purposes in history could be accomplished. On the cross, Jesus suffered for our sins so that we could be made justified, righteous with God. It means that through Christ's death we were made totally guiltless, acquitted completely.

The experience of being called is followed by the assurance of love and forgiveness. It is then, melted by love, that we respond by faith. That too is a gift as we shall see more completely in the next chapter. For now, it is sufficient to say that the offer of God's love in Christ is coupled with the capacity to respond by faith. Augustine said, "God so works out all things, that he works also in us the very willingness by which we believe." And Calvin, following his lead, says, "Election is the cause and keeping of all faith . . . election is in order before faith." Both men were firmly rooted in the Apostle Paul's conviction that "the just shall live by faith" (Rom. 1:17). When we accept what has been done for us, trust our lives to God's love and forgiveness, and surrender our wills to do his will, we have appropriated the justification established for us. In reality, we claim what is already true, finished, completed. We claim what is ours already when we utilize the gift of faith God infuses into us. He's the author of it all! What he demands, He deploys in us.

We have come full circle, with one last golden link. "And whom He justified, these He also glorified." Glorification is what we talked about earlier. It is being conformed to the image of Christ. The aorist active indicative tense is used by Paul in all five stages. It implies an action already completed, consummated, though still to be fully realized; a finished action which is a foretaste; or as some have called it, the "prophetic past." So certain is God's foreknowledge, predestination of us, calling for us, justification of us, and glorification of our character that it is spoken of as an established fact. A fulfilled, yet still to be grasped fully by us, settled matter in the heart of God. I find that terribly exciting!

Consider what it means to be glorified—now, as well as when we reach heaven's experience of being totally like Christ and seeing him as he is. For me, it means that we are the focus of God's attention, grace, affirmation, and persistent maximizing of our lives. We are programmed for growth. No one of us need remain as he or she is. The Christian life is growth in the glory God has given to us which is ever evolving. The glory of God is a person fully alive, living to full potential.

When we think about the wonder of our glorification, we are sent back to consider God's inherent glory. Glorification is God's nature, focused in Christ, entrusted to us. Our glorification is God making us like his Son, the purpose of our life as we explained earlier. In the Old Testament, glory was the term used to express that which people apprehended of the presence of God in their lives. It was God in manifestation. Moses pleaded to God, "Show me your glory!" Ezekiel uses the term to describe the brilliance of the appearance of God. When he saw the *kabod* of God, he was encountered by the person of God himself. *Kabod,* the Hebrew word for glory meant weight, wealth, and substance. A person of *kabod* demanded and compelled respect and honor because of his wealth and dignity. Thus, the awesome power, light, and holiness of God is designated as his glory.

In Christ, the glory of God lived among us. John catches the awesomeness of the incarnation. "And the Word became flesh and dwelt among us, and we beheld His glory, the glory as of the only begotten of the Father, full of grace and truth" (John 1:14). Paul tops that with further praise that the glory of God is Christ, and he shines in our hearts (2 Cor. 4:6). The miracles of Christ manifested his glory. His message imparted the glory of the mind of God for us to apprehend. Christ spoke of his death and resurrection as his glorification.

All of this is recapitulated in our glorification. We are predestined, elected, chosen, and called to die to ourselves and be raised up to a new life in which we are filled with the presence of Christ, God's glory in us. Therefore, he works all things together for our good which is growth in glory. When we glorify God by accepting his love and incredible affirmation, he uses all that we go through to make us sons and daughters, diminutive Christs, to use Luther's audacious description of our destiny.

Now we are ready to clear the ground of the wilted weeds of misconceptions about predestination in the light of this biblical clarity.

First of all, it is not a harsh belief that God created some to be blessed and others to be rejected. This is to deny both the gracious nature of God and the gift of free will. God wants all men and women to know him and respond to his loving call.

Second, the elect, those who hear and respond to God's call, are enlisted not to privilege but to responsibility. An authentic sign that we have accepted our predestined status is that we are convicted by the challenge to share with others what has happened to us. When Paul speaks of Christ as the "first born of many brethren," he is speaking with missionary and evangelistic zeal. The Christians at Rome to whom he wrote about their predestined calling were to be reproducers of what God had done in them. My experience is that those who are lost in "wonder, love, and praise" over their election become truly evangelical in their passion to communicate God's love to others.

Third, predestination fosters true humility. That God has chosen to be our God, that his foreknowledge, predestinating, calling, justifying, and glorification has begun the process of developing our family likeness to Christ, and that our eternal destiny is graciously set—produces a quiet assurance. We look back over our experience of God's love and forgiveness and know that, though unworthy, we belong to him. Our task is not to decide who are among the called, but to spend our lives in thanksgiving.

What more needs to be said? Nothing, other than to question whether we are enjoying who we are because God has chosen to be our God. Have we accepted his acceptance? Are we living courageously in our assurance? Are we relishing the sublime delight of being conformed in the image of Christ? If so, we can say with Paul, "But we all, with unveiled face, beholding as in a mirror the glory of the Lord, are being transformed into the same image from glory to glory, just as from the Lord, the Spirit . . . For God, who said, 'Light shall shine out of darkness,' is the One who has shone in our hearts to give the light of the knowledge of the glory of God in the face of Christ. But we have this treasure in earthen vessels, that the surpassing

greatness of the power may be of God and not from ourselves" (2 Cor. 3:18, 4:6-7, NAS).

Then, can you go on to say that you can live with the
liberating perspective of God's predestined purpose in all
that happens to you? Can you dare to believe that the
painful and the difficult will be used by God, working
them together for the good of our glorification in Christ's
image? Believing that, Paul could say in 2 Corinthians
4:8-10, "We are afflicted in every way, but not crushed;
perplexed, but not despairing; persecuted but not forsa-
ken; struck down, but not destroyed; always carrying
about in the body the dying of Jesus, that the life of Jesus
also may be manifested in our body." The result of predestination is courage. Nothing can happen to us which will
not be woven into God's strategy to bring us to "the fulness
of the stature of Christ."

All that I've tried to say about God's predestined plan
came thundering home to me recently when I read Dr.
Robert Rainy's closing words in a communion meditation
generations ago. The great Scottish divine leaned across
the communion table and flung out the challenge, "Do you
believe your faith? Do you believe this I am telling you? Do
you believe a day is coming, really coming, when you will
stand before the throne of God, and the angels will
whisper together and say, 'Oh, how like Christ he is'?" I
put the book down, so moved I cried. "That's it!" I
exclaimed. That surely is the purpose and power of our
predestination.

But then I heard a whisper. "You don't have to wait . . .
heaven has begun. How like Christ you are becoming!" Do
you, too, hear the angels' whisper?

6

Why Are My Prayers Unanswered?

THE OTHER DAY I saw a fascinating sign in the window of one of those speedy printing establishments which promises to reproduce anything while you wait. The sign said, "Quick printing service for those who want everything yesterday!"

I was impelled by curiosity to go inside to ask the owner about the sign. His response was a classic: "We cater to people who put off until the day after tomorrow what they should do today and then when they want something, they want it yesterday!"

That could also be a description of the way many of us deal with the problem of seemingly unanswered prayer. Some of us put off talking to God on a consistent, daily basis. Then a crisis strikes or an important decision must be made. We tell God our need and want an instant response, answer, action, intervention, or miracle. And we want it yesterday.

But there are also others of us who have experienced what seems to be unanswered prayer even though we have kept up a consistent prayer life. We, too, become impatient when we have asked God repeatedly about a problem or need and are forced to wait for an answer. Waiting becomes excruciating.

In our survey some of the frequently asked questions
dealt with prayer—and unanswered prayer in particular.
Why are some prayers unanswered? Why does God answer some prayers and others take so long? How do I
accept the "no's" of life as God's timing? When will the
problem I've prayed about be taken care of? Do all prayers
get answered? How can I "see" the answer? How do you
know when God is talking to you? The questions seemed
endless. There were hundreds more of which these are
representative. Unanswered prayer is still one of the most
profound problems we all face at one time or another in
our lives. For some, it's a consistent concern.

Waiting is not easy for any of us. Impatience is a persistent problem. But waiting for the Lord to answer our
prayers is the most difficult of all. We begin to feel rejected, let-down, unloved. We pray for guidance, healing,
a resolution of misunderstanding in a relationship, direction for a decision which we must make, the fulfillment of
a deep longing. Then the days drag by. No apparent answer seems to come. What is God up to? Doesn't he know
how urgently we need his help? And then, to complicate
things further, some prayers seem to be answered quickly
and others seem to be unheeded by the Almighty.

We are not alone. The apostle Paul, whose life was
punctuated by spectacular examples of answered prayer,
endured the painful experience of what seemed to be unanswered prayer. In 2 Corinthians 12:7–10, he describes
the perplexing dilemma he endured when he prayed that
a "thorn in the flesh" be removed from his life. He pleaded
with the Lord that it might depart. The prayer was not
answered in the way Paul proposed. The nature of the
"thorn" is not explicitly revealed or divulged by Paul.
Good thing. We all have some thorn in the flesh and therefore all who are afflicted in some way can find comfort and
courage in what Paul discovered.

The word for thorn in Greek is *skolops*. It is used for a
stake, splinter, or thorn. Whatever the imagery, Paul suf-

fered a physical malady which caused excruciating pain. Expositors have variously suggested eye trouble, malaria, epilepsy, insomnia, and migraine headaches. There are good cross-references to support a case for any of these. Paul is not specific. That enables all of us to share in his pain and his discovery. The apostle is as wise in his reservations as he is in his revelations when it comes to personal exposure. All of us can empathize with what he endured by giving the thorn our own personal identification.

Our thorn can be whatever is painful or difficult physically, spiritually or relationally. It is something we've asked to be healed or removed, yet have been forced to wait with no apparent answer to our prayers. For some of us it is a bodily limitation or sickness; for others, a broken relationship; for still others, some unsatisfied dream for our lives.

Whatever it is, identify it for yourself and keep it in the forefront of your mind as we reflect on what happened to Paul. His thorn is a metaphor for anything which causes us sorrow. An infected splinter may be as painful as a stake driven through a limb. What troubles us may seem small and inconsequential to someone else. But to us it is a stake of limitation. Whatever it is, this much must be said: it is ours and why the Lord does not take it away is our personal dilemma.

Note the progression as the apostle deals with the perplexity of his thorn. First there is the instinctive desire to pray, asking the Lord to intervene. Then he experiences the Lord's strength to endure. Finally, there is the peace of abiding, a sublime acquiescense which is in itself a greater answer to prayer than Paul anticipated.

The thorns of life drive us to prayer. Paul relates, "For this thing I pleaded with the Lord three times that it might depart from me." We wonder if "three times" is a Hebraism for many times. That would be true for most of us. We have prayed repeatedly about pain or perplexity wondering if the Lord has heard. But all too often our prayer seems to be a one-way monologue. We don't wait long

enough in quiet for it to be a dialogue. It is as if we made a
telephone call to place an order or ask for instructions and
then hung up before the other person had a chance to
speak. "Hello, Lord, this is what I need. Good-by!"

Not so with Paul. He waited. And listened. What the
Lord said to him has more residual power than the re-
moval of the thorn. Listen! Have you ever heard the Lord
say this to you? "And He said to me, 'My grace is sufficient
for you, for my strength is made perfect in weakness.'"

Did Christ answer his prayer or not? Yes and no. Both.
No, He did not give Paul what he asked for. Instead, he
gave him an infinitely greater gift and assurance. As we
look at the propitious promise in its parts we begin to
appreciate its full impact for us.

"He said." Who? The living Christ! The purpose of
prayer is to persist until we have made a dynamic contact
with the Lord of all life. Christ will not quickly answer if in
the answer we are not drawn closer to him.

"He said *to me*." Prayer is profoundly personal. It is
meant to penetrate into the deepest levels of our inner
hearts. We come to Christ with our requests; He begins a
renovation of our total life. When I go to my internist with
one ailment, he usually wants to give me a total check-up.
He is concerned about my total health and well-being. He
is not quick to give nifty nostrums which merely band-aid
what might be a deeper problem. Since I often use busyness as an excuse for neglecting regular examinations, he
usually responds to my request for a prescription with,
"Why don't you come to my office and let me take a good
look at you?"

Our Lord is no less thorough when we come to him
asking for a speedy answer to some need. He wants to talk
to us about who we are, really, and where we are going
with the precious gift of life. No prayer is unanswered if as
a result of lingering in his presence we can say, "He said to
me. . . ."

And what does he say? "My grace." Pause to savor that!

Grace is his unmerited, unchanging, unqualified love. With that we have everything; without it, whatever else we might receive is empty. We need fresh grace each day. Prayer is the dynamic dialogue in which we spread out our needs and receive healing love and liberating forgiveness. Conversation with the Lord enlarges our hearts until we are able to receive his Spirit.

He alone is sufficient. "My grace is sufficient for you." The word sufficient is *arkei* in Greek. It means that the supply is in exact proportion to the need—never too much, never too little, never early, never late. Christ knows our deepest needs. There are times he answers our prayers by not granting our requests. Dr. James Denny said, "A refusal is an answer if it is so given that God and the soul understand one another." But also, a delay in answering our prayers brings us to the realization that our greatest longing is for the Lord himself. Any quick provision which makes us less dependent on consistent fellowship with the Provider is no answer at all!

And now consider the secret which only the school of what seems to be unanswered prayer can teach. "My strength is made perfect in weakness." Don't forget the meaning of "perfect" in the Greek: end, purpose, intended goal. Christ's strength achieves its purpose in our weakness. The purpose of prayer is not just to make the best of things, but to allow the Lord to use them to make the best of us. Trials and problems give us a grand chance to discover the adequacy of Christ's strength in our weakness.

Often, we want Christ's strength to do *our* will. He waits and puts us through the experience of what we think is unanswered prayer until, more than anything else, we want his strength to do his will. He allows our weakness so that our total dependence is on him and not on our adequacy. Our subtle sin is to decide what's best for ourselves, ask for strength to accomplish it, and then when we've pulled it off, to forget who made it possible. Christ pulls the rug out from under that kind of pride. For a time our prayers seem empty and ineffective. And finally, in confessing our arrogance, we are forced back to his purpose for us and an abundant supply of strength to accomplish it.

That's what happened to Paul. His response to Christ's answer to what he foolishly thought was unanswered prayer is an expression of profound trust. "Therefore, most gladly, I will rather boast in my infirmities, that the power of Christ may rest upon me. . . . For when I am weak, then I am strong" (verses 9,10).

A creative sense of weakness is not only facing infirmities, but daring impossibilities. I am convinced that we should be constantly out on the edge of attempting things which we could never accomplish without Christ's power. We attempt far too little and venture with far too much caution. Christ did not remove Paul's thorn, but he made him "more than a conqueror" in preaching the gospel, suffering persecution, enduring imprisonment, and withstanding hardship. By withholding an answer about the thorn, Christ hammered out a mighty apostle capable of surviving thorny circumstances. His "no" to one thing made possible an obedient man who could appropriate his "yes."

Paul's prayer was answered! The power of Christ rested upon him in a new way from that time forward. The word for rest in the original Greek meant "to fix a tent upon." This is a bold metaphor. The glory of Christ overshadowed Paul. The Lord's promise "to abide in Me and I in you" (John 15:4) was fulfilled. Paul's prayers, for a time seemingly unanswered, were answered by the best of all responses. Christ "abided" in him and he in Christ. No prayer can be considered an unanswered prayer if it denies what we want in order to give us what we need. And our greatest need is to abide.

Remember the old spelling bees? They were a source of both pride and panic when I was a boy in grade school. I can remember the teacher lining us all up in front of the classroom. She would give each of us a word to spell. If we spelled it correctly, we remained standing; if not, we were sent to our seats. It really motivated me to learn my spelling lessons! My keen sense of competition made me desire never to be the first to be sent to my seat. And it was always my hope to be the last person standing. The teacher usually started with little words and worked up to more difficult, complicated ones.

Strange how we remember events in our childhood. I'll never forget the embarrassment I felt one day in third grade when I missed a little word in one of those spell-downs. You could have fried an egg on my red-hot, burning, and embarrassed face. The word given to me to spell was prayer. I sounded it out phonetically in my mind and then spelled it "p-r-e-y-e-r." I did not know then what I know now: that prayer for many is preying on God, a kind of attack, a storming of the gates of heaven for what we want, when we want it, and for our comfort or convenience. It makes all the difference whether our communication with God is spelled with an "a" or an "e."

If I were asked to spell prayer today, I would be sent to my seat again. Little matter. My spelling of it would expose the essence of what Jesus taught us about how to pray effectively and my deepest discoveries about powerful praying.

Prayer is spelled "a-b-i-d-e!" The secret of dynamic, effective prayer is learning to abide. Abiding in Christ and inviting him to abide in us is the sublime purpose and power of prayer. The word abide means to dwell, inhabit, live in, lodge, or rest. When we abide in Christ, we become recipients of all that he has done for us in his cross and resurrection. His abiding in us gives us his indwelling power. No prayer is unanswered if as a result we abide in Christ and Christ in us.

There is a great promise which Christ makes us if we abide. At first it seems to contradict what we've said about unanswered prayer. "If you abide in Me, and My words abide in you, you shall ask what you desire, and it shall be done for you" (John 15:7). The point is that abiding gives us clarity about what to ask. Our desires are transformed in keeping with what is best for us at a particular time. An unanswered prayer presses us to abide until we can ask in confidence.

Christ is for us! He will reorder our priorities, give us strength to endure what he chooses not to change, and courage to ask for what he desires to change. Both what he leaves unchanged and what he changes is perfectly planned for our growth in his grace.

Allow me to draw this into sharp focus with some personal convictions I learned from what seemed to be unanswered prayer.

First of all, I am convinced that Christ knows what is best for me. I have been brought back to that assurance repeatedly. There is no peace until I surrender my circumstances knowing that he will grant me only what will be ultimately good for me. There's so much that I can't see and don't know. Unanswered prayer is really an answer. What I ask for may not have been sufficiently perfected through prolonged abiding. Either the time is not right, or what I've asked for may not be maximum in his plans for me.

Second, I have learned a great deal during the waiting periods. Most important of all, I have found that Christ, not just his answers, is sufficient. Waiting prepares me for what he has prepared and guides me to ask wisely. What is delayed is developed. My prayers are perfected. Relaxing in his presence refines the requests. John Baillie said, "If I thought that God were going to grant me all my prayers simply for the asking, without even passing them under His own gracious review, without even bringing to bear upon them His own greater wisdom, I think there would be very few prayers that I would dare to pray."

Third, I am thankful that the Lord has not answered

many of my prayers! As I look back over the years, and contemplate what might have happened if some of them had been answered when and the way I wanted, I am alarmed. I agree with Longfellow: "What discord should we bring into the universe if our prayers were all answered! Then we should govern the world and not God. And do we think we should govern it better?... Thanksgiving with a full heart—and the rest silence and submission to the divine will!"

Fourth, what I thought was unanswered prayer had led me to discover the formula for creative prayer: ask once and thank the Lord a thousand times that if the prayer is in keeping with his will, it shall be done. I shared that thought with a friend whose prayers for one of his children seemed to go unanswered. When he prayed, fully surrendering the child's future, and released his worried concern with hourly prayers of thanksgiving, eventually the Lord was able to bless the child in ways that exceeded the man's wildest expectations.

And finally, some prayers seem to be unanswered because we ask the Lord to do for us what he's already guided *us* to do for ourselves. Continual asking becomes an evasion of action. Many prayers are unanswered because we have not acted on previously answered prayer. The Lord will not give us new guidance if we have refused to act on what he's told us to do. Often our prayer channel is blocked by disobedience or unwillingness to forgive or become involved in reconciliation. When we pray for people and are not ready to be part of the Lord's answer with costly caring, he waits until we are willing.

An unconfessed sin of the past or an unsurrendered plan for the future will debilitate our capacity to receive. We cannot expect the Lord's "Yes" to today's prayer if we've said "No!" to yesterday's answer. Augustine prayed a prayer that will always be answered: "O Lord, grant that I may do Thy will as if it were my will; so that Thou mightest do my will as if it were Thy will." The first part of that prayer makes possible the second. When we want the Lord's will, and do it when we know it, we will be less troubled with unanswered prayer. We'll be too busy dealing with the marching orders of answered prayer!

What I've tried to say in a variety of ways in this chapter is that there is no such thing as unanswered prayer. What seems to be a delay is a special gift to those of us who want everything yesterday. It gives us the wonderful opportunity to discover the greatest answer to prayer for today. We learn to abide in Christ. He is the answer to prayer. His strength is sufficient. Anything else he gives when the time is right will deepen our trust and heighten our praise. But anything without him is nothing at all!

I will never use the words, "unanswered prayer," again! How about you? Can you join me in a confident belief that all prayers are answered? Can we relinquish our furtive pressure on the Lord, relax and trust him? Are we ready to say that we will receive answers when two things are accomplished: the Lord's perfect timing and our willingness to obey what is implicit in an answer? So often unanswered prayer is simply the Lord preparing us for what he's made ready. We and other people can get in the way, but there will be an answer even for that. A part of the commitment to delete "unanswered prayer" from our language is the commitment to spend prolonged time in intelligent, purposeful, devoted contact with the Lord.

7

How Do I Get More Faith?

RECENTLY, A MAN CALLED to ask me to speak to a group of spiritual adventurers in his community. He explained that many in the group had been turned off by traditional religion and were searching for an authentic faith. Exposing his suspicion of clergymen he said, "We don't want you to preach—just give a witness of what faith means to you personally!"

I knew what he meant but couldn't resist the temptation to puncture his prejudice. "That's what real preaching is. . . ." I responded.

"Yah, I know, but that's not what it usually is. We want you to talk about what's real to you. What is your deepest experience of the reality of a growing faith?"

That hooked me and I said yes. It turned out to be one of the most exciting speaking engagements of my life. I think often of the man's final words as he introduced me to the group. "Dr. Ogilvie, we are ready and we hope you are too . . . tell us how faith really works in your life."

I was reminded of that as I read the hundreds of questions about faith that people submitted. Ninety percent of the questions in this category were prefaced by the phrase "from your own experience." It was as if people wanted to be sure that the biblical and literary objectivity I would utilize in an answer would be coupled with the subjective experience of my own pilgrimage. And so the questions went: "From your own experience, what is faith really?"; "From your personal discoveries, how can I find greater faith?"; "Out of your own life, tell me—how can faith be both something we are to have, to be right with God, and yet a gift from God?"; "As a result of your own walk with God and your counseling of people, why do some have more faith than others?" And here's one that summarizes them all. "Tell me your secret for getting more faith."

My response is a personal witness. I want to share one of the most exciting discoveries of my life. It's based on Scripture, enhanced by what I've learned from the writings of great men and women of the ages. It has passed through the fires of my own experience.

I'm always amazed at the way God deepens my understanding of a truth I'm about to write or preach by a fresh experience of the reality of that truth. In fact, when I finish the outline of my preaching for a year, or the chapter headings of a book, I know what will be the direction of my own spiritual pilgrimage. The Lord usually puts me through whatever is necessary to give a ring of reality to the communication of a conceptual truth from the new discoveries of my own experience.

Faith, for me, has two dynamic dimensions. We cannot have the second if we have not received the first, but to have the first without the second is to miss the adventure of true faith. My understanding of the New Testament is this: there is faith that saves and faith that sustains. Two passages have led me to this conviction.

In Romans 1:16–17 Paul states the purpose and power of his life. His personal witness to the Christians at Rome is, "For I am not ashamed of the gospel of Christ, for it is the power of God to salvation for everyone who believes, for the Jew first and also for the Greek. For in it the righteousness of God is revealed from faith to faith; as it is written, 'The just shall live by faith.'"

Focus on that phrase "from faith to faith." What did the apostle mean? From a study of the total sweep of his teaching, we understand that faith for Paul was a gift. In Ephesians 2:8-9 he says "For by grace you have been saved through faith and that not of yourselves; it is the gift of God, not of works, lest anyone should boast." Some have questioned whether it is grace or faith that is God's gift. I am convinced that he meant both.

Martin Luther said, "Faith is a living, daring confidence in God's grace. It is so sure and certain that a man could stake his life on it a thousand times." The Spirit of God works in our minds and hearts to make clear the grace of the death of Jesus Christ for our forgiveness and the reestablishment of a right relationship with God. He then engenders in us the hunger and thirst for rightness with him, based solely on what he has done for us on Calvary. Then, by the mysterious creation of desire, he gives us the gift of faith to trust our total selves to God's mercy and love. That's the faith which saves. What he desires from us, he inspires in us. Faith is the only basis of righteousness with God. Not works, self-effort or self-justification. Marcus Loane said, "We cannot force ourselves to have faith in God. We are as much in need in this regard as in everything else. Faith can only originate in the soul of man by the gift of God."

What then is the meaning of "from faith to faith"? I eagerly checked the scholars. Charles Hodge said that it is simply another way of saying "by faith alone." C. H. Dodd asserted that it means that righteousness is a matter of faith from start to finish. And Anders Nygren said that it means entirely by faith: "Just as 'death unto death' and 'life unto life' are intensive so faith unto faith may mean 'entirely by faith.'" I much prefer Calvin who said that "from faith to faith" means that we are to advance from one degree of faith to another.

Following that insight, look at 1 Corinthians 12. Paul explains the charismata, grace gifts, of the indwelling Holy

Spirit. He wanted the Corinthians to know all that the Spirit enables in the believers. In verse 3 he says that "no one can say that Jesus is Lord except by the Holy Spirit." Once again this has reference to saving faith produced in us by the Spirit. But then in listing the specific gifts given to justified believers, in verse 9 he lists faith as a special gift of the indwelling Spirit.

Now I think we are getting to the core of the meaning of "from faith to faith." The quality of faith which is one of the gifts of the Spirit is an advanced kind of faith which is a part of the birthright of every Christian. Some have said that Paul meant that different gifts of wisdom, knowledge, discernment, faith, working of miracles, and so on were given to particular people. I am convinced Paul meant that all gifts for all believers were available for the opportunities of ministry. Therefore, this advanced quality of faith is for everyone who is open to the Holy Spirit and costly challenges of service.

Evangelical scholar A. T. Robertson says that this faith is "not the faith of surrender, saving faith, but wonder working faith."[1] This means that those of us who have been given the capacity to trust the Lord unreservedly for our salvation are now afforded a special confidence to believe what he can and will do in our circumstances. Siegfried Grossmann, the German lay theologian, put it this way. "The gift of faith is not the saving faith every Christian has, but rather the special gift of mountain-moving faith ... both the irresistible knowledge of God's intervention at a certain point and the authority to effect this intervention through the power of the Holy Spirit."[2]

This same insight is underlined in the thought of Leslie B. Flynn in his excellent little book, *Nineteen Gifts of the Spirit.* Referring to faith in 1 Corinthians 12 he says, "The gift of faith is a Spirit-given ability to see something God wants done and to sustain unwavering confidence that God will do it regardless of seemingly insurmountable obstacles."[3] These contemporary expositors agree with a great deal of significant historical scholarship that there are in fact two dynamic dimensions of faith.

I know this to be true from my own experience. Years after I had received the gift of faith in Christ, I discovered an advanced quality of faith resulting from Christ, the Holy Spirit, living in me. There's a vital difference between being in Christ and having Christ live in us. Many Christians have trusted Christ for their eternal lives but have little vision to see what He can do with their daily lives. After hearing me preach what I wrote in the previous chapter on predestination a man said to me, "Well, you gave me assurance that I'm going to live forever by God's predestined election; now what I need is power to get through tomorrow!" So say most of us. To do that we need both kinds of faith. We must move "from faith to faith." For me personally that means four things.

First, we are to move from the initial gift of faith to the imaginative faith of a gifted life. After the Spirit enables us to believe the efficacy of the gospel, he wants to give us the gift of believing that he is able to do "exceedingly beyond all that we ask or think." In essence, he wants to give us the imaginative faith to believe all things are possible. The faith of a gifted life sees what others would not dare to expect. This is a special endowment of the Spirit. People who have been open to receive it become vibrant visionaries in spite of the equivocation and timidity around them.

In every situation and relationship, problem or perplexity, the person who has the gift of faith asks, "What does God want?" and has the courage to believe that it will be done. We all live on the edge of some complexity. Most of us expect little from God and are not disappointed. The majority of Christians do not have the lively expectancy which comes from the faith of a gifted life. They had enough faith to accept what Christ did for them on Calvary, but not enough to believe what he can do for and through them today.

When I first became a Christian I was astounded by the amazing grace of God. For the first time in my life I felt loved and forgiven, free to love myself and others, unbound from guilt and self-incrimination. For years after my conversion, I tried to live out my commitment. But it was all self-effort. I read my Bible, prayed, tithed my income, and shared with others as much as I knew of the Lord. There was no question I was in Christ, and if I had died then, I would have known the blessings of eternal salvation. And yet, for daily life, there was the flat striving of my own strength. I could imagine as possible only what I could do in my own wisdom and energy, resources and ability.

You guessed it—the Lord had much more in mind for me than what I could do for him. He wanted me to move on to the faith which would picture what he could do in my life and problems—and dare to trust him for nothing less. Through a series of crises which brought me to the end of my tether, I cried out for help. Haunted by the potential power I saw in others who seemed to be able to envision possibilities and see them fulfilled, I cried out for more faith. At first, God's answer was not more faith, but more of himself. It was then that I experienced the power which had been offered at the time of my conversion, but had not been appropriated. The Lord in whom I had believed, filled my being with his own Spirit. The most remarkable result was a ready-for-anything, nothing-is-impossible, I'll-attempt-anything-God-guides, kind of vision coupled with intrepid faith.

So, in answer to the question, "How do I get more faith?" my response is: receive more of the Holy Spirit! The One who enabled you to believe in the beginning, wants to give you the adventuresome faith to receive guidance as to what he is ready and able to do with the challenges of life in our relationships, in our churches and on our jobs. We were all meant to have the grace gift, charisma, of a daring faith. Then we can pray:

> O God, when the heart is warmest,
> And the head is clearest,
> Give me to act;
> To turn the purpose Thou formest
> Into fact![4]

The second thing I've discovered about the dual dynamics of moving "from faith to faith" is that it is progression from an assurance of eternal life to the audacity of the abundant life. Jesus said, "I have come that they may have life, and that they may have it abundantly" (John 10:10). Over the years, I have come to believe that the Master's offer is a two-part blessing which we grasp with a two-dimensional faith. The life he offers is the grace of reconciliation; the abundant life he offers is the joy of release. We have life eternal in Christ and we have abundant life when he takes up residence in us.

Jesus Christ becomes the instigator of audacity. Does that word audacity surprise you? Don't let it. Check the dictionary. Its primary meaning is exhibiting an unabashed or fearless spirit; temerity instead of timidity; bold; defiant of ordinary restraint. That's the quality of faith I see in the Spirit-filled believers in the Book of Acts and across the pages of history. If the first step of this advanced faith is the vision to see what God wants in us and around us, then surely the second step is the audacity to ask the Lord for what he has revealed in his strategy.

Jesus has called us to be co-creators in the expansion of his kingdom. But he knows how limited is our expectancy. Therefore, he flings out a challenge that only his imputed gift of faith could give us the courage to grasp: "Ask me of things to come concerning my sons, and concerning the work of my hands, command Thou me" (Isa. 45:11). Audacious? Yes! Sublimely so when we realize that he will not act until we ask. It was his decision to trust us that much. But he did not leave us alone with our furtive dumbness, reluctant to claim his promises. He came in his own audacious invasion of fear-bound humanity.

In his own incarnate Word he said, "Ask and it will be given." What shall we dare ask? Well, for openers remember that one of Jesus' most insistent appeals to ask was preceded by an audacious promise indeed. "Most assuredly I say to you, he who believes in Me, the works that I do he will do also; and greater works than these he will do, because I go to My Father. And whatever you ask in My name, that I will do, that the Father may be glorified in the Son. If you ask anything in My name, I will do it" (John 14:12-14).

I have found that "in Christ's name" is a liberating focus for my audacity. That usually clarifies the vision of not only what Christ would do in any situation or relationship, but what he wants us to do. Lillian Dickson, missionary adventurer, doesn't wait around long for an answer. She says, "A knowledge of the need is a call of God!" That has made her audaciously attempt the impossible. Thousands of people in Taiwan and Borneo have been blessed because, in addition to the assurance of her eternal life, she has the audacity of the abundant life. Christ in her gives the vision; Christ around her serendipitously opens doors and provides unexpected resources.

The sure test that we have received the gift of audacious faith is that we can thank God in advance for what he has guided us to ask. George Müller of Bristol, England, had that quality of faith a generation ago. Over a period of sixty years he cared for more than 10,000 orphans. He started with two shillings in his pocket and received over five million dollars through the years. (That would be more than ten million now). There are hundreds of stories about his faith-ministry. One stirs us particularly. One day when he had no food to feed hundreds of hungry children seated expectantly at the breakfast table, he prayed,

"Father, we thank Thee for the food Thou art going to give us." After a pause, a knock came at the door. It was a baker who said that he had been awakened at 2:00 A.M. and was compelled to bake bread for the children. Shortly after, a milkman knocked at the door. He said, "My milk wagon just broke down in front of your place. I must get rid of these cans of milk before I can take the wagon in for repairs. Can you use the milk?"

Müller writes that thousands of times they were without food or funds and their needs were met. He never made appeals. He believed God that if he knew the need, he was perfectly capable of making that need known to the people who had resources to help.

Stories like that quicken our faith. They also disturb us. It's difficult for most of us to be that dependent. Or to reach out beyond our own capabilities or resources. And so our lives are built around what we can do for God rather than what he can do for us.

It's in the realm of financing guided ventures of ministry that I have learned to accept and experience this gift of audacious faith. The Lord persistently presses me out into adventures where the need for financial support is beyond discernible resources. He has always been faithful. "What the Lord decides, He provides!" is the motto of my life.

It works in the church. At each stage of a congregation's life there is a next step to be taken. Expansion of mission, church growth, evangelism, staff development, new programs, building facilities, visionary budgets—all require the persistent question, "Lord, what do You want?" Not, "What will the congregation give, or who will do the work, or how could we ever do that?"—but simply, "Lord what do You guide?" The great need of the hour in most churches is for officers and members who will ask that question, plan in keeping with the answer, and believe God for the provision. But that kind of audacity will be the result of the fresh infilling of the Holy Spirit and the engendering of the gift of audacious faith. More than the gift of faith for eternal life, it is the special gift of faith for the abundant life.

I've experienced this "faith-beyond-faith" in my relationships. When I am most worried or concerned about a member of my family or a friend, I've learned to take that person to God in prayer. "Lord, give me a vision of what You are ready to do in this person's life." Often he gives me a picture of growth, change, or development which seems humanly impossible. But then I feel the stirring of his Spirit within me, equipping me to believe it shall be so. And then I am given freedom to thank him that in his own way and timing it shall be so.

I know my readers well enough to know that some of you are thinking, *Wait a minute, Lloyd, how is that any different than wishful thinking and projecting on to God what you want for a person or some situation?* It's very different. The key is in asking God for the vision of what he desires to do. Then we can have a bold faith in asking for what we know he wants. "What about when people resist or circumstances work against what God wants to do?" Given our freedom of will, that's a real and dangerous possibility. At this point we are given even deeper faith to know that God will use even stubbornness, rebellion, and resistance—and use it for a person's growth and his glory. That quality of faith I do not have in myself. I must ask for it. And I've never asked without it being given.

That leads me to the third aspect of the dual dimensions of a dynamic faith. Growing "from faith to faith" also means moving from faith which is our pedigree to faith which gives us pertinacity. That's another word we don't usually use about faith, but it's meaningful. Pertinacity means persistence, tenacity of purpose, unyielding, incessant, adhering to a pursuit. The Holy Spirit's gift of faith gives us indefatigable patience in unresolved tensions. This kind of faith is beyond the pedigree of belonging to God's forever family; it's the development in us of his family likeness.

One of the greatest attributes of God is his faithfulness.

That faithfulness was displayed in the character of Christ. And Paul tells us that one of the manifestations of the Spirit of Christ in us is the fruit of faithfulness (Gal. 5:22). In between the vision of what he wants, the prayer of bold faith to ask for it with thanksgiving, and the fulfillment, there is the waiting period where we need pertinacious faith. Hebrews 11:1 describes faith as the "substance of things hoped for, the evidence of things not seen." In the Greek substance really means assurance and evidence means conviction.

Note the dual dynamics of faith again. We are given an inner assurance which actually envisages what the answer will be—and the conviction intellectually and emotionally that it is on the way. Perhaps you are in one of those waiting times right now. The Holy Spirit himself is the Author of assurance and conviction. His presence keeps us from giving up and his word of comfort gives us hope. Inadvertently, through his work in our minds and emotions, our pedigree becomes pertinacity!

There is a four-letter word which is the key to the fourth aspect of "faith to faith." It's the undeniable evidence that we have both dynamic dimensions of faith. The word is risk. We are to move from a faith which redeems to a faith that risks. Faith is a risky business. It is raw trust in God's power to see us through. Our fear of risk often makes us resist, and then miss, the faith-vision God's Spirit dramatizes in our minds. But a life without risk is no life at all. It's a risk to love, forgive, dare to hope, and launch out into new ventures he guides. A woman said, "I've avoided risks all my life and now I am old and all I have is a million 'what might have beens.'" How sad—and how like millions of people, many of them Christians.

But that does not have to be true. Have you ever asked for the dual dynamics of the gift of faith? If you have never experienced the joy of God's love and forgiveness, and are unsure of your eternal life, ask him for the faith only he can give. If you've admired the freedom and assurance of Christ-confident people wondering if it could ever happen to you, risk your life, ask for the one thing that can make you right with God forever: the power of faith. He's more ready to give than you are to ask.

And to those of you who already have that essential gift, are you ready to move on the audacious, pertinacious faith that asks for clear visions from God, attempts great things for God, and risks everything with God? We all stand on the precipice of a bold next step. We cannot dare without moving from faith to faith. Right now ask the Holy Spirit to fill you. Suddenly you will know that all that he guides is possible. In God's name, risk something . . . risk you yourself!

There's a wonderful story about a first grade teacher who stood at the door bidding her pupils good-by as they moved on to the second grade. "Teacher," one of the little boys said. "I sure do like you. I'd like to stay in first grade forever, but I've been promoted. Boy, I wish you knew enough to teach me in the second grade."

We laugh at that and then the parable hits us. In the school of faith, it's time to move on. And the Holy Spirit who gave us the gift of a primary faith knows more than enough to give us a powerful faith.

8

Is It a Sin to Doubt?

A PLEASANT, SURFACE conversation with a brilliant intellectual at a party suddenly took on an unexpected dimension of depth. "Do you ever have doubts?" the research scientist asked intently. "Of course," I responded. "Doubt can be creative as the prelude to intellectual and spiritual growth. The crucial thing is discovering what to do with our doubts."

He had not anticipated my response. Knocked off guard for a moment, he confided that he had left his church a few years before because he was told it was a sin to doubt. He had drummed himself out of the corps because, even though he believed in Christ, he had doubts which beleaguered his scientific mind. "What do you think—is it a sin to doubt?"

"That depends," I answered with empathy, "on whether your doubt is dynamic or debilitating. There is an authentic doubt which delineates the demarcation line of where we need to grow. And then there is an arrogant doubt of settled resistance. Dynamic doubt takes place in the context of fellowship with God; debilitating doubt holds him at arm's length." I went on to explain that the issue is what we do with our doubts. The most important thing is to see them as the positive edge of our spiritual pilgrimage, tell

God about them, and ask for the gift of wisdom to discern deeper truth in both our understanding and experience. I challenged the man to a thirty-day experiment. "Get back into prayerful communion with your Lord in spite of your doubts and ask for the gift of wisdom. In communion with him, dare to doubt your doubts!"

It worked. At the end of the month, he came to see me. "You were right," he exclaimed, "I was holding God at arms length with my doubts. Telling him about them has broken the bind. I had put him on the judgment stand when I needed him most as an advocate in the battle for assurance against doubt. Sure, I still have doubts, but now I want to see them as a sign that there's a next step to be taken." When we prayed together, the intellectually gifted man reaffirmed his faith and made a commitment to doubt his doubts.

I have related this man's story because I believe there are millions of Christians who are disturbed by doubt. When doubt invades our minds, a vicious cycle begins. We see it as a denial of our faith, feel separated from our Lord, and soon begin to doubt ourselves and our relationship with him. When we need him most, we feel our doubts are a roadblock. A sense of distance develops. But who moved? Not God! He is ready to help us turn the doubt into wisdom.

Johann Wolfgang von Goethe once said, "Give me the benefit of your convictions, if you have any, but keep your doubts to yourself, for I have enough of my own." I don't agree with that. I want to put it differently: give me your doubts. Be honest enough to admit them. Our Lord is pressing us on to new growth. Our doubt is our human response. He can take our struggle with doubt and give us the gift of faith to ask for wisdom.

A young graduate student was filled with doubts. He believed in God but doubted the extent of his intervention and influence in our lives today. "Wonderful! I salute you!" I said to him. "Your doubts are not bad. But unless I miss my guess, your doubts about God's intervention relate to some area in your life where you need his power to invade your inadequacy." He admitted that was true. The grip of general doubt was not broken until he trusted that situation to God, confessed his doubt, and dared to use the faculty of doubt to doubt his doubts.

So many questions submitted about doubt express a profound need to deal with how to overcome this haunting disability. It robs many people of courage and companionship with our Lord. I think there is an edge of doubt in all of us about some aspect of what God can or will do in our lives. I reach out to the doubters. This chapter is meant to be of both personal and practical help to those battling the problem of doubt. It follows naturally from what we said in the last chapter about faith. I want to share how the gift of faith can be given in the battle with doubt so that we can receive wisdom as the antidote to our doubt.

This is what James offered the early church. In the first chapter of his epistle, he gives us the cause of doubt, the cure of doubt and the confidence which displaces doubt:

> My brethren, count it all joy when you fall into various trials, knowing that the testing of your faith produces patience. But let patience have its perfect work, that you may be perfect and complete, lacking nothing. If any of you lacks wisdom, let him ask of God, who gives to all liberally and without reproach, and it will be given to him. But let him ask in faith, with no doubting, for he who doubts is like a wave of the sea driven and tossed by the wind. For let not that man suppose that he will receive anything from the Lord; he is a double-minded man, unstable in all his ways (James 1:2–8).

At first reading this seems like further condemnation of doubt rather than remedial help. Not so. Deeper study of the words and their context actually helps us to know what doubt is and how to confront it.

Consider first the real cause of doubt. The early Chris-

tians to whom James wrote were facing trials which tested
their faith in the sufficient adequacy of God to meet their
needs. They had been pressed out onto the edge of doubt
which revealed their need to grow in their understanding
of, and reliance on, God's providential care. They believed
in God, but trials had fastened a doubt about what God
could do. Doubt is the spiritual condition which invades
the valley between our problems and the realization of
God's power. It is usually emotional and spiritual before it
is intellectually articulated. We become uncertain of him in
our trials, question his knowledge of our need or inclina-
tion to act, and then entertain intellectual questions about
his nature, will and way. When life brings us to the condition of doubt of God, we make him our enemy rather than
our friend. When we most need him, we are filled with
doubt.

But the trials of life do other things to us which result in
doubt. They wear us down and sap our energy. Life,
people, our surroundings and problems seem gloomy and
forbidding. Exhausted with coping, we begin to doubt
ourselves and then God. Do you know what I mean? Remember a time when you became so run down physically,
and then emotionally, that your resiliency to hope was depleted? I think the same thing happens in thousands of
diminutive ways that allow doubt to block out our confidence. We become like Elijah and wonder about the sovereignty, as well as the sympathy, of God. We cry out: "It is
enough!"

At a time like that the last thing we need is self-
condemnation or judgment from others upon our doubt.
Attacking the doubt or even the trials which brought us to
it, does little to help. What we need is to admit the doubt to
God and reach out for the real cause. At that point we
reject the pattern of trying to run our own lives on our
own energy and understanding.

There's a further implication of trials for doubt that we

must consider. Often some trial in the past has filled us
with a profound lack of trust in God. When our prayers
have not been answered on our time schedule, or when
we've asked and the answer is not what we wanted, doubt
pervades our future praying. The same is true when we
have suffered some physical or emotional difficulty in the
past. We blame God and doubt becomes the attitude of our
lives. "If he could allow that to happen, how can I believe
in him now?" is the persistent expression of uncertainty.

Behind so much respectable intellectual doubt is a hurting heart. Others will usually argue with a person about
the content of the conceptual doubts rather than reach
deeper into the condition of hurt which needs love and
understanding. Of course, we must begin with an intellectual doubter by taking his doubts seriously, but the
solution does not usually lie in some lucid explanation of
doctrine. Rather it lies in a loving expression of concern
about his needs as a person.

I think of one of the most articulate agnostics I ever met.
He enjoyed arguing about doctrine. He could wrestle the
most brilliant of Christian teachers. Because he kept the
adult Bible classes he attended in turmoil, I decided to take
him on, not for a debate, but for friendship. After months
of lunches and visits, I discerned a problem in the man's
early experience as a boy in Sunday school. He had felt
rejection of his questioning mind. Added to that, his pious
parents, who had the words but not the music of the faith,
had little love for each other or for their son. He had
decided that Christians were fakes and that their lofty beliefs had little relevance.

Now the man was in trouble in his own marriage. He
needed to discover how to receive and give love. I touched
a raw nerve when I stopped arguing with him and witnessed of what love had done to transform my own self-
image and heal the hurts of the past. We used the scientific
method to establish the assumption that we need love and

that, in spite of loveless Christians we had known, God was essentially love. Then we went on to experiment with asking God for his love and the power to communicate love.

It was when the man asked for help in loving his wife unselfishly that the debilitating doubt focused in intellectual questions was lifted. At that point he was no longer just a thinker in quest of intellectual certainty. Rather, he stopped holding God at bay. Over the years, he has discovered that doubt can be the fortuitous sign indicating he is ready for more growth, rather than a device to resist God.

The cure for doubts about God is the wisdom of God. Doubt is a sure sign that we need deeper experience of who God is, how he works in our lives, and what he is ready to teach us. Wisdom is God's intelligence entrusted to us, providing supernatural knowledge, discernment and insight. It is more than human sagacity or I.Q. The gift of wisdom maximizes all levels of intelligence. If doubt in life's trials leads us to complexities beyond our capacities, we are encouraged by James to ask for wisdom.

"If any of you lacks wisdom, let him ask of God." The Greek word for "lacks" is *leipetai* from *leipō*, meaning to be destitute or fall short. Actually it comes from an ancient banking term meaning to have a shortage of resources. Doubt alerts us to the realization of a spiritual overdraft, an insufficiency to face life's questions, concerns and difficulties—as well as unresolved intellectual problems. The word for ask, *aiteō*, is in the present active imperative, implying that we should "keep on asking." The word for wisdom is *sophias*, which is practical and applicable knowledge. It is important to distinguish that it is not just knowledge, *gnōseōs*, but wisdom, knowledge which is gained in actual relationships and situations. It is the quality of understanding which makes a person astute in discerning God's nature and seeing his handiwork in our lives and in the world.

When Solomon ascended to the throne, succeeding his

father David, he asked for one gift from God—an understanding heart. "Now, O Lord God, Thy promise to my Father David is fulfilled, for Thou hast made me king over a people as numerous as the dust of the earth. Give me now wisdom and knowledge, that I may go out and come in before this people; for who can rule this great people of Thine?" (2 Chron. 1:9-10). And God blessed the young king with special wisdom then, and all through his life. He was able to make decisions, build a kingdom, unravel knotty problems, and set a clear course because he was willing to depend on God for wisdom.

The secret of Solomon's wisdom is given in Proverbs 1:7. He says pointedly, "The fear of the Lord is the beginning of wisdom." Here fear means awe and wonder, dependence and praise. The first three chapters of Proverbs eloquently describe the wonderful gift of wisdom. The way to wisdom is found in Proverbs 3:5-7: "Trust in the Lord with all your heart, and do not lean on your own understanding. In all your ways acknowledge Him, and He will make your paths straight. Do not be wise in your own eyes; fear the Lord and turn from evil."

In the New Testament, wisdom is sublimely focused in Jesus Christ. Paul clearly describes him as the incarnate wisdom of God, "Christ the power and the wisdom of God" (1 Cor. 1:24) "Who was made to us wisdom from God" (1 Cor. 1:30). In Colossians the apostle boldly asks that his fellow believers in Colossae be filled with the knowledge of God's will "in all wisdom and spiritual understanding" (Col. 1:9). He also identified wisdom as one of the gifts of the Holy Spirit (1 Cor. 12:8).

What this means to us is that God has revealed his wisdom in Jesus Christ. When we ask for wisdom in our doubts, we are drawn into closer union with Christ himself. The more we know of him, the more we will be able to find answers to our questions and resolution of our doubts. Added to that is the power of his indwelling Spirit in us. From within, he infuses the tissues of our brains with the gift of wisdom. We will be given a profound insight and understanding previously impossible with our human capacities. With this wisdom will also come the patience to endure trials in the sure confidence that nothing can ultimately hurt us now or for eternity. We will have the inner calm to wait for the unfolding of perception for the problems which otherwise would be a potential for doubt.

The apostle John pointedly tells us how this happens. The source of wisdom is an anointing of the Spirit of Christ. We will be singled out, blessed, set apart and both covered and filled with his Spirit. "But the anointing which you have received from Him abides in you, and you do not need that anyone teach you; but as the anointing teaches you concerning all things, and is true, and is not a lie, and just as it has taught you, you will abide in Him" (1 John 2:27). Wisdom is given us as we abide in Christ and he abides in us. What we receive from him is beyond acquired skills, deeper than insight alone, and more profound than learning. Our minds can receive his mind, our emotions can be infused with his love, and our wills can be fired to discern and do his will. We no longer need be distressed with doubts. We can receive the precious gift of wisdom which will give us the Lord's perspective and power.

And it works. When we open ourselves and ask for the mind of Christ, we are entrusted with powers of understanding way beyond our own. We are led to truth and given depth-perception of its meaning. The Bible opens up to yield its unlimited truth. Prayer becomes an opportunity for thoughts to be implanted which we would not have discovered with years of research. But equally crucial, we are given a new disposition toward our doubts and fears. Now we can ask God to use them for our growth and for sensitive listening and help to those around us who are tempted with doubt.

James says that wisdom is given to all who ask of God "who gives liberally and without reproach." The Greek word *haplōs,* from *haplous* meaning "single," is the word which is used to translate Jesus' Aramaic word in Matthew 6:22, "If your eye is single (RSV), good (NKJ), clear (ASV)." The word may also be rendered "generous, gracious or liberally." Perhaps a combination of both "singleness" and "liberally" comes close to what James meant. My understanding is that God gives us wisdom which is single— unique for our specific needs—and generously beyond anything we might expect or deserve. And he gives it without reproach. There's no "I told you so," or "Why did you wait so long?" or "Well, here's the wisdom you asked for—you don't really have it coming with all your doubts and uncertainties—but here it is anyway." There's no lecture with the gift. He waits patiently until we ask and when we do, he is more ready to give than we have been to ask.

Next James tells us how we are to ask in verse 6. "But let him ask in faith, with no doubting, for he who doubts is like a wave of the sea driven and tossed by the wind." At first that seems like a "Catch 22." How can we ask for wisdom to replace our doubts if we are beset with doubts when we most need wisdom? That throws us back on the thoughts we had about faith in the previous chapter.

Faith is the primary gift—before wisdom. Remember we cannot produce faith; it is engendered by the Holy Spirit. All we can do is admit our need. And even that is a result of the Spirit's activity. So my sense of this challenge by James is that the Spirit works in us giving us an urgent desire and hunger for God which supersedes our doubts. Then we become more sure of God's love than we are of our doubts. That's when we can doubt our doubts and ask for wisdom. We don't need to spend the rest of our lives being tossed to and fro like the waves of the sea driven back and forth, churned up by the wind. Our double mind, fractured by doubt, can become as single as God's liberality.

I know this to be true from my own spiritual and intellectual life. There have been times when doubt has disturbed my peace. I did not doubt God's existence, but I did doubt his power for problems and people. And then, when I least expect it, by the mysterious moving of the Spirit in my mind and heart, I begin to doubt those doubts and sense a longing to find a more intimate fellowship with the Lord. I want him more than the false security of the doubt. Then I am given the faith-courage to ask for a hearing heart of wisdom. He has never refused that prayer which he himself motivated. The gift of greater wisdom helps me see through the darkness of whatever caused the doubt. But most of all, I am filled with the inner light of God's presence and new confidence, vision, and hope begin to flow.

What Amelia Burr said of a friend, we can say of the Lord.

> I do not know what makes the tides
> Nor what tomorrow's world may do,
> But I have certainty enough,
> For I am sure of you!

9

What Is a
Born-Again Christian?

I WANT TO ASK YOU a very personal and pertinent question. It may surprise you that I think I know how you will respond before I ask. The experience of working with people over the past twenty-five years, coupled with the statistics of countless surveys and inventories made by eminent pollsters like George Gallup, tell me that your answers will fall into three distinct categories. If each of you could make an honest, anonymous response, I am convinced that one third of you will answer "Yes!"; one third of you will respond "I'm not sure"; and one third of you will say, "No." The question is, "Have you been born again?"

Notice that I did not ask, "Are you a Christian?" or "Are you a church member?" or "Are you a good moral person?" My question is whether you've had a definite, vital experience of spiritual rebirth. The great need among church members, religious people, as well as agnostics and authentic inquirers, is for a transforming new birth experience.

I am aware that raising this question leads to real communication difficulties. The third of you who say yes may respond with ho-hum familiarity. You may have missed the secret of your rebirth for recurring renaissance. The other two thirds may be defensive. Those of you who are either unsure or resistant may have turned off the possibility because of the attitudes or esoteric exclusiveness of those who claim the experience.

Born-again Christianity is big news in America today. It has captured the attention of the press, merited headlines, and become a topic of conversation everywhere from church parlors to cocktail parties. Prominent political, entertainment, and sports personalities who have claimed to be born again have dilated the American consciousness. The shocking thing is that many of the people who extol the joy and peace of being born again have been related to Christianity and the church prior to their metamorphosis.

Added to this is the fact that the polls I referred to before were not markedly different among church and non-church people. The answers of those who were sure they had or hadn't been born again, and those who were unsure, were essentially the same among those actively involved in a church as among those who have no formal relationship with a church!

This fact has aroused a disturbing question. What were these church members before becoming born again? How could they be a part of a church, work for good causes, live respectable lives, and never have been confronted by the challenge to be born again? And what about those who claim to be born again, but are not in a church? This says something about institutional Christianity as well as something about all three groups.

The organized process of receiving church members and the progressive nurturing program of the local church can be guilty of trying to encourage people to grow in a life they have never begun! The anesthetization process can disguise or even obliterate the need for a radical beginning which is specific and crucial. Also, the crisis which creates a sense of need may not come at the time when a person accepts Christ as Savior, or is confirmed in the faith. When that crisis does hit, a person may feel that though he or she knew about Christ, he or she had never really met him personally. It is then that a vague identification with Christianity, a bland self-help moralism, or a bootstrap independence is replaced by an intimate, impelling, inspiring relationship with Christ.

The hundreds of questions submitted about what it means to be born again came from the two thirds who are either unsure or defensive. "Why all this emphasis on being born again?" people are asking. "Must I be born again to be a Christian?" others query. And "Do I have to become like some born again Christians I know to become born again?" still others demanded. But most challenging of all were those who confessed, "The people who claim to be born again seem to have a spiritual power I don't have. How can I find what they have experienced?" All of the questions demand a straightforward response. I want to answer by describing what it means to be born again, how to be sure, and what results.

To do that I want to clear away the brambles of misunderstanding and layers of confusion by going back to what Jesus actually said. There's no better way than to do an exposition of John 3 and the Lord's encounter with Nicodemus. The natural unfolding of the account gives us a progression from the universal need for rebirth, to the crisis which brings us to it, to Christ's explanation of how it happens, and then to what we can do to cooperate in being born again.

We all need to be born again. Nicodemus' character, stature, position, learning, and religious life puts us all on level ground. How very clever of John to select this leading Pharisee's conversation with Jesus to proclaim the necessity of rebirth! We can be sure that Jesus talked about the necessity of being born again with many others. Out of the treasure chest of countless interviews, encounters and confrontations, John selects the one with Nicodemus so that however good or bad, spiritual or unspiritual we may consider ourselves to be, what Jesus said to him needs to be said to us. The point is that a dynamic relationship with God is not the result of what we have done, learned, or accomplished.

Nicodemus was one of more than 6000 Pharisees in Israel, known as the *chaburah,* the brotherhood. As such, he had pledged himself to spend all of his life studying, observing and enforcing every detail of the Ten Commandments (as well as the scribal laws and oral tradition which annotated and explained the application of the Commandments). He was an impeccable moralist, seeking perfection in absolute obedience to all the rules and regulations. His learning (probably under Gamaliel the great teacher in Israel who also taught Saul of Tarsus) had steeped him in tradition and the Scriptures encompassed in the Torah, the Law and the Prophets.

John tells us he was a ruler of the Jews, meaning that he was one of the thirty-five Pharisees who, along with thirty-five Sadducees, made up the high and ultimate court, the Sanhedrin. As a Pharisee, he looked forward to the coming of the Messiah, longed for the coming of the kingdom of God which he perceived in political terms, and was fiercely patriotic. His whole way of life had made him fiercely defensive of the Law and tradition.

Nicodemus had something more, however. He had a longing for new truth and an inquiring mind which was open to what God was doing, as well as what he had done in Israel's history. He had observed Jesus' miracles, had listened to his message, and had wanted to find out who he really was. Setting aside caution and propriety, he came to Jesus to see and hear for himself. There is much made of the fact that he came by night, suggesting that he came secretly so as not to have his interest in Jesus exposed to the Sanhedrin. That's to miss the fact that the evening hours were set aside by the Pharisees for study and reflection. John's reference to the hour of the visit underlines the seriousness and intensity of Nicodemus' purpose.

The first thing we learn from this background on

Nicodemus is that, on a human level, no one could have had finer religious credentials or a more impeccable character. However perfect our performance, however advanced our spiritual learning, however much we have read and memorized the Scriptures, and however diligent our search to know God, we still need what was missing in this outstanding man. He knew about God but did not know God personally!

Secondly, a crisis brought Nicodemus to a realization of his need. There are two kinds of crises: the crisis precipitated by a problem and the crisis brought on by a potential. Jesus himself was the cause of the crisis in Nicodemus' life. What he had heard and seen of the Master had created a disturbance within Nicodemus. Here was the power of God being manifest in word and deed. It brought both shock and awe to the Pharisee. To one whose life was devoted to preservation of what God had done, there was the shock of God's imminence. Awe aroused by what he observed created a desire to experience the same present power of God in his own life. John's record of what Nicodemus said to Jesus surely is a capsule of a longer expression of his admiration and wonderment: "Rabbi, we know that You are a teacher come from God; for no one can do these signs that you do unless God is with him." Quite an accolade!

It tells us that the Pharisee discerned the undeniable evidence of God working in Jesus. His statement borders on messianic recognition. I have always wondered if Nicodemus is not really saying, "Are you the one?" Also, his wistful acknowledgment that God was with Jesus is clearly a desire to find for himself what he observed in the Lord. His veiled statement is really, "Rabbi, I need you and want to know you."

Then, as now, Jesus Christ precipitates a crisis. It is the crisis of potential for our problems. He disturbs us not only with how inadequate our lives have been, but with how great we were meant to be. In his presence we sense our impotence and yearn to experience his power; we feel our need for love and his unlimited love for us; we face the broken pieces of our fractured lives and long to know his unbreakable peace. When we read the Gospel in which his majestic Person is vividly described, or when we meet a person in whom he lives today, a crisis is created. We feel a combination of emptiness, loneliness, and lack of fulfillment, coupled with an irresistible pull toward him. And he will allow whatever it takes to bring us to the place where we cry out, "Lord, I need you! All that I have learned, accomplished, and acquired on my own has not filled the emptiness I feel when I am confronted by You and what I see You have done in the lives of people who really know and love You."

Jesus' response to Nicodemus must have been a lightning flash of challenge followed by a thunderclap of disturbance in the sensitive soul of the Pharisee. The shock and awe he had felt observing Jesus was nothing in comparison to the turbulence created by what Jesus said to him about his own spiritual condition. Jesus did not acknowledge the accolade paid to him by the Pharisee. Instead, with divine discernment, he cut to the core of the religious man's empty soul. "Most assuredly, I say to you, unless one is born again, he cannot see the kingdom of God." The word for "again" in the Greek means "from above" as well as "a second time." Both are implied. The miracle of a totally new and radically fresh beginning is induced by God and is nothing less than starting all over again.

Nicodemus' question about how a man could enter his mother's womb to be born again and his later question, "How can these things be?" expose a deeper question. What he is really asking is—can a person after years of living, conditioning, habit forming, mind setting, ever start all over again?

Now Jesus hammers home the essential truth. "Most assuredly, I say to you, unless one is born of water and the

Spirit, he cannot enter the kingdom of God." The key is what Jesus meant by the kingdom of God. Perhaps the unrecorded part of this conversation includes what Jesus reinterpreted to be the meaning of seeing, that is, understanding and experiencing the kingdom of God. In the context of his total message and life, we know that the kingdom of God meant the reign and rule of God in the mind and heart of a person. It included his relationships, responsibilities and all of life in society. It was not political, nationally exclusive to Israel, nor a return to the glory of the past. Rather it was knowing God personally and living in faithful and obedient response to his guidance and will. No Jew, even one as famous and accomplished as Nicodemus, could enter into that sublime union and power without an absolutely new beginning.

The words, "born of water and the Spirit," press the point. Water baptism was the rite of initiation for a proselyte into Judaism. In effect what Jesus was saying to Nicodemus was, "Unless you are willing to become a novice again, you cannot enter into true fellowship with God." The Pharisee's learning and experience qualified him for the old idea of the kingdom of God, but not the new. "That which is flesh is flesh, and that which is born of the Spirit is spirit."

Think of flesh as a synonym for humanity. Humanly we could enter a political, military or geographical kingdom of God's rule. We can by human effort accomplish a great deal in social causes and programs. In fact, what we are able to do without God in our own strength is sometimes a roadblock to discovering what he can do in and through us. Goodness keeps us from grace, religion from regeneration, effort from entering the true kingdom. That happens only when God's Spirit creates a longing, a realization of our emptiness, and a dominant desire in our spirit.

Jesus illustrates how this happens to bring about the miracle of birth from above, from God's Spirit. The movement of the Spirit in the human spirit is like the wind.

I have always imagined that the trees rustled with the blowing of the wind while Jesus was talking to Nicodemus. "Listen to the wind, Nicodemus. You cannot explain where it came from or where it is going but its power and evidence are undeniable. The wind of the Spirit began gusting through your heart and mind when you saw what I did and heard what I said. Now God himself is blowing out the self-confidence and legalistic assurances of the past. It is God's Spirit himself who is creating the desire for rebirth and actually producing the willingness for the new beginning in you."

What does that mean for us? It tells us of the mystery of the new birth. The Spirit of God is the prime mover. He is impinging on me as I write this and on you as you read it. Suddenly there is the stirring you cannot explain, the restlessness, the dissatisfaction you now feel with your past life, the new compelling loneliness for deeper meaning and purpose. Perhaps life has fallen apart in some way, maybe your relationships are filled with discord and lack of satisfying love, or possibly you are feeling the bland boredom of the sameness of life.

The wind is blowing. Like a sailor on the sea, you can't explain the mysterious movement, but you can hoist the sail. The ceaseless action of the Spirit is stirring you. Just as the sailor knows the wind that fills the sails, so we know that right now the Lord has decided to fill the sails of our hearts to move us from where we've been to where he wants us to go. The wind is blowing on you! Don't resist it. Turn your keel into the wind and catch its power.

The very thing Jesus is talking about was happening to Nicodemus, for he asked, "How can these things be?" His first question had been one of confronting the impossibility; this second question asks how to appropriate what he now acknowledged as a possibility. How does this happen? Jesus answers by telling Nicodemus that it is exactly what had been promised by the Scripture. This the Pharisee should have known. "Are you a teacher of Israel, and do not know these things?" Jesus asks.

The obvious reference is to the promises God made through Ezekiel. "A new heart I will give you, a new spirit I will put within you" (Ezek. 36:26). The learned leader had forgotten. Then Jesus goes on to give him the secret of how the promise is being fulfilled in himself and what he came to do. He boldly speaks of himself and the Spirit as one. There is an undeniable messianic assertion in the plural of verse 11: "Most assuredly I say to you, We speak what We know and testify what We have seen, and you do not receive Our witness." The New King James correctly capitalizes the plural pronouns. It was as if Jesus said, "The new heart promised so long ago is why I came. Through what I will do you will be given a new heart to be filled with a new Spirit—God Himself. What you see happening in Me will then happen in you!"

Then in rapid-fire order Jesus predicts the cross and gives Nicodemus an undeniable revelation of his messianic mission. "God so loved the world that He gave His only begotten Son, that whoever believes in Him should not perish but have everlasting life." The love of God in Christ is the motivating power of the new birth. The cross melts down our resistance and assures us that Christ died for us. There cannot be a new birth without forgiveness for an old life.

It was not until Nicodemus stood on Calvary watching Christ die that he remembered what Jesus had said. That windy night he had become a secret disciple of the Lord. He had defended Jesus in the Sanhedrin when the vicious anger mounted against him. And he was with Jesus when he died.

Imagine what he felt when, along with Joseph of Arimathea, he prepared the Lord's body for burial in Joseph's garden. He had brought the myrrh and aloes and tenderly wrapped the nail-pierced body of his friend in the linen strips. Did he remember then that the Lord had predicted what would happen on that day? Christ was lifted up, indeed!

Then picture what must have happened on Easter morning. The news that Christ had risen sealed Nicodemus' belief that he was who he said he was that night. I've always counted Nicodemus among the followers of the Lord during the days of waiting between Calvary and Pentecost. I'm sure he must have been among the 120 who waited in the Upper Room (Acts 1:15). When Christ returned in the power of the Holy Spirit with "a rushing of a mighty wind" all that he remembered Jesus had said about the wind came true for him. On Pentecost Nicodemus was reborn.

Now we can see the progression of being born again with undeniable clarity. First, the promise, then the cross to make it possible, and then the gift of a personal Pentecost to make it a reality. Jesus' teaching about the new birth, his death to ensure the forgiveness of the past, and his infilling power are the three great gifts he offers us. And what can we do to cooperate in being born again? Accept his diagnosis that our deepest need is to be born again; receive his complete forgiveness for all that is past; and surrender our new, ready, and receptive hearts to be filled with Christ's Spirit.

Then your rebirth will issue forth into revision. The focus of your life, the purpose of your every waking hour, and the commitment of your now-willing will is to know and do *his* will. You will have a new set of heart eyes to see the kingdom of God, to realize his will and way in all things. Out of your reborn heart will flow the rivers of living water Jesus predicted. Each river will be one of the fruits of the Spirit Paul enumerated. Out of your words, attitudes, countenance, action and new life will flow love, joy, peace, patience, kindness, goodness, faithfulness, gentleness, and self-control.

10

Why All This Talk
About Commitment?

THE MAN'S QUESTION was really a statement: "Do you have a church of *committed* Christians?" The adjective of emphasis caught my attention. I suspected that, more than discuss my congregation, he wanted to tell me something he had discovered. So I responded with a question, "Can you be a Christian and not be committed?"

That gave my new friend the opening he was waiting for. He launched into an exciting description of what had happened to him. After years of believing in Christ and being a leader in his congregation, he had made an unreserved commitment of his life to him. He had discovered the secret of Christian freedom and joy in the transformation of his will.

At a deeper life conference, he had been confronted with the challenge to surrender the control and guidance of his life to the Lord. A closing "commitment" service had given him an opportunity he claimed had never been offered him through all the years of his active churchmanship. He had heard the gospel preached for two decades but said that he never had been confronted with the necessity of turning his will over to the Lord's will. When he did, he realized the ingredient he had been missing. Not only did he now *know* the Lord in whom he had before only

vaguely believed, he now received the daily power to utilize the opportunities of life that before had masqueraded
as problems.

No wonder he asked about the commitment of my
members. The passion of this man's life is now to share
with other traditional church people what a difference
commitment has made in his life. I was happy to tell him
about the many members of my church who are deeply
committed. We talked about how important it is to make
commitment a part of the preaching and teaching of the
church and an essential dimension of introducing people
to Christ. I am gratified by the large number of people in
each of our monthly new members' classes who find release and power through a commitment to Christ. Also, I
am delighted whenever he raids the ranks of bland, cultural Christians and confronts them with the necessity of
committing however much they know of themselves to
however much they know of him.

In the previous chapter we discussed what the Lord offers us. The gift of rebirth and the infilling of the Spirit
are his part in our transformation. Commitment is our
part in realizing all that is offered to us. It is an act of the
will in which we yield total control of our lives and turn all
our relationships and responsibilities, the problems and
the potentials, completely over to the Lord. The purpose
of this chapter is to probe the depths of what that means.

Among the hundreds of questions which focused on
commitment, here are some that are representative. What
part does commitment play in our response to God's
grace? How is commitment different than just having
faith? What part does the will have in becoming and growing in the Christian life? How can I be sure I've become a
committed Christian? I can't pinpoint any day or hour
when I committed my life. Is commitment a "once for all
and ever" thing, or must it be done again and again? Please
explain the jargon some people use when they say they are
"committed Christians."

Once again we turn to the Bible for God's answer to our urgent questions. The Bible has many salient passages concerning commitment, but there is one I find most helpful. It gives us a basis for considering many of the others. It is Paul's affirmation and assurance given to Timothy in 2 Timothy 1:12. "For I know whom I have believed and am persuaded that He is able to keep what I have committed to Him until that Day." The verse offers a two-part blessing: intimacy with the Lord and great freedom through commitment. One enables the other but the first cannot grow in depth and worth without the second. Actually, they are so closely intertwined that they are dependent on each other. We could not make a commitment unless Christ first invaded our lives with his love. But believing must be coupled with an initial and oft-repeated commitment for us to know him profoundly.

Note the context of Paul's grand assurance. The apostle is reminding Timothy of what Christ has done for him. He witnesses to the power of the gospel which has transformed his life, the companionship with Christ which has sustained him in suffering, and the relentless hope which spurs him on in faithfulness in prison. Paul's commitment to Christ is based on Christ's commitment to him with everlasting love. The words, "what I have committed to Him," can also be rendered, "what He has committed to me." Both can be a correct translation from the Greek. It was the "Savior Jesus Christ, who abolished death and brought life and immortality to light through the gospel" who appointed Paul to be "a preacher, an apostle, and a teacher of the Gentiles." For that reason he could suffer and never be ashamed.

The Lord is wholly committed to us, and our response is to be unreservedly committed to him. He commits to each of us the total gift of both abundant and eternal life. Our commitment is to accept his love, forgiveness and guidance—and then surrender our will to him. His response to our commitment is to keep what we have committed. The word "keep," *phulaxai* in Greek, means to guard against robbery or loss. The word for "committed" is *parathēkēn,* from the banking term for deposit. The deposit of our life in the bank of heaven is secure. More than an F.D.I., a Federal Deposit Insurance, it is an E.D.A., an eternal deposit assurance. When we commit our assets and liabilities to Christ, our eternal status is accepted and secured. Equally so, when we commit our daily needs to him, the unlimited resources of our Lord are unleashed to multiply our investment with strength and courage. He promised also to "work all things together for good," replacing our liabilities with the assets of his Spirit.

Because Christ is able (that is, has all power) to keep us and all our concerns secure, we can with Paul make these four triumphant assertions: I know, I believe, I am persuaded, and I have committed. A study of Paul's life and our experience indicates that the progression is actually in a slightly different order. Paul first believed, then he committed his life, then he knew Christ personally, and then he became totally persuaded of his sufficiency for suffering.

My own experience is that I believed in Christ long before I committed my life to him. It was through a surrender of my life that the static of my resistance was tuned out and I could receive the impact of his personal presence. But that was only a beginning. Each day in the thirty-two years I have known Christ, I have been persuaded afresh by the fact that he is able to keep the problems I have committed to him.

My great concern is for the millions of Christians today who believe in Christ as their Savior, but have not made him Lord of their lives. To believe in the existence of a person is one thing; to know that person in a profound, personal relationship is something far greater. Paul's experience on the Damascus road convinced him that Christ was alive. That experience would have been enough to change Paul's misguided passion to stamp out the followers of the Way. But it would not have produced the bold apostle of grace. I am convinced that Paul's commitment to Christ made it possible for him to become the man who out-lived, out-cared, and out-dared the world.

Christ had all that there was of Paul. He was born again, filled with the Spirit, *and* he was committed. That initial commitment was renewed daily whenever he accepted impossible tasks and was confronted with excruciating circumstances. Belief became personal knowledge through commitment.

It is a tremendous assertion to say that we really know anything or anyone. We are ready to listen to anyone who can say that he or she *knows* in any area of intellectual or interpersonal experience. So few people are sure of anything today. There was no lack of certainty for Paul. He knew whom he believed, was thoroughly persuaded of his knowledge, and the key to that confidence was that he was a thoroughly committed man.

From his own life and ministry, Jesus himself shows us the power of commitment. His persistent prayer and constantly repeated "Thy will be done" shows us the way commitment unleashes the power of God. His final words on the cross, "Father, into Thy hands I commend my spirit," had been expressed in essence all through his life. But on the cross especially they became the promise of what commitment can mean for us. Christ went to the cross in full confidence that God would raise him from the dead. He laid down his life in complete trust. During his ministry he seldom spoke of what he must do without also affirming what God would do by raising him up on the third day. Now, as King, the resurrected, victorious Lord of all, he has the power to "keep" our lives and needs.

We commit our lives and then our daily concerns in this same confidence. Our initial commitment is indeed our crucifixion. It means a death to self and the willful control of our personalities, plans and purposes. All this comes with the assurance that the Lord will resurrect a new person with new power and passion. Salvation is totally his gracious gift. He prepares us by showing us our need. He makes the gospel a personal word of love, forgiveness, and assurance to us. Then he gives us the gift of faith to respond, believing that we are predestined, appointed, called. His Spirit impinges on ours seeking entrance and indwelling. He reorients our minds and infuses our emotions. The will to commit ourselves is left to us. We are not saved by our commitment, but our commitment enables us to grasp and realize what has been offered to us. The will is like a thermostat: it opens our lives to receive the offer of new birth and the gift of the Spirit.

Before writing this next paragraph, I pushed back from my desk to meditate. I spent a long time thinking about all the people I have known through the years who were ushered into the adventure of life in Christ through making an unreserved commitment. Some of them made a commitment at the time they were introduced to Christ. What astounded me as I reflected were the many Christians I've known who did not take this initial step of commitment. So many of them were what I would call religious people. The renewal of their parishes came as church officers, church school teachers, committee chairpersons, and consistent attenders deposited their lives for the Lord's keeping power. Now they are no longer trying to keep the faith, as if it were something to be clutched and preserved. They are *being kept* in dynamic relationship with the Savior.

This need to commit ourselves to Christ frankly recognizes that we do have free will. We say yes or no to the offer of salvation as well as the Lord's offer of power for our perplexities. Commitment combines elements of faith, trust and dedication, but is something more than all three. There are people who have received the gift of faith and will live forever. They trust the Lord for wisdom and strength, and have dedicated their money, time and talents to him. But they have barred him from the citadel of their wills. They have not let go at the core of their volitional nature. Until this happens, the Christian life is struggle and strain. There is no inner peace.

Once we acknowledge that the Lord has chosen us, we must make a choice. The Lord loves us regardless of our commitment. But only as we commit our minds, souls, and bodies to him, does his love become real to us. Until he has all that there is of us, we are missing out on the complete blessing of salvation.

I am convinced that it is a sublime expression of his love for us that he entrusts to us the power of choice made specific by definite commitment. This is followed by countless further commitments as we grow in fellowship with him. He allows us the will to be sure we are sure. That means three areas of commitment—our lives, our concerns and our challenges.

Everyone of us should be able to identify the time when we committed our lives to Christ. I can remember vividly my own experience in college. Through the years there have been times of deeper and repeated relinquishment of my will to Christ resulting in closer communion with him. And no day goes by without some challenge or crisis which forces me to let go of my control.

Particular times stand out in my mind as watershed days. I will never forget the time in seminary when I was in debt and was forced to give up my hope to go on to postgraduate school. After months of trying to work it out for myself, I finally surrendered my future to the Lord, giving up the dream of studying in Edinburgh, Scotland. A few days later, Ruth Palmer, an educator in the Kenosha, Wisconsin, school system when I was a boy, called to see how I was doing. When she learned of my need, she made me an interest-free loan from her carefully acquired savings. This she allowed me to pay back over the first ten years of my ministry.

Or, I think of the time early in my ministry when success and popularity became more important than the gospel. I ran out of power. The Lord graciously waited until I was at the end of my tether. Then he received me back into intimate communion through a recommitment of my life to him. He became the only meaning, message and motive of my life. Each new parish, sermon to preach, project to launch, conference to lead, or book to write brings me to that painful, but eventually sublime moment of surrender. When my wife, Mary Jane, was ill with cancer, we both individually, and then together, had to be brought to the crisis point of committing the illness and our future to the Lord. Raising my children presented a constant need to commit their needs and my relationship with them to him. But these are examples from the past.

Presently, commitment of my needs to the Lord is the only way I am able to survive in the pressures of a busy parish, a national television ministry, and the opportunity to write. Often life fills up, frustration sets in, and burnout is a frightening danger. I find myself neglecting my wife and others dear to me. Times of recreation and relaxation are missed. Prolonged time for personal prayer and Bible study to nurture my own soul is edged out by busyness. And then a strained relationship or physical exhaustion alerts me to the realization that I'm running my own life again. It is then that I go back to reclaim the reorienting verses which have helped me through the years: "Commit your way to the Lord, trust also in Him, and He will do it . . . rest in the Lord and wait patiently for Him . . ." (Ps. 37:5,7) and "Commit your works to the Lord, and your plans will be established" (Prov. 16:3).

There is a picture of E. Stanley Jones on the wall of my study. I look at it often when life drives me to a fresh commitment. Behind the immense effectiveness of this tireless warrior for the Lord was the secret of a vital commitment which took place some years after he began his ministry. "I laid at Christ's feet a self of which I was ashamed, couldn't control, and couldn't live with; and to my glad astonishment He took that self, remade it, consecrated it to Kingdom purposes, and gave it back to me, a self I can now live with gladly and joyously and comfortably."

Years ago I had a chance to ask Dr. Jones if that crisis was ever repeated. His answer was yes. He told me that life can be "awfully simple or simply awful" depending on whether each day and each situation is committed to the Lord. Daily surrender, moment by moment, was Jones' secret.

That leads us to the third kind of commitment. It is the secret of success in living out what we believe had been committed to us to do. No venture is accomplished without commitment of our inherent talents and Christ's imputed gifts. When we feel led to dare to attempt something, it requires clearly established goals, tireless effort, and complete dependence on the Lord's power to pull it off.

No athlete sets a new record without constant practice and preparation. There are no great, long-term marriages which have not required the commitment of both husband and wife. Marriage requires the hard work of mutual adjustment, forgiveness and effort to discern and do what love requires. The significant accomplishments in scientific research are the result of endless hours of committed investigation. It takes testing and repeated failures to discover a hidden truth or power. Battles are won, movements begun and sustained, programs for human welfare launched and accomplished because of the commitment of an individual or group who believe that what needs to be done can be done.

I am convinced that the Lord offers each of us a challenge which we must be committed to do. Often it changes as we and the circumstances around us change. What is it for you—right now? What seemingly impossible task is before you? If you are sure it has been given to you to do, have you committed yourself to do it by the talents you already have and the spiritual power the Lord will give you? It will be accomplished. Don't give up! The final stages of success are always preceded by disappointment and discouragement. Press on—victory is near. Our task is to be faithful to the vision the Lord has committed to us—the final result is up to him. If we have "deposited" the goal, it is being multiplied by the investment of "interest" from the Lord. We were created to be co-investors with him. Dare to risk the commitment of all you have.

What does all this mean to you? If we were face to face in conversation, I would look into your eyes to discern whether you have that joyous assurance of a person who is up to date with the Lord with a commitment of all that you are and have. Some of you may never have made an unreserved commitment and cannot say you really know Christ. Why not now? Others of you may be feeling the tension of trying to exist with areas of your life still not relinquished to the Lord. Why not now? Still others of you may be wrestling with problems or frustrations which await solutions through a complete surrender of them to the Lord. He waits patiently to act until you give the needs to him. Why not now? And what about that challenge for which you were born? Indeed, why not now?

The freedom of a committed life is at the core of what Joshua challenged the people of Israel to do. "Consecrate yourselves, for tomorrow the Lord will do wonders among you" (Josh. 3:5). Then we can say with assurance: I believe, I commit, I know, I am persuaded.

11

How Can Christ Help Me
When I'm Tempted?

HAVE YOU EVER wondered what might have happened if Jesus had not won his battle with Satan in the wilderness at the beginning of his ministry? I have. It has prompted me to consider what would be written about Jesus if he had given in to temptation. It might go something like this:

I want you to meet the greatest man who ever lived. He was the founder of the most powerful religion in history. Throughout his long life, he ministered in Palestine, but his influence reached the then-known world. Three great accomplishments early in his ministry have become the motivation and message of this religion. He performed three miracles which are the basis of what is called the threefold way to self-fulfillment through the immediate, the expedient, and the temporary.

The first of these three spectacular feats took place when he turned stones into bread in the wilderness. He had taken forty days to think through the strategy of his leadership. To focus the attention of his mind on how he could do this, he fasted for forty days. At the end of it, he was famished and weak. The flat stones of the wilderness reminded him of the loaves of bread of his time. He used his power to transform them into bread. It tasted like bread and satisfied his hunger. Since the hungry masses were on his heart, he continued to produce this miraculous bread and distributed it to them. That gained him a loyal following made up of fanatical supporters. The first tenet of this religion comes from this: God's power exists to satisfy our wants.

The second miracle was performed to increase the following of those who had been fed by the bread into a world-wide movement. The great leader knew that he had to impact the whole world in his lifetime. He decided to perform a physical feat which would shortcut the long process of getting the attention and absolute allegiance of the world. Since what he did is recorded in the annals of Hebrew, Roman, and Greek history, this indicates that he accomplished his purpose.

The records of the event differ slightly, but eyewitness accounts state that this popular leader astonished his followers and became the most renowned personality of his time by climbing up to the pinnacle of the Temple in Jerusalem. It was the corner of the plateau where Solomon's Porch and the Royal Porch met at Mt. Zion. There was a sheer drop of 450 feet into the Kidron Valley. Millions of people from all over the world saw him defy the laws of gravity. He leaped off the pinnacle. People watched him fall. They were breathless and stunned when, just before he hit the ground, a mysterious power intervened and he landed safely on his feet. Some say they even saw angel wings undergird him and make his landing secure. The wondrous event is the source of the second tenet of this religion: man's will can be accomplished by God's power.

The result of this was the third great human accomplishment. The leaders of the world all sought this leader's friendship. He became a trusted and revered guest in the courts of the kingdoms of the world. Kings and princes sought to be identified with him. His advice on political and military matters became the lesson for the longest period of peace on earth. It lasted all through the influence of his long 120-year lifetime.

This accounts for the third emphasis of this religion: compromise is the condition of peace. Through the ages, however, the followers have found that the meaning of this leader's influence has not reproduced the temporary peace he was able to develop during his lifetime.

At the time of his natural death from old age, he was buried in a magnificent temple. People have visited this site for two thousand years. In the great hall beside the tomb which contains his bones to this day, there are three symbols of the religion he founded: flat stones to remember that he temporarily solved the problem of human hunger; a carving of the pinnacle of the Temple, memorializing the leap of human courage; and a monarch's scepter, reminiscent of his influence over people of power. Smaller replicas of this central temple in Jerusalem have been built all over the world. The one strange thing which often disrupts the worship of this great man of history is a hideous, satanic laughter which some say can be heard.

Startling? Alarming? Bordering on blasphemy? Perhaps. And yet, this unsettling "what might have been" forces us to grapple with the meaning of Jesus' victory over temptation and his power to help us with our temptations. Suddenly, an oft-repeated Scripture verse leaps from the pages of Hebrews with new meaning: "For in that He Himself has suffered, being tempted, He is able to aid those who are tempted" (Heb. 2:18). In the wilderness, all through his ministry, and in Gethsemane our Lord met the constant onslaught of Satan to keep him from the reason he came: the cross and the sacrifice for the sins of the whole world.

Jesus Christ, the God-man in whose nature the divine and human were blended into perfect oneness, won the battle over temptation. He was God with us, engaged in a struggle with Satan and the powers of evil. He was also the new Adam beginning a new creation, the first completely obedient Man in the midst of a disobedient, fallen creation. "God was in Christ reconciling the world to Himself." The cross was his central purpose and passion. Satan's attacks were to tempt him to substitute, shortcut, and subliminate that awesome destiny of Calvary.

If our Lord had been thus beguiled, something like I have just described would have happened. Jesus of Nazareth would have been a revered personality of history, but not the triumphant Savior of the world. But because he won, the cross is now our assurance of forgiveness, the blessing of eternal life, and the power for our victory over temptation. He suffered and was tempted, indeed! Now he is able to aid us when we are tempted. The word "aid" in this Hebrews text in the original Greek is *boēthēsai*, from the compound verb, *boētheō*, (*boē*, a cry, *theō*, to run) to run at a cry, or call for help. As we are tempted, Christ runs to help us when we cry for help.

The words of the gospel hymn communicate the intensity of his empathy: "No one understands like Jesus." No one else can, for no one else has been through greater temptation than he went through for us. He runs to our cry for help in the midst of temptation with words of comfort and courage. "You are not alone. I understand. I know what you're going through. I've faced it myself. I'm with you all the way. Because I won, I am able to help you. Beloved, you are being tempted because you belong to me. You are the moving target of the evil one because you have given your life to me. Trust me and I will give you power!"

Just as Satan tempted Jesus to evade the cross, so too, all our temptations are to avoid our ultimate dependence on what he did for us on the cross—and to take up our own cross as the basic motive and message of our lives. The issue of Jesus' testing was his obedience to God. We are called to be his obedient disciples. Our basic purpose is to know and do his will. Once we have committed our lives to him and he has taken up residence in us, we can count on being tempted. These temptations in their many forms will all be aspects of the temptation he faced. What he said and did in response to Satan, he enables us to say and do today. His power is available to help us battle through to deepening levels of obedience. In our Gethsemanes when we are tempted to bypass the cross, we can say with him, "Not my will, but Thine, be done."

The temptation of turning stones into bread is the temptation to substitute something for the cross. It is difficult to say, "Nothing in my hand I bring, simply to the cross I cling." We are constantly tempted to justify ourselves. It is not easy to admit that we are sinners saved by grace alone. We want to be honored because of what we do for the Lord, accepted because of our moral achievement, and cherished because of what we can accomplish for him.

Sharply focused, our turning of stones into bread is the temptation to put our trust in secondary things. We look to our perfection, status, personality development, or influence. We try to gain life's security from something other than the cross.

Our insecurities and anxieties expose the impact of this temptation to substitute for the cross. We become overly dependent on the approval of people because we deny the love offered to us through Calvary. People's acceptance becomes far too important. We allow their affirmation or lack of it to control our security and peace of mind.

Jesus' answer to Satan is our only defense when this temptation beguiles us. "Man shall not live by bread alone, but by every word that proceeds out of the mouth of God." This forthright quotation of Deuteronomy 8:3 calls us back to intimate communion with the Lord in prayer and meditation on the Scriptures as our security. The cross calls for raw trust on the grace of God. When we are tempted to put our confidence in anything else, we are being given the opportunity to see the substitute for what it is and obediently trust in Calvary alone.

The second temptation is to take a shortcut around the cross. It is to take things into our own hands—to do God's work on our power. We tempt God by demanding signs and wonders. "If you do this for me, I will obey!" As the first temptation is to depend on a secondary substitute for our satisfaction, the second temptation is to put what God can *do* for us before what he *is* for us. That's always rooted in self-doubt. Satan's effort to dislodge Jesus' confidence in who he was and what he came to do was opened with the unsettling "if." "If you are the Son of God. . . ." If! He knew who he was. Satan uses the same strategy on us. If you are a Christian, prove it! Self-doubt is his treacherous weapon. If he can get our attention off the cross and our eternal security through Christ's love and forgiveness, then we will spend our energies on trying to prove to others that we are truly Christian. A never-ending cycle of self-justification begins, resulting in pretense and posturing. Our efforts at perfectionism, rather than Christ, become the focus of our lives. The point is that we don't have to *do* anything to prove that we belong to the Lord. When *doing* is wrenched from *being*, we are in trouble. Our only task is to grow in a profound, intimate relationship with the Lord. Then we will be motivated to do his work by his power, under his moment-by-moment guidance.

Competition between Christians to know and do more is a subtle variation of this second temptation. Satan knocks us off balance when we take our measurements from other people rather than from Christ. We pattern our lives on what others have done rather than the special and unique calling we are given. Pastors play the numbers game. Church people tell of spiritual experiences, not always to glorify the Lord, but to establish their image. All of us are tempted to ask "How am I doing?" in a million different ways. Raw dependence on the cross is blocked out in trying to measure up to the expectations of others. Before long, Satan has us where he wants us: we become intoxicated by pride or self-condemning remorse. Proving ourselves proves nothing—except that the cross is not enough for us.

But there's an even more dangerous aspect to this second temptation. What Satan wanted Jesus to do was not only to prove his authenticity as Messiah, but to test God to do a miracle on the Master's demand. The crucial thing is that God did not guide Jesus to affirm his anointed destiny in this way. He was sent to perform a bigger miracle than that! The cross and the resurrection make leaping off the pinnacle of the Temple look like hop-scotch by comparison. That would have been a shortcut indeed. A mere spectacle was denied so that a cosmic sacrifice could be made for the whole world—followed by a *true* miracle of all time.

This has so much to say to us. We are tempted to ask God to act miraculously to meet our wants on our timetable—and according to our specifications. Satan tempts us with impatience with God and his providence. The Lord is more concerned about our real *needs* than he is about our *wants*. What he denies us or delays is always to get us to the place where what we want is what he knows we need. He will never give us anything which will be a shortcut to realizing the miracle of our own cross and resurrection. The secret of the abundant life is death to ourselves and regeneration through a personal experience of the uplifting power of the resurrection.

A person who lives in the ambience of that transforming miracle is not constantly demanding evidences that the Lord is able. And the amazing thing is that his life is a succession of serendipities of miraculous interventions. But not according to his demand or agenda. Jesus astonished people by his mighty works not because he demanded that God act for the validation of his ministry or his own assurance. Rather, he was in complete harmony with the Father's plan and purpose.

There is a "what have you done for me lately?" syndrome among Christians today. We've misused the deep peace which comes from surrendering all our needs to the Lord with full assurance that he will act in a way that will bring us closer to him. When we give him the glory for what he has done, we become open for what he is prepared to do. Calvary and Easter are followed by our personal Pentecost. In fact, anything else he does for us is to bring us back to this ultimate act of mercy and liberation. What more does he need to say or do?

Often our pride in our service for the Lord, the gifts of the Spirit we have evidenced, the answers to prayer we have received, the miracles done through us, become a source of false security and a leverage on others. Satan is delighted. The more he can get us to talk about our superior spirituality, the more he can demote us to a place of having to out-do our own past accomplishments.

A further implication of this temptation lies in our distorted efforts to communicate our faith to others. Jesus' question in the wilderness was how God wanted him to accomplish his messiahship. Ours is how best to share with others the love and forgiveness his obedient life and death and resurrection now affords. How can we help people?

Satan is ready with easy shortcuts. He wants to keep our self-justifying anxiety level high so that we will try to side-step the Lord's strategy for loving people.

The cross, on the other hand, calls us to profound caring and sharing. As we have been forgiven, we are called to forgive. The indefatigable grace we've received is the only basis of really becoming involved with people and identifying with their needs.

Cross-oriented evangelism challenges us to develop profound relationships in which we can be Christ's love to people we want to help. It means vulnerability. Our time, schedules, plans, privacy, and resources are surrendered in our effort to be available, interruptible, and open. Whatever we do for people is in preparation for that tender, Spirit-created moment when they want to discover for themselves the Lord who has motivated our sacrificial concern for them.

Satan would have us avoid that sacred encounter at all costs. He would convince us that changing people's circumstances will transform their characters. Or he is delighted when we use manipulation, coercion, or criticism to get people to be or do what we want. All are shortcuts to the slow but ultimately effective cross-motivated love which earns the right to lead people to the cross.

Almost every day I talk with people about their concerns for others in their lives. They are troubled by their problems and hang-ups and want easy solutions and quick remedies. It is easy to wring our hands in consternation or smack our lips in criticism, but there is no substitute for prayer, personal involvement, and patient trust that the Lord will bring the person to a realization of his or her need of his love and forgiveness. Leaping off the pinnacle of some temple will not help. *Being* the love of the cross to bring them to the hope of the cross seldom fails.

The third temptation is the most beguiling of all. We need to expose it, ridicule it, and laugh at its absurdity. Think of it! Satan offered the kingdoms of this world to the Word through whom all things were created. The ludicrous thing is that they were his already. What could Satan offer the Son of God? "He was in the beginning with God. All things were made by Him, and without Him nothing was made that was made" (John 1:2-3). Christ had come to reclaim his creation and begin a new creation. The price of this redemption was the cross so that his people would know they belonged to him and not this world. Satan could not offer Christ any power. Christ was and is "the wisdom and power of God" (1 Cor. 1:24). What Satan could offer was the support of earthly power to accomplish Christ's work. Jesus resisted the temptation. He would do God's work on God's power. Again, the cross of Calvary was followed by the lasting hope of Easter.

Satan is no less persistent with any person in whom Christ lives. He constantly tries to get us to want what we already have. The way he does it is to offer facsimiles of grace, assurance, and power. He offers us things, popularity, positions of power, financial security. None of these is

wrong unless they become subtle substitutes for our relationship to Christ. His answer to Satan becomes our best
defense: "Away with you, Satan! I will worship and serve
only God."

In both Hebrew and Greek the words for worship and
service are interrelated. Both *abodah* in Hebrew and *latreia*
in Greek imply labor, servitude and service. The use of the
word "service" to describe worship in the contemporary
church has its roots in this. A pastor ended a service by
saying, "The worship is over and now the service begins."
This is clever but incorrect distinction. Our worship is our
service, and our service in the world is also our worship.
The Anglo-Saxon use of the word worship comes from
"worth-shape," to give ultimate worth. All this focuses the
question—Is God the only One we live for, serve, and
glorify in all of life?

It is shocking to note how closely connected in both tone
and intent were Christ's words to Satan and Peter. "Away
with you, Satan!" he said to Satan. He said, "Get behind
Me, Satan" when the disciple tried to dissuade him from
the cross (Matt. 16:22–23). Peter's ambitions for himself,
centered in the Master, had become a tool for Satan's
equivocation. We too can be on Satan's side when anything
or anyone becomes more important than Christ and his
cross. And Satan's trick is to try to convince us that he can
give us some temporary satisfaction which will meet the
emptiness or need inside us which only the Lord can fill.

Paul's assurance to the Corinthians exposes the foolish-
ness of thinking that we need what Satan temptingly offers. "For all things are yours . . . the world or life or death,
or things present or things to come—all are yours. And
you are Christ's, and Christ is God's" (1 Cor. 3:21–23). If
we make that conviction the basis of our lives there results
a conversion of our desires. When we want what the Lord
has already given us, we can rebuke the forces of evil.
"There is nothing you can offer which I don't have in
abundance—now and forever."

There is no temptation I have ever faced which could not be placed into one of the three categories of Jesus' temptations. All temptations are to evade the cross in one way or another. Make a list of your temptations, put them into one of these three groups, and let Christ help you. Temptation introduces us to the real struggles inside us. The issues of our divided loyalties are exposed.

When we are tempted we are aware of a new need for the Savior. He runs to us the minute we cry out for help. He is able! Paul knew that. "No temptation has overtaken you except that which is common to man; but God is faithful, who will not allow you to be tempted beyond what you are able, but with the temptation will also make the way of escape, that you will be able to bear it" (1 Cor. 10:13). Christ and his cross are the way of escape. He won his battle and from within us will help us win ours.

12

Why Are
Some Christians
So Dull?

I WAS ALARMED BY THE large number of questions which articulated concern about the ho-hum lack of enthusiasm and excitement in some Christians and many churches. What caught my attention, and eventually created a separate category for these questions, was repeated use of the word "dull." They expressed as much an indictment as an inquiry.

Here are some of the questions which illustrate the grouping I called, "Dull Christians." Why are so many Christians dull? What makes so many churches so dull? What can we do about the gray dullness of so much of institutional Christianity today? Why is church work so often dull? How can I keep my faith aflame and not settle for the drab dullness I sense in so many Christians and experience in most churches? Shouldn't we be able to expect that Christians be interesting, and not dull people? I've lost the glow of my initial faith—how do I get it back? Believing all we do, why is Christianity so grim and dull for so many? How do you keep your faith from becoming routine and dull?

The use of the word "dull" reveals the confusion of people about their own faith. It also shows their consternation concerning others and contemporary Christianity.

The questions forced me to get in touch with some feelings and fears of my own. The last adjective I would ever want to be descriptive of me or my church is dull.

The variety of the uses of the word make it all the more disturbing when applied to Christians or Christianity. A cutting edge which has lost its sharpness is dull, blunt. Intellectually, a dull person is sluggish, listless, lacking in perception and responsiveness. In the emotional realm, dullness is the opposite of acute or intense, incapable of passion and purpose. Such a person lacks vitality, brisk- ness, energy. A dull personality is boring, wearisome, obscure, uninteresting. Other uses of the word are equally denigrating. Dull also describes lack of luster, brightness, illumination. A dull sound is one that is indistinct, muf- fled, and unclear.

On the basis of this etymological excursion into the meaning of dullness, we are forced to define what is meant by a dull Christian. An authentic encounter with Jesus Christ should have an observable intellectual, emotional, volitional, and physical impact on our personalities. These result in volitional decisiveness in following Christ as Lord. This illuminates the countenance with sparkle and zest. A dull Christian is one who lacks burning intellectual convic- tions which infuse into him emotional warmth and vitality.

Dull churches are made up of dull leaders and mem- bers. They are traditional instead of triumphant, bland rather than exciting, grim without grace, cool rather than full of conviction. The cutting edge of the gospel has been dulled with impersonal preaching and teaching. People's deepest needs are unmet and what's said and done is often irrelevant to the real issues of living in the real world. The great wonders is that we put up with it!

What a picture! Pious clergy voices drone classical theories with little contemporary application. The worship is characterized by lifeless singing and prayers to a distant and aloof Lord. This lack of vitality in the life of the church and its program is like a marriage without affection.

I am constantly amazed at how many Christians are bored with their local churches. Why? Knowing Christ and growing in him are meant to be exciting. He is interesting, stimulating, impelling. The Scriptures are anything but dull. The Christianity of the New Testament is a thrilling adventure. There's nothing tepid or tedious about life in Christ.

How then, echoing the questions people have asked, can Christians drift into dullness and their churches become powerless purveyors of faithless familiarity? How does it happen? Are dull Christians simply people who were dull before becoming Christians and just remain uninteresting and unenthusiastic people? But what about those whose excitement for Christ has been bleached and starched by the rigors of religion? And nothing is more alarming than to see a fun-loving, affable pagan become grim and pious with the pretentious mask of spirituality and the lackluster jargon of some brand of religious posturing.

Sometimes the dullness can be blamed on the lack of power in the pulpit. Other times it is church officers who have not kept their faith alive. Often the problem is programs which maintain traditions rather than care for people and equip them for contagious witness in the world. As a friend of mine described a conference he attended: "Dull, dull, deadly dull. Dull people, arguing about dull resolutions, to perpetuate a dull, culturally imprisoned, tradition-bound institution." A church officer said at a time of spiritual monotony in his church, "We ought to engage in a building program to get the people excited about this church again." As if Christ, the gospel, and changing lives were not enough! A Christ-centered church filled with Christ-possessed Christians is meant to be a fellowship throbbing with new life—thrilling, energetic, dynamic. And the rebirth of our churches begins with you and me.

Dullness in a Christian is simply lack of fire! A vital, consistent relationship with Christ fuels an unquenchable fire in us. Then we can become enablers of a very different quality of church. We will become what Calvin called the fellowship of the flaming heart.

The experience of two of Jesus' followers on the road to Emmaus on the evening after the resurrection gives us an example of how he can transform dullness into dynamic delight. A careful study of Luke 24:12–35 shows us the way the Lord fans the banked embers of a dull faith into a flaming fire. Once again, a faithful exposition of a biblical passage answers our questions. What the Lord did that day in the hearts of these two men exemplifies the greatest need of the hour today. Picture the incident; get inside the skins of these discouraged disciples; allow to happen to you what happened to them. Here is a drama in three acts. The concluding act can't be appreciated without the first and second.

It was as if their feet were filled with lead as they trudged the dusty, rock-strewn road from Jerusalem to Emmaus. Discouragement dogged their steps as they shuffled along. They felt as if the weight of the whole troubled world were placed back on their impotent shoulders. As a part of the fellowship of the followers of Jesus of Nazareth along with the appointed disciples, they had felt the lifting of that world of care. With Jesus they had experienced hope, witnessed the power of God in his mighty works, and anticipated the ushering in of the promised kingdom of God to Israel. Oh, how they had grown to love him, need him, delight in him! And then their hopes dashed around them as he was arrested, tried, and crucified.

Surely they must have watched from a distance as their beloved Master writhed on the cross. Perhaps they had helped Joseph of Arimathea and Nicodemus take his body down from the cross. Tenderly and lovingly they may have placed it in the tomb in Joseph's garden. Along with the disciples they had waited in the Upper Room during the excruciating, fearful hours of Saturday, wondering, grieving, aching with despair. And then they had been shocked by the news that the tomb was empty and Jesus' body was gone.

When the women returned to the Upper Room with the news, their "words seemed like idle tales, and they did not believe them" (Luke 24:11). The account in Luke implies that these two men must have left the assembly at that point and made their way out of the city, seeking the quiet of the countryside, away from the sorrow, pain, mounting tension, and anxiety. They were emotionally spent, depleted, devoid of the capacity to hope again. A walk to Emmaus, perhaps their home, would quiet their nerves and give them a chance to talk out what had happened.

There is nothing more tragic than a knowledge of Jesus' message and a witness of his crucifixion without an experience of his resurrected presence. Oscar Wilde captures what must have been the mood of those men as they talked with one another along the road, their shoulders slumped in remorse, their heads down in diminished dreams.

> We did not dare to breathe a prayer
> Or give our anguish scope
> Something was dead in all of us,
> And what was dead was hope.

Then suddenly there was a Third Person with them on that road. The resurrected Lord drew alongside them. It is significant that they did not recognize him. They had not really heard his promise to rise from the dead and, therefore, had little expectation. Dullness indeed! Dulled by their lack of hope they did not remember that he had told them he would rise and would be with them always. How could they have failed to recognize his voice, his undeniable radiance? "What manner of conversation is this that you have with one another as you walk and are sad?" he asked.

One of them named Cleopas responded with consternation that this stranger did not know what had transpired in those cataclysmic days in Jerusalem. To help the follower get in touch with his feelings the compassionate Christ pressed him to explain. "Concerning Jesus of Nazareth," he said, "who was a Prophet mighty in deed and word before God and all the people. . . ." The disciple then went on to explain the events of Jesus' trial and crucifixion. His hopelessness could not be dispelled even by the rumor that the tomb was empty.

At this point the Lord interrupted with an incisiveness which must have shocked them. "O foolish ones, and slow of heart to believe all that the prophets have spoken! Ought not the Christ to have suffered these things and enter into glory?" It is fascinating to note that the Greek word used to translate Jesus' Aramaic word for "slow" is an old word for one who is dull.

The Lord was deeply concerned that these two followers had not been listening all through his ministry as he repeatedly told them about his death for the sins of the world. They had not heard that his resurrection was the ultimate vindication of his victory over death. The most they could say about him was that he was a prophet mighty in deed and word.

How could they have missed his message? Why did they not expect to meet him resurrected, alive, powerful to help? But before we become too critical of them, we must ask what we have heard, how much we expect, how little we hope. We hear but have not heard. Dullness!

But Jesus is not dissuaded by the dullness in these would-be followers on the Emmaus road. Instead, he carefully led them through the Scriptures explaining from Moses and the Prophets the truth concerning himself and what he had come to be and do. We can only imagine what it must have been like to hear that sweeping account of the preparation for the Incarnation, Atonement, and Resurrection victory.

When the three reached Emmaus, the men were so moved by what they had heard that they asked the "Stranger" to stay with them. "Abide with us, for it is toward evening and the day is far spent." And even though he had indicated that he was going on, the Lord who always responds to an invitation to linger with us, went into their home and joined them for supper.

That's when it happened. The Guest became the Host! When he broke the bread for them, their dullness was dissolved. Feel the realized excitement; imagine the surging wonder. They knew it was Jesus, the Christ, their Lord and Savior. He was right there with them! Was it that they saw the nail wounds in his hands? Or was it the way he broke the bread that reminded them of how he had broken and multiplied the loaves to feed the five thousand in Galilee? Little matter. They recognized the resurrected, victorious Lord!

What they exclaimed to one another after Jesus departed from them is very pointed for our concern about dull Christians in this chapter. "Did not our heart burn within us while He talked with us on the road, and while He opened the Scriptures to us?" Their dullness, slowness of heart to trust and expect, had been replaced with a burning heart.

What did they mean? Prolonged pondering and prayer and meditation upon this passage lead me to this definition: a burning heart is one in which the dry kindling of unrealized, unexperienced truth is set ablaze with flaming conviction. This transforms doubt into daring, coolness into warmth, unwillingness into commitment, and a cloudy countenance into radiant joy. Now excitement, enthusiasm and courage pulsed through the minds and bodies of those followers who became bold by beholding the risen Lord. In the words of a friend of mine, their "soul desire became the sole desire."

What a contrast they are now to the dull people they had been when the Lord invaded their moody discouragement along the road a few hours before! No wonder they could not wait to return to Jerusalem to tell the eleven disciples in the Upper Room. Their feet had wings on them as they ran back to Jerusalem. I have often wondered if they paused briefly at the spot where the Lord had met them on that road. Imagine how they might have looked at one another, laughing with uncontainable excitement, grasping each other, bursting with joy! And then, when they reached the apostles, there was certainly no dullness in their exclamation, "The Lord is risen, indeed!"

This stirring account gives us four crucial ways Christ can transform dullness today. He is not satisfied until we can all say, "Oh, how my heart burns within me!" He wants that for every preacher before, during, and after he or she preaches. He wants to set every church officer's heart afire with that kind of decisive encounter as a basis for leading congregations toward the goal of being the "fellowship of the burning heart." He offers nothing less for every church member as he dispels the darkness with his "I am with you always."

In the light of this account, "dull Christians" is a contradiction of terms! We have seen the "before and after" picture of those two men. What happened in between gives us the charter for enlivening burned-out Christians and bringing renaissance to the church. The Lord calls us all to be on fire. He wants us to be radiant, passionate disciples. Here are the four ways the One who is the baptizer with fire makes us part of the fellowship of the flaming heart.

First of all, Christ himself comes to us just as we are. Don't miss the fact that our Lord took seriously the dullness of those two men. He knows and cares about whatever it is that has cooled our spiritual ardor into dullness. So often the reason for our dullness is that we bypass our real needs. Our faith becomes a lifeless, uneventful, dull ritual and routine if we do not allow Christ to indwell us. We can worship, work in the church, pray our prayers, study the

Scriptures, even witness to others, and not confess and relinquish our deepest hurts and hopes. The Lord came to those men on the road and forced them to articulate how they were feeling.

The Christian faith becomes exciting when we are consistently invaded by the surprising presence of the Lord. He will not allow us a bifurcation of the spiritual and the personal. He intrudes on the real you and me, the persons we are in our secluded aloneness. Dull Christians are those who have not allowed the Lord into the unresolved problems and frustrations of their lives.

My own experience is that when I open myself to the Lord's serendipitous interventions, my relationship with him becomes exciting again. Enthusiasm for Christ and the gospel burns within me as a result of the fresh grace I have received in what I had thought were impossible situations. For me, the most powerful preparation for preaching in addition to prayer and study, is a profoundly personal experience of seeing the Lord take situations or relationships relinquished to him and bring unimagined blessing out of them.

As I write this, I am ablaze with gratitude for answered prayer in several crucial relationships. But Christ himself has been the answer! If I had closed off those needs, continuing to pray general prayers and doing the work of ministry, eventually I would have experienced tragic ineffectiveness, blandness, and lack of fire in my personal and professional life. Just as in any human relationship, when anything is unexpressed or hidden, the relationship eventually becomes strained, or what's worse, coolly accommodating. The same is true for our relationship to the Lord.

Substitutionary secondariness results. We major in minors. We become concerned with details rather than the dynamic of Christ himself. We become fussy about churchmanship and forget the Lord of the church. Form becomes more important than function. We argue theology, become empassioned over some esoteric aspect of Scripture, emphasize the things which divide rather than unite, and take pride in our performance rather than realizing the Lord's power.

The reason for the dullness in many churches is a failure to allow the gospel to be personal. We preach and teach without touching the raw nerves in people and pointedly sharing personal illustrations from our own and other's experience of what a particular text or truth can mean in people's lives today. In so doing we skim over both heads and hearts. When church officers are loved and cared for as people, their fellowship together is transformed.

The great need in church renewal is for leaders who are up to date with the Lord, allowing him to meet their needs. Often the most courageous advancements in a parish occur after a time of revival among the officers. And this is marked by honesty and openness about personal problems or frustrations. When a church officer has had an Emmaus road experience with the Lord, by allowing Christ to deal with an area of his or her life at home, at work, or in the inner recesses of the heart, an entirely different attitude of expectancy is displayed in church work. Often church officers expect little for their churches because they are experiencing little in their personal relationship with the Savior. The same is true for all of us.

The first step to a burning heart is to believe that right now as you are reading this, the resurrected, living Lord is drawing nigh. I am more sure of that as I write this than I am of my next breath! Does he have all of us? Are there areas where we've resisted his intervention? Have you been amazed in the past few days because of some relationship or problem he's taken over and transformed? If not, there's something wrong. Dullness is on the way. Life in Christ is meant to be a continuous succession of miracles, small and big. The more we are in touch with needs in ourselves, others, and our world, and trust the Lord for his power, the more on-fire we will become. Christ himself is the fire of the burning heart!

That leads to the second thing we discover in this account of the Emmaus road appearance. The burning heart is the result of listening to the Lord talk to us about himself. The men in our passage exclaimed that their hearts burned as Christ talked to them on the road. And what did he talk about? The Scriptures and what they proclaimed about him. The emotional feeling of the burning heart is always the result of an intellectual conviction: that of who Christ is and what he has done for us.

Think what it must have been like to hear the Lord's Bible study that day on the Emmaus road! He traced the red line of redemption through the five books of Moses' Pentateuch and then in each of the major and minor prophets. I believe he taught the two men that he was the Passover Lamb. He showed them that the sacrifices of ancient Israel begun in the wilderness were now fulfilled in the sacrifice of Calvary. He was Israel's scapegoat, the unblemished sacrifice, the blood of atonement. All the ancient rites, rituals, and ceremonies were but a foretaste of him.

How gently he contradicted the idea that he was only a prophet. Rather, he is the One of whom the prophets spoke in longing anticipation. He is Isaiah's Immanuel, suffering servant, and Prince of Peace. He is Jeremiah's "Branch of righteousness"; Ezekiel's "Plant of renown" giving shade, and shedding fragrance; Daniel's stone cut without hands; Hosea's dew to Israel, blessing like a lily, rooted like the cedars of Lebanon with unqualified love in spite of the failure of Israel's fickle heart; Joel's "Hope of His people, the Strength of the children of Israel"; Amos's "plowman overtaking the reaper" bringing judgment and grace; Obadiah's deliverance; a greater than Jonah; the "turning again" of God's redemptive love signaled by

Micah; the publisher of peace anticipated by Nahum; Habakkuk's Anointed going forth for salvation; the purity of truth in Zephaniah; Haggai's true Zerubbabal rebuilding the house of God; Zechariah's King over all the earth, the "only One"; and Malachi's "Sun of righteousness."

We can understand why the hearts of those men burned! The impact of Jesus' teaching was clear: the sovereign God of all creation had come to them in Christ. The Creator had appeared to recreate a new people and to begin a new creation. Jesus enabled the Emmaus travelers to think magnificently of God and what he had done through him.

A mind alive to new truth results in a heart ablaze with new excitement for the Lord. A consistent, daily study of the Scriptures is one of the most powerful ways the Lord talks to us. He focuses our need and then answers through the passages we study. When we come to the Bible with an open mind, sincerely asking for the Lord's truth to meet whatever we are facing, he speaks to us. Then we are ready for receptive prayer.

Prayer is listening to the Lord. When we are silent, patiently waiting, he talks to us. He floods our minds with insight and wisdom, guidance and discernment. So often people ask me, "What do you mean—the Lord talks to you?" There is only one answer: when I become quiet and really want to hear what he has to say about my life and ministry, he speaks. I do not hear voices. I don't need to. The thoughts he places within my mind are like spoken words, and yet, they are more powerful than an articulated sound.

I have never been disappointed. Alone and in my solitude, he speaks to me. X-ray vision and insight into people and situations are given. Mistakes and failures in my life come because I acted or spoke precipitously without waiting on the Lord. But even in the failures, when I return to him seeking forgiveness and a new chance, he shows the way. When there seems to be no immediate answer in some situation I've surrendered to him, this is a sure sign that I'm to wait.

My heart burns within me both when he clearly speaks and when his silence cautions me to wait. In times of heart-ache as well as thanksgiving, intimacy with the Lord brings healing and hope. There can be no lasting antidote to dullness which does not consistently include prolonged listening.

The third thing that we discover about the burning heart in the Emmaus road account is that it produces in-clusive warmth expressed in genuine fellowship. Note this: the two followers did not say their hearts burned within them but that their heart, singular, *kardia* in Greek, burned within them. Dull Christians are usually not in-volved in deep, supportive *and* remedial fellowship. The Lord came to make us one with him and with one another. There is a unified heart the Lord wants to set on fire. Dullness is a sure sign that we are trying to go it alone. The sure evidence that we have received Christ's indwelling Spirit is that his flame sets fire to the kindling waiting to be lighted in another's heart.

Each week I receive hundreds of letters from all over the country. They come from people in deep spiritual trouble. Most of the people are not in any consistent fellowship. My advice, after showing them how to turn their trouble over to the Lord and to listen to him, is to encourage them to find a band of believers in their church, where they work, or in their neighborhood with whom they can read the Bible, share concerns and problems, and pray for one another. Worship services inspire, preaching uplifts, teaching classes instruct, but we all need times with fellow-adventurers. Then we can process what is happen-ing to and around us as well as the intellectual truth we are discovering. When we are challenged to talk through what we are thinking and feeling, and then hear others pray for us, our hearts burn brightly. We all need to be a link in the chain of love.

The fourth aspect of the burning heart is discovered in witnessing. Their experience with the risen Christ sent the two men back to Jerusalem to share their joy. They could not contain their excitement. Christians who have experienced the burning heart must give away to others what they have received. Our heart fires are fueled by serving people and sharing Christ with them. Communicating Christ's love is to our burning heart what oxygen is to fire. It is a fact of experience that our faith becomes dull if we are not telling others what the Lord has done for us.

The first thing we need to do is ask the Lord for the people he has arranged on our agenda. Then, expressing the warmth of Christ in us, we can enter into deep, caring friendships with them. We are called to be servants in our witnessing. When we serve people by listening and loving, we earn the right to deep relationships. As the friendship deepens, there will be increasing opportunities to share what Christ is doing in our lives. Some great challenge or problem in the other person's life will eventually emerge. This is the Lord's open door to help that person to give his or her need and whole life over to Christ.

Anyone who feels dullness creeping in must ask certain questions: Have I been willing to care and share? Have I asked the Lord for opportunities? Am I open to listen and be the kind of friend others can trust implicitly? Have I been vulnerable to share what Christ has done in my own needs? Have I been loving enough to be incisive when the time is right?

The final point I want to make draws all the above four aspects of a burning heart into sharp focus. Whenever I read this passage, I am amazed at how close those men came to missing the realization of the risen Lord and the gift of a burning heart. Luke tells us that as they "drew near to the village where they were going . . . He indicated that He would have gone farther." The Lord would have gone on if they had not detained him with the urgent request, "Abide with us." He will not force himself upon us. He waits to be wanted.

Having answered the questions about dull Christians and churches, the further question must now be answered by each of us. Am I dull? Is my faith exciting and enthusiastic? Contagious? Impelling? We Christians don't have to be dull. We can receive a burning heart. Christ will do for us what he did there in that humble home in Emmaus. Invite him to abide forever. You'll be a flaming Christian then. Be sure of that! And then you can be his flame to ignite your church.

13

Is It Possible
To Change
Human Nature?

"YOU HAVEN'T CHANGED a bit!" an old friend exclaimed after a good, long visit. My immediate, inadvertent, blurted response surprised me as much as it did him. "Oh, really?" I said, "That's very disappointing!"

We both laughed. I hadn't seen the man in years. What he said had been intended as a compliment. He had wanted to affirm certain beliefs which he had observed to be intact. Then, in response to my reaction, he went on to say something I will cherish as long as I live. "The thing that hasn't changed a bit," he said, "is your commitment to change." I really liked that. The motto of my life is: "I am not what I used to be and, thank God, I'm not what I'm going to be!"

From that personal perspective I want to consider the question asked in a variety of ways by so many: "Can human nature be changed?" The question has been asked by two groups of people—those who are impatient with their own progress and those who are frustrated by the lack of progress in others.

When trying to answer an honest query, we need to ask three questions: who asked it, why did they ask it, and how serious were they about wanting an answer?

Why does it take so long to become mature in the Christian life? Why do I battle the same old problems? What does God expect—perfection? How can I overcome old habits and ways of thinking? Just how new is the new creation in Christ? When will the battle be over?

Obviously these questions were asked by people who were disappointed in their own progress and wondered why growth is so difficult. But an equally large group of questions was asked by people who were disturbed by the lack of progress in the personalities and habit patterns of people around them.

Do people ever really change? Why am I constantly disappointed in the way people act and what they say? A wife asked, "How can I live my faith with someone who is not a believer and does not want to be?" A father put it this way, "I am discouraged with my children—how can I change them? Is it too late?" A college student queried, "Does becoming a Christian make any difference? If so, why are so many Christians unchristian?" And a church officer inquired, "Why is it so many Christians never move into a lifelong love affair with Jesus Christ so that they can say unreservedly, 'My passion in life is to know and serve Christ'?" Why so many unfruitful Christians? Why do Christians struggle with the same problems as others who don't believe?

Really, these questions we ask about others are no different than those asked by people concerning themselves. If they knew the answer for their own lives, they would not have asked it about others. The essential question is—How can I change and help other people to change?

What still another person affirmed and asked focuses all the questions about the potential of human nature to be changed. He put it this way: "William James said, 'The most exciting discovery of our generation is the discovery that we can alter our person by altering our attitude of mind.' How can I most effectively use this power to become the person God wants me to be? I believe that change in my life is a lifelong process to be savored, enjoyed, and exploited!"

We respond positively to the gusto of that man's adventuresome quest for growth, but end up with the same question: How can we alter the attitudes of our minds? His question, like all the rest, betrays an essential distortion. It is focused in the personal pronoun, I.

How can we change ourselves or others? My response is that we can't. Only Christ can change human nature. And how he does it is the triumphant note of Paul's hymn to love in 1 Corinthians 13. For me, verses 9 and 10 sound this assurance of hope. "For now we know in part and we prophesy in part. But when that which is perfect has come, then that which is in part will be done away." We are all in transition, capable of being more than we are. We are on the way to the perfect. You will remember in our study of knowing God's perfect will, "perfect" means "end, purpose, and intended goal." Paul's goal in his hymn to love is to describe how this takes place. In essence it describes Christ himself and the person we can become when his Spirit resides in us and controls our natures. Human nature can be changed by the indwelling power of his Spirit.

But from what to what? That presses us to a definition of human nature and why it needs to be changed. Our word "nature" comes from the Latin root "to be born." It means the innate, essential traits and characteristics of a person or thing. Human means that which pertains to, or is characterized by, man or mankind. Human nature, then, could be defined as the composite of assets and liabilities with which we were born. These are shaped, but not essentially changed, by our environment and the influence of significant others throughout our formative years.

We were endowed at birth with intellect, emotion, and will, housed in a physical body. We enter the world with a need to be loved and a potential to learn how to love. This is the implanted need for God. Only he can love us as much as we need to be loved.

There is also a liability with which we enter the world, however. We are born with a blemish: an innate selfishness and self-centeredness. This liability is constantly at variance with our assets. The conditioning of our environment and the impact of others can seek to channel it creatively, but cannot change it. It is part of our fallen creation, an inherited distortion of the Lord's original intention. Another word for it is sin. It robs us of the Lord's purpose for our human nature. Humanness.

The incarnation of God in Christ is both an affirmation and a reclamation of humanness. God came to transform the blight on our nature into a blessing. Christ's life and death had cosmic ramifications. It was to begin a new creation made up of people who were set free from the compulsion to focus the need for love on self. Christ was not only the divine Mediator between God and man, but the model of humanness as it was originally intended to be. His death on the cross was both an atonement for man's sin, and a reconciliation of mankind's estrangement from God. Now, as our resurrected, victorious Lord, he has the power to break our bonds of self-centeredness and transform us to be able to live the genuine humanness he exemplified.

The goal of human nature is to be fully human. The glory of Christ is a person fully alive, reaching full potential, recreated in his image. Whatever we do to escape our humanness ends up in some form of inhumanity. Selfishness and self-centeredness make us less than the human beings our Lord intended us to be. The only way to change human nature is to remove the distortions which keep us from true humanness. Our fallen nature is in rebellion against our Creator. We seek to run our own lives with no center of control. This results in the pride, anger, hostility, and competitiveness which are signs of inhumanity. When Christ takes hold of a life, he makes the person more human. It is the devil's game to try to convince us that we should try to escape our humanity. Treeness is the purpose of a tree; the glory of a rose is roseness. And what is the glory of a person? It is wholeness of personhood: a healed, released, loved, and loving person. What we call change in human personality is really liberating that person from those things which cause him or her to be inhuman. True humanness is the result of allowing Christ to love us, daring to love ourselves, and creatively loving others as gifts from him.

So when we speak of changing human nature, we are talking about more than personality modification. Nothing less than a transformation from self-centeredness to Christ-centeredness can change human nature. The inhuman things we do are the outward expression of the inhuman person we are. A genuine experience of Christ's love will make us more human!

I talked to a man last week who said, "I wish I were not so human in my reactions! How can Christ help me to be more spiritual?" There's the basic distortion. It took a lot of deep conversation to help him understand and accept the fact that true spirituality is humanness. What he meant was that he wanted Christ to help him deal with the inhuman expressions of his selfishness. His inherent liability was at war with his assets. The God-given gifts of intellect, emotion, and will were all focused in on himself and his little world. His family training had given him the Christian ethic and vague idea of spirituality. But he had no power to live the ethic or to love others. He had just enough religion to keep him from Christ. Like so many cultural Christians, he needed a profound healing of the liabilities of human nature. I am thankful that healing has begun. There's a good chance he will allow the Lord to make him human!

I am convinced that this was what Paul was seeking to communicate to the Corinthians. He gives us the secret of how human nature is transformed. That which is in part, our inhumanity, can increasingly attain the goal of authentic humanness.

It is exciting to expound 1 Corinthians 13 in that context. The key to a new nature is love. Paul knew that from his own life. He is one of the finest examples of the power of Christ's love to change a personality from the core. His encounter, and subsequent union, with Christ enabled a new creation in which the old passed away and a new person emerged. His education and training had produced a legalistic, hostile man. He was loveless and judgmental. His immense intellect was passionately committed to rules and regulations. Anger flamed within his heart. Pride dominated his attitudes. Tradition was his security, issuing in defensiveness.

The Pharisee who met Christ on the Damascus road was desperately in need of a nature transplant. And that's what happened. His encounter with Christ, and the fourteen years of preparation for apostleship which followed, shaped a new man to preach the good news that Christ can change human nature.

Even after his conversion and years of growth in Christ, Paul was a man in transition. He discovered that the process of changing human nature is the result of Christ-centeredness and Christ-confidence. Progressively he grew toward perfection as he relinquished control of his nature to Christ. He became more and more like the Savior. An inhuman religionist became a human being! He became capable of receiving and communicating profound love. First Corinthians 13 is not only a biographical description of Christ, it is also Paul's own autobiography. Most important of all, it can be our story, a description of the person we were meant to be and are becoming.

The first thing Paul establishes is that an exchange of religions is no substitute for the transformation of our natures into Christ-likeness. In the first three verses of this stirring description of a new humanity, the apostle warns against substituting anything for growth in a love-infused nature. The danger of the secondary manifestations of Christian piety could preclude love as the basis of the Christian life. Paul saw the danger of Christianity becoming one more religion in a very religious world.

That's the reason he begins with the supremacy of love. Our initial experience of Christ can become more important than our continuing growth in him. The gift of prophecy can be paraded without the evidence of becoming like Christ. We can understand mysteries without growing in the mysterious process of character transformation. The accumulation of knowledge can preclude a liberating, growing knowledge of Christ. Working miracles can become more important than allowing Christ to work a miracle in our nature. He wants to astound the world with the miracle he has performed in us. Then we will be able to help people experience Christ's love and the transformation of their own natures. That will begin in the love they receive from Christ through us. Our service to them can never substitute for personal, giving, forgiving, accepting love. Feeding the poor is part of our responsibility, but it should never take the place of offering the Bread of Life. Even martyrdom, giving our body to be burned, without love profits us and others little.

So often we think that to become a Christian we have to take on some kind of superpious spirituality. What ends up is not humanness, but an escape from it. That's the reason so many of us Christians ask the question, "After I gave my life to Christ, why was I no different?" It's because we started off on the wrong track. We went off to perfectionism on our own strength, rather than fulfilling our purpose by Christ's power. The only way we're transformed is to put our eyes on Jesus Christ, fasten on him, draw into him, abide in him, and then inadvertently we become like him. And as we become like him, we don't become some superpious, angelic being hovering between heaven and earth. We become human beings—softened, perceptive, feeling, caring, empathetical and, most of all, loving.

Paul goes on to give us the secret of becoming this kind of person. The reproduction of Christ's nature in us enables authentic humanness. Verses 4 through 8 of this magnificent hymn of love (1 Cor. 13) describe what love is and what it is not. The secret of understanding this passage is to replace the word "love" with "Christ" in the phrases which describe what love is. Those verses which clarify what love is not are a description of inhumanity in need of love to produce humanness.

Take the positive description of the love Christ offers first. "Love (Christ) suffers long and is kind." These words are a salient summary of the nature of God exposed all through the Old Testament and sublimely imparted in Christ.

The term "suffers long," *makrothumei* in Greek, is a combination of *makros,* "long," and *thumos,* "passion." When combined with "kind," *chrēsteutai,* meaning gentle in behavior, we have a lovely picture of God's attitude and essential nature. Other translations render the phrase, "patient and kind." The basic meaning is that our Lord is infinitely compassionate in his enduring grace toward us.

Patience is the power to suffer long. Kindness implies empathy and understanding, forgiveness, and a constant flow of second chances and new beginnings. There is nothing we can do or say which will make the Lord stop loving us. The loving-kindness of God is indefatigable. He offers us his acceptance, waits patiently for our response, and suffers through our long and repeated rejections. He has all eternity and can wait for us to come to the end of our own wilful rebellion and finally turn to him for help. When we do, the same long-suffering patience is reproduced in us. Our inhuman impetuousness is replaced by patience with ourselves and others.

Kindness flows from this. The kindness of God is expressed in his indefatigable willingness to forgive us. The experience of his forgiveness in Christ frees us to forgive ourselves. That heals the inhuman judgmentalism which denies us the warmth and graciousness of a Christ-inspired humanness. Our initial experience of the cross breaks us open to the flow of love and our oft-repeated need to be forgiven keeps us tender and accepting toward others. Our human nature is returned to its original glory: to be to each other what the Lord has been to us.

We begin to rejoice in truth. Honesty with God and one another becomes the consistent, dependable expression of our nature. The objectionable dishonesty of duality—being one thing and pretending another, saying one thing and meaning another—is replaced by an inward and outward unity. We love the truth, speak it, and live it. The inhumanness of escaping reality is replaced by a genuineness. People will be able to say, "What you see is what you get," in their relationship with us.

Christ's love in us enables a passion for integrity. As the Living Bible translates it, "Love rejoices when truth wins out." One of the things in human nature which troubles all of us is our tendency to dissemble and pretend. Christ in us gives us the power to return to the glory of our humanity as it was intended to be. We can be honest about our mistakes, failures, and inadequacies. Most of all, we can be ourselves—the loved and forgiven, unique and very special miracle of the Lord.

When we realize how gracious he has been to us, his character is manifested in us so that it "bears all things, believes all things, hopes all things, endures all things." This is patience and kindness in action producing a truly positive personality. Negativism is replaced by the confident belief that the Lord will use all things, in us and others, for the accomplishment of his purposes and our growth. Negativism is our inhuman experience of lack of faith. We become positive people when we accept our humanity and the Lord's power. Negativism is caused by trusting in ourselves and others and being disappointed. We fail others and people fail us. A grim attitude results. We become negative because we expect from others and ourselves what only God can do. A positive attitude is the result of complete trust in our Lord's faithfulness.

Can negative people change? Yes! A profound experience of Christ's love followed by an infilling of his presence frees us to trust him and not ourselves and others. He is the One who replaces the inhuman negativeness with a genuinely human trust in his truth and power to bring good out of evil.

From within us he bears the hurts, gives us the courage to believe that his power will triumph, produces the daring capacity to hope in spite of what happens to disappoint us, and engenders an endurance through life's problems and frustrations. It is not that we do it on our own to glorify him; he glorifies himself in us, giving us the capacity to do what we could not do on our own.

Now consider what Christ in our human nature is not. Most of the things people questioned could be changed in human nature are in Paul's list.

Love does not envy. Again insert Christ's name in the phrase. Christ does not envy. Why? Because he has all power in heaven and earth. What does he lack? Nothing! So, too, a person in whom Christ lives begins to love himself or herself as loved by him. Our life is filled with praise for the person he has enabled us to be. Comparisons motivating envy and jealousy are swallowed up in a new delight in our Christ-filled nature. Envy is a sure sign of an unstable state of grace. We have not accepted the love Christ offers us nor enjoyed the wonder of our specialness.

Parading ourselves results. We have to blow our own horn if we have not answered the trumpet call of the Lord's grace. We will drop names until we feel the power of the Name. We will have to convince others of our goodness until the goodness of the Lord is our security. There is no need to tell people how great we are if we know that any greatness we have is a gift. When we have the Lord's approval, we don't need to puff up ourselves to win the approval of others. Our purpose will be to brag on the Lord, not on ourselves.

A Christ-possessed human nature, healed by love, becomes sensitive to others. It "does not behave rudely." Rudeness is the wrong thing, said or done at the wrong time. It puts others down, ridicules them. Christ in us gives us empathy to feel what others are feeling and to give encouragement. Self-centeredness, "seeking our own," is just the opposite.

Christ helps us get inside people's skin to feel what they are feeling and give them a boost and not a burden. We are given the patience to endure with people in their problems and shortcomings, knowing that the Lord is at work in them. Christ in us is not provoked to irritation and sharpness. Within us, he whispers, "Can you do less to this person than I have done for you?" That replaces exasperation with exoneration. Christ never gives up on us and we cannot give up on others.

It is inhuman to be insensitive. It is human to be sensitive. Someone said to a friend of mine, "Why are you so sensitive?" And the man retorted, "Well, I want to know why you're so insensitive." Rudeness is insensitivity. It's saying and doing those things that hurt another person. Not thinking about what we're going to say before we say it—blurting out all of the hurting things that cut and tear and distort. And then we say, "Oh, well, I'm only human." Oh, no, don't say that! Say, "Oh, I'm only inhuman. God didn't intend it that way. He wants me to be filled with love and become sensitive."

But press on. Paul next tells us that love thinks no evil and does not rejoice in iniquity. Christ frees us from the inhuman gloating over people's failures. The little word "thinks" is an accounting term in Greek, meaning to keep records. Love, Christ in us, does not keep a ledger of what people have done to hurt us or themselves. Christ's love gives us the power to forget mistakes, sins, and failures by remembering his gracious forgiveness. So often I talk to people who are a computer filled with the memory statistics of the wrongs of the past. Our inner beings become a garbage dump of mistakes and heartaches. That was not the Lord's original intention for our human nature. That's why Jesus put such a high priority on forgiveness—his forgiveness of us, our forgiveness of ourselves, and each of us of one another. It is inhuman to store up the past hurts.

The other day a man was delighted to tell me about the failures of a mutual friend. He was rejoicing in iniquity! He went on in almost fiendish delight while covering his tracks with an attitude of concern. What he was saying was exposed as destructive gossip when he was asked, "What have you done to help this man? Does he know that you love him and will not let him down regardless of what he's done?" The telling reality is that the gloating gossip has some things in his own life that, if exposed, would make this other person's failure small by comparison.

Can Christ change the flaw in this gloater's nature? Yes, the inhumanity of his rejoicing in others' iniquity can be healed. But he will have to have his own heart broken by the things that break the Lord's heart—in himself as well as others. A divine pity must transplant his petulant delight in the mistakes of others.

It won't be easy. My friend must go through a profound experience of forgiveness to bring him back to humanness. But in the Lord's good time. I believe the process was begun that day when several of us told him we would not be part of the character assassination which he was attempting. He was shocked. Love leads to decisiveness, but always on the Lord's timing, and carefully guided by him. Witnessing the inhuman capacity to think, store up and tabulate evil, made the rest of us in the group examine ways we might be doing the same thing. The danger of thinking evil about people and rejoicing in their failures is that we form an image of them which locks them into the very pattern we abhor.

Contrast that with Paul's assurance that "love never fails." It won't quit; it goes on forever. The Lord won't give up on us. His purpose is to make us perfect, like himself, accomplishing our awesome goal of being truly human. And when we are, we are progressively reformed into his image and likeness in preparation for the time when we leave this stage of eternal life for the next. Then the perfect will be fully formed.

In the meantime, we are in transition. The childishness of inhuman behavior is being transformed to mature personhood in Christ. That's what Paul meant by saying, "When I was a child, I spoke as a child, I thought as a child; but when I became a man, I put away childish things." It would be a denial of our destiny to remain a child forever. Most of the things we abhor in ourselves and others and long to have changed, are the child in us which has not grown up to the fulness of Christ. But Christ will not leave us children in our human nature. We will continue to be changed in preparation for the perfect—our ultimate goal and purpose—to live with him forever.

"For now we see in a mirror, dimly, but then face to face. Now I know in part, but then I shall know just as I also am known." We will know Christ as fully as he has known us through the years. Faith gives us the assurance that what has been, has been forgiven; hope presses on into the future with confidence; and love, Christ himself, is the power to be fully human in the present.

Can human nature be changed? Yes. In fact it is the only thing which can be changed, really. All other seeming change is rearrangement. Christ changes people to become what they were meant to be. Like him. For now and for eternity. We are not what we were, and praise Christ, we are not what we are going to be!

14

How Can I
Forgive and Forget?

THE MAN HAD BEEN through a painful divorce. His wife had left him for another man, leaving his ego bruised and his hopes for the future shattered. He was a burning cauldron of unforgiven memories. A mutual friend asked me to see him. "He has a heavy cross to carry with all those unresolved hurts," my friend said empathetically. "I'll be happy to help," I responded, "but his cross is not those memories, but forgiving them."

When I visited with the man, the essential task was to help him face the fact that his wife was not coming back and that he had to dare to live again. Self-pity had been refortified in him by our mutual friend who had tried to comfort him by encouraging him to accept the tragic thing which had been done to him as his cross to bear. This distortion of both theology and psychology had become deeply rooted and was not easy to dislodge.

There was little breakthrough until the man realized his own need for forgiveness and his calling to forgive and forget what had been done to him. The truth which caught his attention and became the focus of a new beginning was that his cross was forgiving and not just carrying the hurts. I asked him to write out all that needed to be forgiven and then sign it "forgetfully forgiving" with his name.

This man's need was focused in many different ways by people who submitted questions about forgiveness. The difficulty of forgetting as a part of forgiveness was expressed by both those who needed to be forgiven and those who needed to be forgiving.

Here are some of the questions of those longing to realize forgiveness. How can I be sure I'm forgiven? Does God have a memory? When I'm forgiven does he still remember what I've done, or is it completely erased? Why is it difficult to ask for and accept forgiveness? Can God help a brooder?

And then those who were grappling with the costly need to forgive: How can I forgive and forget? Why do I still remember what has been done to me by others even after I say I have forgiven? If God's love is unconditional and his forgiveness undeserved, why does Jesus say that we can't be forgiven unless we forgive? Why am I seemingly powerless to forgive? Why do I insist on storing up anger, seemingly incapable of dissipating it? If I know I'm forgiven, why is it difficult for me to forgive? We are told that God completely forgets our sins when we seek forgiveness: why then do I harbor memories of past hurts?

Ever ask any of those questions? We all have. Forgiving ourselves, others, and groups is a continuing problem for most people. And yet, our mental health, as well as our relationship to Christ, is dependent on being forgetfully forgiving. The cross is the secret of victorious loving. Not only Christ's cross and its assurance that we are forgiven, but the cross he challenges us to take up daily and carry, following him.

Our cross has been identified through history as everything from our discipleship to the difficulties we have to endure. We hear people refer to people, physical pain, and excruciating circumstances as the cross they must bear. Referring to the problems of life we say "Well, that's my cross, I guess!" or to other people's vicissitudes, "He's got a heavy cross to carry through life!" I want to suggest that we've missed the point. When we rediscover and experience the essential purpose and power of Christ's cross, we can begin to accept and appropriate the demand and dynamic of the cross given to us.

Some exposition of Scripture will help to make this clear and will answer our questions about forgiveness.

Imagine the shocked alarm on the disciples' faces when Jesus sounded the amazing call to follow him. "If anyone desires to come after Me, let him deny himself, take up his cross daily, and follow Me" (Luke 9:23). The cross was an ignominious form of execution employed by the Romans for the most abhorred of criminals and political insurrectionists. The condemned person would have to carry the crossbar, the *patibulum,* to the place of execution where the vertical stake, the *stipes crucis,* was firmly planted in the earth. The criminal's hands were nailed to the *patibulum.* It and his body were then lifted until it was socketed into the *stipes crucis,* forming a "t" shaped vertical rack. The feet were nailed to the *stipes crucis,* and the condemned was left to writhe for hours, sometimes days, until he died— usually by suffocation when the lungs collapsed, or from a heart attack because of the unbearable pain. No wonder the disciples shuddered when Jesus said that he must face his cross and that following him meant taking up a cross.

The only way to understand what he meant is to grapple with his perception of his own cross and then, in the light of that, the disciples' cross. Jesus knew who he was and why he had come into the world. He was the Lamb of God come to take away the sins of the world. The prediction at his birth was undeniably clear, "You shall call His name Jesus, for He will save His people from their sins" (Matt. 1:21). As the disciples began to realize that their Master was none other than the Messiah, he began to teach them about his death on the cross. His teaching was clear: he would be the Suffering Servant, the Sacrifice, for the sins of the world. Atonement and forgiveness would be the purpose of his death.

Then he called the disciples to take up their crosses daily and follow him. Did he mean that they were to go to Jerusalem to share his fate? Did he imply that following him would mean martyrdom? Or was there something even deeper impacted in the impelling command to take up a cross and follow him? I think so.

My thesis is that Jesus' perception of his death was a cosmic forgiveness and reconciliation by God and the crosses we are to take up are to extend through history the powerful efficacy of that forgiving love. Being a disciple may mean suffering, or even martyrdom, because we belong first and always to the Savior. But also, our diminutive Calvarys are those times when we forgive and forget what people do and are, not only to themselves and others, but to us.

We may be called to die for our faith, but in the meantime, one thing is sure, we are to "die daily," to use Paul's words, in giving up our judgmentalism and becoming mediators of forgiving grace. Our ministry of forgetful forgiveness is inspired and sustained by three things: our calling, the courage to accept our calling, and the comfort afforded us in our calling. Christ not only calls us to take up our cross, but reminds us that we can't take it alone!

Forgetful forgiveness is the apostolic calling given to every Christian. Matthew 10:38-40 amplifies the Luke passage and links our forgiveness of others to the nature of God and to our calling to be extensions of the incarnation. "And he who does not take his cross and follow after Me is not worthy of Me. He who finds his life will lose it, and he who loses his life for My sake will find it. He who receives you receives Me, and he who receives Me receives Him who sent Me."

For me, that means that as God sent Christ into the world to expose his forgetful forgiveness on the cross, so, too, we are sent to reproduce the implications of that cross in our relationships. God sent Christ; Christ sends us. An apostle is one sent. "As My Father has sent Me, I also send you" (John 20:21). But notice what we are sent to do in this post-resurrection commission of the Lord and the power available to accomplish it. "Receive the Holy Spirit," he offered. The Spirit of the living God will come within us to provide the instigating impetus to do for others what he's done for us. "If you forgive the sins of any, they are forgiven them; and if you retain the sins of any, they are retained" (John 20:22,23). We are part of the apostolate of hope with the keys of the kingdom. The authority entrusted to the disciples after Peter's confession on the road to Caesarea Philippi earlier in Jesus' ministry is now our apostle's authority and awesome opportunity. "I will give you the keys of the kingdom of heaven, and whatever you bind on earth will be bound in heaven and whatever you loose on earth will be loosed in heaven" (Matthew 16:19).

In Christ we receive none other than the Father. And through us, people are to receive his measureless love in Christ. We are to be Christ's forgiving forgetfulness to the people around us. That means the gift of a bad memory when it comes to our own or others' sins. The Scriptures are full of references to God's forgetfulness when it comes to our sin. "I, yes, I alone am He who blots away your sins for my own sake and will never think of them again" (Isa. 43:25 TLB.). "For I will forgive their iniquity, and their sin I will remember no more" (Jer. 31:34). "For high as the heavens are above the earth, so great is His lovingkindness toward those who fear Him. As far as the east is from the west, so far has He removed our transgressions from us" (Ps. 103:11,12). "If Thou, Lord, shouldst mark iniquities, O Lord, who could stand? But there is forgiveness with Thee, that Thou mayest be feared" (Ps. 130:3,4). And then that magnificent assurance from Nehemiah's prayer: "Thou art a God of forgiveness, gracious and compassionate, slow to anger, and abounding in lovingkindness; and Thou didst not forsake them" (Neh. 9:17).

In the light of this we can appreciate what it means for Jesus to say, "He who receives Me receives Him who sent

Me." This is forgiving love incarnate. But with equal impact we now understand His word, "He who receives you receives Me." That's what is involved in taking up our cross. It is the awesome calling of *being* His forgiveness. Don't miss the obligation and the opportunity: our cross is our call to forgive—regardless!

But how can we do that unless we receive fresh forgiveness ourselves? The courage for our calling comes from renewed experiences of being forgiven ourselves. That's where the "daily" renewal of our calling to take up the cross is provided. Yesterday's forgiveness is not enough for today's sins and failures. When we are moved by "amazing grace" for our own mistakes, we will have fresh grace for others. Jesus put it pointedly, "But to whom little is forgiven, the same loves little" (Luke 7:47).

The context of that truth is the contrast between judgmental Simon and the woman who had been forgiven greatly and anointed Jesus at the Pharisee's banquet. Simon lacked realized forgiveness and loved little. The broken woman had received undeserved forgiveness and could not love enough. The courage to forgive and forget is the overwhelming, daily experience of undeserved, forgetful forgiveness from our Lord. He has totally forgotten our former sins! That alone fuels the fires of warmth and acceptance of people. There is a tenderness in people who have kept "short accounts" with the Lord, seeking daily forgiveness. In spite of anything, they can take up their cross as courageous forgivers.

I know this to be true in my own life. When I become critical and judgmental, withholding healing forgiveness, it is a sure sign that I am in need of grace in my own life. When days drift by without my repentance, I put down my cross and for a time miss my calling to be a reconciler. Then comes the Lord's whisper in my soul, "Will you not forgive as I have forgiven you?" Do you ever have times like that? I know you do.

So many people who submitted questions on this topic

expressed the problem of not being able to feel forgiven even after hearing repeatedly about the Lord's forgiveness. This difficulty is usually related to our inability to forgive ourselves. A deep-seated pride is often the cause. We play God when we refuse to forgive ourselves as much as he does. We fear losing control over our own lives. Holding ourselves in the contempt of unforgiving self-negation is our way of keeping control. We become brooders, down on ourselves. And eventually we get down on others. Our attitudes become cold and cautious. A fracture in our relationship with the Lord results and deepens until our prayers are ineffective, the joy of living drains away, and we become critical, negative people.

Taking up our cross and denying ourselves means the total reorientation of life with the self no longer at the center. We give up our rights to run our own lives. That includes the right to be the imperious judge of our own worth. Nothing negates our calling to be forgetful forgivers more than being locked on the dead-center of withholding forgiveness from ourselves. We sidestep the meaning of Jesus' cross and are immobilized in taking up our own cross and following him. We evade responsibility by rendering ourselves as incapable of being forgiven. It is like getting sick to get out of an obligation. Sometimes the decision to be sick is so subtle we don't even know that we've done it. People are sympathetic and let us off the hook. In the same way we compensate for ourselves by condemning ourselves. How could God expect any courageous loving and forgiving from a person like us? With all we've done and been, what right do we have to offer forgiveness to others?

And yet, the Lord never gives up! He comes to us relentlessly with daily offers for us to deny our right to be our own gods, accept him as Lord of our lives, allow him to be our judge and crucified forgiver. Taking up our cross always spells crucifixion of ourselves. Our Calvary is to die to self-control. And that includes angry judgments of ourselves and others manifested in a petulant unwillingness to forget what the Lord has forgiven.

Alexander Pope said, "To err is human; to forgive, divine." A Christian who has died to himself is ready to be the channel of the divine nature. Jesus continually warned that we cannot be forgiven if we do not forgive. "And whenever you stand praying, if you have anything against anyone, forgive him, that your Father who is in heaven may also forgive you your trespasses" (Mark 11:25).

Our channel is clogged when we bury in our memories what people have said and done. I am constantly stabbed into spiritual alertness by Jesus' cutting words at the end of the parable of the unforgiving servant who refused to be as gracious to his debtor as the king had been to him. Who can escape the alarming implication of the judgment given the unmerciful servant? "So My heavenly Father also will do to you if each of you, from his heart, does not forgive his brother his trespasses" (Matt. 18:35). The unsettling point is that we cannot receive what we will not give. The ebb and flow of forgiveness is receiving and giving in order to receive more.

The faces of countless Christians come to mind. Because they will not forget as a part of forgiving, they are stunted in their growth in receiving and transmitting the divine nature implanted by the Holy Spirit. Recently, a woman shared the meager, stingy level of her willingness to take up her cross. "I'll forgive, but there's no way I can or will forget!" That's just another way of saying she will not forgive. What was done to her by a life-long, trusted friend was deplorable, to be sure. Letting go of that hurt is a spiritual matter of life and death. Her relationship with the Savior is in jeopardy. She is in danger of closing him out of her life when she needs him more than ever. She is on the edge of making one of the greatest discoveries and steps of growth in her life. The good news is that she was open to discover how to forget when she realized what could happen to her soul if she didn't. What she has finally faced is our last point. She could not forget without the Lord's help.

The comfort of our calling to take up our cross in forgetful forgiveness is that we don't have to take it alone. The same Savior who called his disciples to take up their crosses and follow him, did not carry his cross alone to Calvary! Simon of Cyrene was conscripted into service to carry the heavy crossbar the final steps up Golgotha. Why, looking back on that gruesome day, was Matthew so careful to include this in his passion account? To show the humanity of Jesus? Or is there something more . . . much more . . . intended for us? Surely Jesus could have carried that cross alone. The One who performed miracles and healed the sick was not lacking in power to carry his cross! There's a profound meaning here for us. If Christ was willing to be helped to carry his cross, should we refuse help in carrying ours?

We will never be alone to carry our crosses if we accept his uplifting help. In the context of our emphasis that our cross is forgiving and forgetting, that means that he can and will give us the healing of our memories. He's done it for me countless times. I've seen it happen in thousands of people with whom I have prayed that the gift of a divine amnesia be given. When we believe that nothing is impossible for the Lord and tell him of our inability to forget, he is ready to blot out all the anguish and pain of a debilitating memory. Paul challenged the Colossians to nail their sins to the cross. The same should be true for our memories. In ancient Greece, a nail driven through a charge list against a person and displayed publicly, meant exoneration. The apostle maximizes the imagery by calling the Christians to do the same. Nail it to the cross! When we do, the same love exposed on Calvary floods the tissues of our memories, expunging the remembrance of harbored sin—our own first, and then those of others we have hoarded so dangerously.

Let the forgiving, forgetting love of Christ's cross give

you a sublimely poor memory as you take up your cross. Make your own list of past hurts and failures which you have been unwilling to forgive to the healing extent of forgetting. Feel the submerged anguish for one last time as you take up your cross.

Is the load too heavy? Is the burden of forgetful forgiveness too big for you? Is the weight of carrying that cross unbearably demanding? Jesus never gives us more than he will help us carry. Even now as we surrender the pride of aloof judgmentalism and commit ourselves to be a forgiven, forgiving mediator of grace, he comes to lift the cross he has given to us. He is the eternal forgiveness of God with us. Can you feel the lifting of the weight? The secret of victorious loving is that the cross Christ calls us to take up and follow him, he helps us lift by the power of his own cross.

> When in affliction's valley
> I'm treading the road of care
> My Savior helps me to carry
> My cross heavy to bear
> My feet entangled with briers
> Ready to cast me down
> My Savior whispers His promise
> "I'll never leave you alone."
>
> *Anonymous*

Take up your cross of forgetful forgiving, but remember you can't take it alone! And the good news is that you don't have to. Christ is able!

15

What Can I Do
with My Moods?

Moods. We all have them. Good moods and bad moods. Glad, sad, and mad moods. They make us feel just great, or just blue. Elated or deflated. Because of them, we have sunny days and gloomy days—hours of self-confidence and hours of self-pity.

Moods are the temporary feelings which dominate our state of mind. They are capricious, whimsical, tyrannical. Our dispositions and our attitudes are often controlled by them. The people around us are blessed or blamed.

The old folksong could be our theme: "Sometimes I'm up and sometimes I'm down. Oh, yes, Lord." And our problem is how to get up when we're feeling down. What can we do with our negative moods? So many people have asked. Controlling their moods is an unconquered frontier for many Christians. So often our moods contradict our faith, mock our witness, and cause havoc in our relationships. We say and do things we abhor. Our low moods sap our energies and immobilize our creativity. Can Christ help us conquer bad moods and moodiness?

That's what a friend of mine wanted to know. He had been through a difficult, pressured time. It left him physically and emotionally depleted. A depressed mood engulfed him and tyrannized his disposition. Expressing concern, I asked him how he was doing. "Well, joy's certainly no option!" he said grimly.

His words tumbled about in my mind. I knew what he meant. In his negative mood, he could not imagine expressing joy. Though he was a Christian, his mood, not Christ, was temporarily lord of his life. And yet, what he said, expressed differently, is really the only viable antidote for his moodiness.

"You're right!" I said. "Joy is no option. It's your responsibility."

That shocked him. "You talk about joy as if it were a duty," he retorted, obviously piqued that I was not more sympathetic with his mood.

"Right again!" I responded. "We don't have to be victimized by our moods. We have a duty to the Lord, ourselves, and the people around us to battle through to joy. A moody Christian is a contradiction of terms."

What I went on to explain to my friend is the essence of what I want to share in this chapter. It comes in response to the many questions about what to do with our moods. It is one of the most crucial discoveries I continue to make in my own spiritual pilgrimage. In down moods, bad moods, bland moods, and moody times, I've discovered that I can and must battle through my moods to joy. I have decided not to surrender to the ups and downs of my moods. Joy is not an option.

There are four scripture passages which have helped me personally and have become the basis of my theory about joy to change our moods. The first is a promise, the second an assurance, the third a challenge, and the fourth an admonition. Nehemiah promised, "The joy of the Lord is your strength" (Neh. 8:10). Jesus assured us of his joy. "These things I have spoken to you, that My joy may be in you, and that your joy may be made full" (John 15:11, RSV). Paul challenged the Philippians, "Rejoice in the Lord always. Again I will say, rejoice!" (Phil. 4:4). And the apostle admonished the Christians in Rome to "Never take vengeance into your own hands, my dear friends, stand back and let God punish if he will" (Rom. 12:19, PHILLIPS).

All four Scriptures were spoken to liberate people who faced a mood of depression. Nehemiah's encouraging words were spoken to the Jews who had rebuilt Jerusalem and its walls after the exile. At a celebration of the completed work, Ezra's reading of the law of Moses caused remorse and not rejoicing. The people realized that not only Jerusalem, but their moral and spiritual lives needed to be rebuilt. The objective standard of God's commandments brought a mood of mourning and self-condemnation. Nehemiah broke the bind of the mood with a trumpet call. "This day is holy to our Lord. Do not be grieved, for the joy of the Lord is your strength." The reading of the law was meant to bring the people back to complete trust in the Lord. He had been their strength in rebuilding. And now he would bless them with joy to break the spell of their negative attitudes toward themselves. These were caused by their realization of what he had destined them to be and what they had done with his calling.

In the Upper Room the night before Jesus was crucified the mood was grim and gloomy. The disciples were overcome with grief because of what Jesus had told them about what was ahead of him. Judas had been identified as the betrayer and the Lord had tried to help the others understand what he must go through. Everything he said that night was to dispel the depressed mood which had captured the emotions of the disciples. The antidote of his joy was offered. "What I've tried to explain is so that my joy may be in you," he said in essence. What they obviously did not understand then, later became a source of comfort and courage. After the resurrection, Christ's joy became the pervading mood of the disciples in spite of the most depressing circumstances they had to endure around them.

Paul discovered the secret of this joy to heal his moody disposition. After his conversion, the dominant note of his message was joy. Christ had broken the bonds of his moods and made him a joyous apostle in the midst of discouraging difficulties. His epistles are filled with challenges to rejoice. Three times in his letter to the Philippians, each to offset an aspect of their mood of negativism, Paul told the people to, "Rejoice!" And then to the critical, condemnatory, judgmental spirit which was dragging down the effectiveness of the church at Rome, he gave an admonition which tells us how to find joy. He told them that judgment and punishment were up to God.

Considered together, these passages help us understand the cause and cure of bad moods and moodiness. Negative, down, bad moods are caused by circumstances, condemnation and conditional love. They are cured by confrontation, confession and commitment.

The spiraling, downward descent into the morass of a bad mood begins with our perception of what's happening to or around us in our circumstances. A mood is an emotional interface between reality and our response to it. When things don't go the way we've planned, when people don't measure up to our expectations, or when we've done or said things which disappoint us in ourselves, we are susceptible to moodiness. It's our defensive mechanism of trying to regain control. We get down on ourselves, others, or life in general. Before we know it, we feel an overall gloominess, glumness, dissatisfaction, self-pity, and sometimes despondency. All this leads us into a whirlpool of destructive introspection.

All this comes because of condemnation. A bad mood is a way of punishing ourselves or others. It is playing God. We take judgment into our own hands. Think of the way we do it to ourselves. One of the most destructive breeding grounds of negative moods lies in our critical self-evaluation. If we have done too much or too little, or said something better left unsaid, or are reminded of what we should have said, or realize our sins of omission or commission, we take over the responsibility of punishing our-

selves. "Why did you do that? Why didn't you find time to
do that? With what you believe, how could you have
reacted the way you did?" With parental, self-condemning
hostility we say to ourselves, "Self, why don't you shape
up!" An angry mood is sure to result. What are the things
you find cause you to be impatient and eventually condemnatory of yourself?

The same thing happens in our relationships with the
people around us. We often think our moods are the only
way we can express how we feel. Thus we revert to sulking,
silence, or sarcasm. This happens because we have taken
the responsibility of punishing others for what they said or
did or failed to say or do. A warped sense of justice grips
us. People must pay! Our punishment is meted out by
what we withhold of ourselves. We back people into a
corner until they take responsibility for our mood and
admit whatever we've decided was the crime against us.
We do all this to gain and keep control.

An even more disturbing cause of moodiness is our
judgment of life in general—even of God. The more I
study human nature, the more convinced I am that our
moods are often an expression of our displeasure with the
way God is running the universe—particularly our part of
it. We can't convince him of our desires, he won't march to
the beat of our drum, and he doesn't do what we want
when we want it. This idea that our moods may be our
petulant response to God's providence may shock some of
us. But who else can we blame, ultimately, when things
don't go according to our schedule and we swim around in
the swamp of self-pity?

Paul said, "Never take vengeance into your own hands,
my dear friends: stand back and let God punish if he will."
This stabs us awake to what we are doing in our moodiness. Moods are a form of vengeance against ourselves,
others, life, even God himself. When we need God the
most, we make him the enemy. And most dangerous of all,
we follow the contemporary psychological ambience of

mood-indulgence. We have come to think of our moods as our private possession. Whatever they are, they are ours and it's our right to feel however we feel. We forget that our moods are like deadly germs. They become epidemic in our homes, offices, churches, and among our friends. One person with the virus of a bad mood can radically distort the peace and happiness of others. Worst of all, moods become a habit. They become manipulative behavior modifiers.

Condemnation results in conditional love. Whenever we've taken the responsibility to judge ourselves or others, we will withhold the love both we and they desperately need. Our moods are a self-imposed lack of self-esteem. If we feel bad in our down moods, and continue to reflect them on ourselves, it's a sure sign that we have not loved ourselves sufficiently. If we took small doses of poison each day which caused a debilitating effect on our bodies, we would be called self-destructive. Our moods do nothing less to our emotional and spiritual health.

I talked to a woman whose depression had lasted for weeks. She nursed her mood like a cherished possession. "Do you enjoy your mood?" I asked. "Of course not!" she said indignantly. "You apparently don't like yourself then," I suggested. That disturbed her. She explained again the legitimate complaints she had which were causing the moodiness. They all seemed justified to her. But the only one being punished was herself. Then we talked in-depth about the conditional love expressed by her self-imposed imprisonment in her mood.

For different reasons, a young man was facing the same problem. He could not forgive himself for something he had done. A moodiness hit him. The cause was his unwillingness to forgive himself, even after he had asked God to forgive him.

Conditional love for others can cause the same frustration.

One man I know literally controls the people around

him with his moods of criticism. No one ever measures up. He seems incapable of giving affirmation. And it's all done in the name of religion. His wife expressed the feeling of many of us who know and care about him. "Whenever I'm with him, I feel like I've done something wrong and that I'm responsible for his sour mood." When I confronted him with what he was doing, he was amazed. I was not surprised to discover how critical he was of himself. He had never quite met his father's standards either. The sins of the fathers . . . indeed! It was not easy to help him see what his moods were doing to his family and friends. It took a profound experience of God's grace in a time of failure to finally break the bonds of his condemnatory spirit.

Reflect for a moment on what our moods do to our relationships in friendship or marriage. Here's a good inventory to discover what our moods are doing:

Do we ever feel misused, misunderstood or mistreated?

In response, do we ever withhold communication, affirmation or approval?

Are we able to express our perception of what has or has not happened and leave the punishment to God?

Have we ever, do we often, resort to a mood as our way of expressing disapproval?

Have we, or are we right now, using silence, sulking, or sarcasm as an expression of our critical or condemnatory feelings?

The tragedy of coercive bad moods is that eventually we are the ones who suffer. Moods meant for others always boomerang. They fly back and hit us in the soul. They cut off the flow of God's grace. We become all the more miserable. Prayer is stifled and joy is a stranger to us. And yet, for a Christian, joy's no option.

That presses us on to the cure of moodiness. As negative moods are caused by our perception of conditions, condemnation, and conditional love, just so battling through to joy means confrontation, confession, and commitment.

Confrontation means getting in touch with the mood,

analyzing its causes, and admitting responsibility for it. No one or no situation can control our moods without our permission. It is often helpful to ask, "Why am I feeling the way I am? What contributed to this? How did I get run down physically or emotionally to the place that this mood captured me?" Dare to be ruthlessly honest.

The next step is confession. This means not only telling our Lord about our mood, but confessing our need for him to help us experience fresh grace and express joy. In every time of moodiness we need the infusion of grace, the Lord's unmerited and unlimited love. Joy is the result of grace. It is the emotional expression of the experience of God's presence and power. Whatever the cause of our dark mood, the brightness of grace can dispel the darkness. We all desperately need to know that God loves us and will not let us go.

The cross is the source of our victory over our moods. It is the sublime assurance that there are no limits to the Lord's forgiveness. But also, there is nothing too great for him. The grace which flows from Calvary into our hearts gives us the assurance that there is power available to us. Our God can bring good out of all we go through.

When we battle through our moods back to grace, our feeling of being loved cuts the taproot of the condemnatory spirit which pits us against others and ourselves. When we open the floodgates and grace surges into the negative, parched places of our souls, we suddenly are overcome with joy. How can God, knowing all about us, love us still? How could he care about what happens to each of us? And yet when we confess our mood to him, he heals the anger, self-pity, anxiety or emotional depletion which has caused the mood.

Then we can commit the problem to him. If confrontation of our mood has exposed the cause of the mood and confession has surrendered it to the Lord, commitment means that we can dare to act differently. How would we feel, respond, relate to others if we did not have the bad mood? Picture it and thank the Lord that it shall be so.

"Trust in the Lord with all your heart, and do not lean on your own understanding. In all your ways acknowledge Him and He will make your paths straight" (Prov. 3:5,6).

The joy of the Lord becomes our strength. God's Spirit is joy. Christ incarnated that joy and promised us nothing less than his own joy. A bad mood is a signal that we need his indwelling presence. Christ is joy. The fruit of his Spirit is ebullient, ever-flowing joy.

That leaves us with a choice and an awesome responsibility. We can decide to change our mood! When a mood seeks to dominate us, we can make a decision of the will to be different. If we follow the process of analyzing the cause, we can also follow the prescription for the cure. The Lord has entrusted us with the jurisdiction of our moods. Saul had a problem with himself for which he chose to blame David. So too we have a problem with ourselves; we blame others. Our bad moods simply do not work. They are ineffective and hurt ourselves and everyone around us. The question is, "Who needs it?"

Whenever I'm tempted to coddle a bad mood, I think of Annie Johnson Flint. She is one of my favorite poets. Her grand and glad thoughts came in the midst of suffering. If anyone had a right to bad and low moods, she did. She lost her parents early in life, had to work hard for her education, and was never free of financial worries. As a young woman she endured the encroachment of arthritis which worsened until she was completely crippled and physically helpless. And yet she gave to the world poems of joy. The secret was in her experience of God's grace. Her indefatigable courage was based on the fact that God's love has no limits. His grace cannot be measured. His power goes beyond the boundaries set up by man. That assurance was expressed in this mood-changing poem:

> God hath not promised
> Skies ever blue,
> Flower-strewn pathways
> All our lives through;

God hath not promised
  Sun without rain,
Joy without sorrow,
  Peace without pain.

God hath not promised
  Smooth roads and wide,
Swift, easy travel
  Needing no guide;
God hath not promised
  We shall not bear
Many a burden,
  Many a care,

But God HATH promised
  Strength for the day,
Rest amid labour,
  Light for the way;
Grace for the trials,
  Help from above,
Unfailing sympathy,
  Undying love.

With that conviction, we can confront, confess, and commit our moods to the Lord; receive fresh grace; and express a contagious joy. Joy's no option!

16

What's the Secret of Being a Confident Person?

A LETTER FROM ONE of our television viewers forced me to rethink what it means to become a truly confident person. The fact that she identified herself as a Christian made her need and question all the more urgent.

"I was browsing in a bookstore recently," she wrote, "and was startled by the title of your recent book, *Congratulations, God Believes in You!* 'He's got to be kidding!' I said to myself. 'How can God believe in me—I don't even believe in myself!?' "

She went on to explain her battle with low self-esteem and lack of self-confidence. There was not a time she could remember when she felt really good about herself. Even when good things happened to or around her, she could not enjoy them because she felt they were just a prelude to some new disappointment. She said she had purchased and read the book, but it was very difficult to let the good news that God loved her sink through the protective layers of her self-negation. I called and asked her to come in to see me.

I was astonished when the woman walked into my study. She was attractive and carefully groomed. I checked my appointment calendar to be sure she was the same person who had written that negative letter of self-deprecation. No mistake in appointments. The outwardly polished woman who sat across my desk was the same woman who had confessed her struggle with self-confidence.

As she told me her life story, I realized why she had worked so hard to build a protective shell around her inner insecurity. Childhood had bruised her self-image badly and teen years had deepened the hurt. She was determined not to let anyone into her hidden self.

Now in her thirties, she had a picture of herself which completely contradicted the lovely person she really was. Helping her become a confident person was not easy. Her belief in Christ had not resulted in emotional healing. The breakthrough did not come until months later when she discovered the difference between self-confidence and Christ-confidence.

What she experienced is what I want to explain in this chapter. Working with this woman, and so many others like her, has reminded me that lack of self-confidence is a problem we all face at times—for some, all of the time. Our confident exteriors can be misleading. We dare not take anyone for granted. Inside may be a very insecure person with little confidence. Many people may be Christians who have the words but not the music of healing faith.

The many questions about confident living I received in our inventory of people's most urgent questions can be summarized and focused in these two which echo the need of the woman I just described: "How can Christ make me a more confident person?" And, "What do you do when, even though you're a Christian, you've lost confidence in yourself?" In response, I want to consider what confidence is, what self-confidence is all about, and what it means to become a Christ-confident person.

The word confidence is a combination from the Latin root. *Con* means "thorough, altogether"; *fidere* means "faith" or "trust." Confidence is altogether faith. Complete trust. It is a response to something that is constant. It requires someone who is consistent and, therefore, reliable. Confidence is linked to dependability.

Our minds are like computers. We have a data bank in

the tissues of our brains which holds the memory factors of previous experience. Our confidence is dependent on what's been stored up in our computer.

For example, we have confidence in the laws of nature because of their constancy and consistency. If you are seated while you're reading this, you probably have confidence in the chair in which you are seated. You have sat in that chair many times without it collapsing. This experience assures you that you are not likely to land on the floor at any moment. You are seated confidently.

We don't spend our every waking moment thinking about gravity. But a lifetime of experience convinces us that we are held to the earth by gravity and only by the force of a jet engine can we defy it briefly. And none of us would be tempted to refresh our confidence in gravity by leaping out of an airplane without a parachute!

We're not surprised by either the sunrise or sunset. We are confident that the constancy of the earth's revolution around the sun will be consistent. Nor are we amazed by daily exposure to the scientific insights we have come to take for granted. Experience of their verity has made us confident of them.

But confidence in other people and ourselves is a different matter. People are neither consistent nor constant. They don't always do what they've promised and their own lack of confidence often makes them negative about us. If they happen to be our parents, or significant others during our formative years, the impact of their lack of affirmation may leave an indelible scar on our self-esteem.

Self-confidence is a precious commodity enjoyed by very few. It is the result of thousands of positive image-building experiences which enable the computer to read out, "You're super. You're of value. You can be sure of yourself." Our psyches can just as easily be dominated by the memories of failures, inadequacies, and frustrations. We are what's happened to us. Our confidence in ourselves is colored by previous performance.

Think of that in relation to our confidence, or lack of it, in the performance of our bodies. If we are highly trained in some athletic activity, we probably have developed consistency and constancy. Recently, I watched Johnny Miller win the Los Angeles Open. Confidence exuded from his face and body as he stepped up to hit the ball or sink a putt. He didn't appear insecure or uneasy. Years of practice had grooved his swing and given him incredible accuracy.

Hugh Downs says that he feels completely confident when he walks into a studio. And yet, recently on his program, "Over Easy," he shared that it was not always so. Years of hard work gave him the assurance that he could trust his innate gifts. Now his relaxed style, like Miller's swing, can be depended on to be reliable.

My own experience of preaching confidently without notes didn't happen overnight. It began one Sunday morning twenty years ago when I walked out to my car with robe, Bible and complete manuscript to be read, in hand. I put the Bible and manuscript on the top of the car while I hung the robe inside. Forgetting the Bible and manuscript, I started the car and proceeded to drive off. The manuscript was distributed page by page down the seven blocks to the church and then scattered irretrievably by the wind. When I reached the church, I realized that I had neither the Bible nor the manuscript! The congregation was waiting. There was nothing to do but preach without reading what I had written. It went so well that I tried it the next Sunday. I found that my mind could retain what I had memorized and that God would help me. Now years later, I feel confident enough to preach without notes. But the confidence would be shaken if for a month of Sundays I forgot what I wanted to say!

I don't have that confidence in some other areas of work or life. As a skier, I lack confidence because of too little experience and too many falls. There are other areas as well where my confidence is limited. Like most people, I have insecurities from failures in certain situations and with particular kinds of people. In those cases, I have few good memories of reliable competence to call on.

These homely examples lead us to the heart of the matter. Self-confidence is based on the reliability of the self. But if the negative experiences of the growing years, or the lack of esteem from others, have deprived us of feeling good about ourselves, we may spend the rest of our lives devoid of self-confidence. And even the most secure person can endure hardships and failures which shake his or her confidence.

The problem with self-confidence is that the self is not either consistent or constant. Now we are at the core of the issue. We all blow it too often to be worthy of "altogether faith." We collide with life's difficulties and seeming impossibilities. Often, we find that we are inadequate and insufficient when faced with the needs of people. We realize we can't love selflessly. The stress of life robs us of peace of mind. Pressures mount. Disappointments engulf us. We realize we don't have what it takes.

The reason is that we were never meant to be self-confident. We were created for a relationship with the Lord. He alone can give us an authentic, lasting confidence for living. His ability can fortify our disability. He is the same yesterday, today, and tomorrow. What he has done, and is ready to do for us, provides the constancy and consistency which motivates the complete, "altogether faith" of genuine confidence. It is the confidence of knowing our ultimate destination is assured and all our needs getting there will be met.

That's the confidence-building assurance of the "He is able!" assertion in Hebrews 7:25. "Therefore, He is also able to save to the uttermost those who come to God by Him, seeing He ever lives to make intercession for them." Confidence does not come from "I am able," but from "*He* is able!" The Greek word "able" here is *dunatai* from *dunamis,* meaning "power." All power in heaven and earth belongs to Christ. That power saves us and sustains us.

The author of Hebrews compares Christ as our High Priest with the historic Levitical priesthood. The priests could make only sacrifices for the sins of the people. Christ was *himself* the Sacrifice for the sins of the world. He has the power to save us because he is our salvation. He saves us to the *uttermost.* The Greek word is *panteles,* to the end of time. This encompasses all the exigencies of life. He has saved us from darkness and brought us into the light of truth; he lifted us from alienation to citizenship in the kingdom of God; he liberated us from guilt to pardon; he took us out of the slavery of self-centeredness to freedom; and he healed our fears and gave us peace of soul.

The word "save" has a fascinating progression in Scripture. In the Old Testament the Hebrew root meant "to be wide" or "spacious" or "to develop without hindrance" and then "to have victory." Salvation implied safety from danger and deliverance from enemies. The pages of the Old Testament are a history of the saving work of God. "God is salvation" becomes his name.

In the last centuries before Christ, salvation was identified with the coming of the Messiah who was to subdue Israel's foes and establish the kingdom of God on earth. But there was a deeper problem from which the people needed salvation. Sin, focused in rebellion and the pride of self-will, required a greater deliverance. The prophets exposed it and yearned for an atonement of the alienation of God's people they described so vividly.

And then he came. In time, on time, with the power to save for all time. Jesus. His name dramatized his destiny: "He will save His people from their sins." To the uttermost. Calvary was the place. He is able to save because he was God in limitless love, suffering for our separation, pride, and rebellion.

What does that have to do with confidence? Everything!

The only thing that can transform the memory bank of our inconsistencies and inadequacies is the profound experience of healing love. Christ is able to save us from self-condemnation. We are of uttermost value to him. That's why he "ever lives to make intercession" for us. True confidence is built on the assurance that our Lord knows what we need, provides for us according to his perfect timing, and intervenes to help us.

Alexander Maclaren summarized the confidence engendered by our Lord. "Jesus Christ, regarded as the High Priest, meets the deepest wants of every heart, and fits the human necessity. . . . He is the answer to all questions, the satisfaction of all our wants, the bread of all hunger, the light for our darkness, the strength for our weakness, the medicine for our sickness, the life for our death."[1]

Christ-confidence replaces self-confidence as we realize his ability in spite of our disabilities. He is able when we are unable. Zwingli, the reformer, put it pointedly, "Our confidence in Christ does not make us happy, negligent or careless, but on the contrary it awakens us, urges us on, and makes us active in living righteous lives and doing good. There is no self-confidence to compare with this."

The words confidence and boldness come from the same root in Greek. Christ-confident people have a boldness in living. The Book of Acts illustrates this. The fourth chapter is one of the most exciting examples. That quality of life the Sanhedrin observed in Peter and John, which identified them with Christ, was boldness. "Now when they saw the boldness of Peter and John, and perceived that they were uneducated and untrained men, they marveled. And they realized that they had been with Jesus" (Acts 4:13). The word for boldness, *parrēsia*, means "intrepidly daring, free to speak, unafraid of anything or anyone."

The boldness of Peter and John was not rooted in self-confidence, but in Christ. Their experience of him was utterly reliable. They had been with him in his ministry, death and resurrection. His message had unlocked the truth. His death was an assurance of their salvation. His resurrection was a final validation of the ultimate power of God. His presence in them as indwelling Lord was the motive power to attempt anything he guided.

Boldness was what the leaders of Israel remembered about Jesus and then were amazed to find reproduced in the apostles. It should be the undeniably evident quality of Christians in every age.

John later exposed the source of their Christ-confidence when he wrote to give strength to the early Christians. He reminded them that if their hearts condemned them, God was greater than their hearts. "Beloved, if our heart does not condemn us, we have confidence toward God" (1 John 3:21). He foresees the lack of confidence which comes as we recognize our failures and inadequacies. What he's really talking about is the inefficiency of self-confidence. We condemn ourselves for what has not been to the extent that we cannot grasp what can be.

When we put our trust in the Lord's forgiving acceptance, however, we no longer need to judge our adequacy. We shift the center of our confidence from self to Christ. But that's dependent on intimate communion with him. Prayer becomes the revitalizing, renewing source of our confidence. "And this is the confidence (boldness) that we have in Him, and if we ask anything according to His will, He hears us. And if we know that He hears us, whatever we ask, we know that we have the petitions that we have asked of Him" (1 John 5:14, 15). That's the reason for the remarkable confidence we see spread across the pages of the New Testament.

The basic conviction which undergirds true confidence is that the Lord hears and answers prayer. He reveals what is best for us and gives us the power to do it. The more we trust him, the more our inner computer stores up memory factors which read out "He is able!" in life's challenges.

The assurance of my life after thirty-two years of companionship with the Lord is that what he does is for my delight, what he gives is for my growth, what he withholds is for my deeper willingness to trust him and base any confidence I have on him alone. I can expect anything, hope for everything, and fear nothing. Paul's motto is mine, "I have confidence in the Lord" (Gal. 5:10). And Peter's assurance is my theme, "Through Him (Christ) you have confidence in God" (1 Pet. 1:21).

William James wrote, "As the essence of courage is to stake one's life on a possibility, so the essence of faith is to believe that possibility exists." The more we know Christ, the more confident we become. The possibility of his power becomes a reality.

Recently, I rushed to the airport to take a plane to Detroit. Forgetting that all the country does not enjoy the mild winter weather of California, I neglected to take along an overcoat, muffler and gloves. Totally unequipped, I arrived in a Detroit blizzard. There was nothing to do but go to a department store and buy what I needed.

Perhaps it was because I had not worn gloves often in the past ten years that I was fascinated by the illustration my new gloves gave me. Without the insertion of my hand, the gloves were listless, inanimate, motionless. When they received my hand, the gloves were alive, vital, energized. Our self is like an empty glove. It is meant to be filled in order to fulfill its purpose. When we invite Christ to fill our self with himself, we become confident and bold. We no longer need to say with William E. Henley "I am the master of my fate, I am the captain of my soul," but are able to say,

> I cannot do without Thee
>   I cannot stand alone;
> I have no strength or goodness
>   Nor wisdom of my own.
> But Thou, beloved Savior
>   Art all in all to me
> And perfect strength in weakness
>   Is theirs who lean on Thee.

Author Unknown

And lean on him we must if we are to become truly Christ-confident. Each of the memories that contribute to our lack of self-esteem and confidence must be replaced by a transforming experience of his faithfulness.

Lack of self-confidence is a blessing if it leads us to Christ-confidence. He always comes through. He will not forget or forsake us. He is ultimately and momentarily available. The secret of lasting confidence lies in his indwelling resourcefulness. Then in the words of John Denver, we can "reach for the heavens and hope for the future and all that we can be and not what we are."[2]

17

How Can I Find
a Strategy
for Stress?

A COUPLE OF YEARS AGO, I had an opportunity to address a group of pastors in Korea on the assigned topic of the pressures and problems of leadership. A translator was assigned to me for the occasion. To introduce my topic and to establish communication, I told several humorous stories about stress. The translator tried valiantly to put the stories into the Korean idiom and identifiable situations. There was no laughter or response. Finally in frustration he said to me in English, "No more funny stories; they understand; please give your message!" The audience burst out in laughter. Apparently, most of the group understood English. The tension eased as I joined in laughing at myself.

The translator's advice is especially well taken for the thrust of this chapter. All I need to do is mention the word stress and we all can identify. Every one of us experiences stress, knows that it is one of the major causes of physical and emotional sickness in our society, and longs to find some innoculation against its virulent contagion. Right at this moment either we are under stress, are deeply concerned about loved ones and friends who are suffering its debilitating effects, or are inadvertently the cause of stress in those with whom we live and work.

The questions submitted about stress were pointed. What should be the Christian response to stress? If I am a Christian, why do I still have stress? Why are some Christians unstable intellectually and emotionally? How do I get beyond a yo-yo Christianity of ups and downs? Why is it that some people are able to take life's strains and stresses and others seem to fall apart? How can I find a strategy for stress?

We've all asked these questions—about ourselves and others. There's no need for "funny stories" to establish mutual understanding. I live with stress and so do you. But years of wrestling with the problem and trying to help others grow through it have led me to some convictions about how to find strength in the midst of stress.

My prescription for stress is based on a great word used by the apostle Paul. It comes at the beginning and end of the vibrant epistle of hope communicated to the Christians at Rome. Paul opens and closes Romans with this word. It is an antithetical word promising the antidote to the stress in which the Christians were living.

All that Paul writes in Romans about the sovereignty of God, the plan of salvation, the sublime adequacy of the cross for human sin and suffering, the resiliency of resurrection living, and the power of the indwelling Spirit, can be capsulized by this one word. The Greek word Paul used is *stērizō*, translated into English in the New King James as established. Its meaning is "stable, strengthened, firmly fixed on a firm foundation." That's what Paul wanted for the Christians at Rome. To help them find it motivated his desire to visit them and the reason for his epistle: "For I long to see you, that I may impart to you some spiritual gift, so that you may be *established*" (Rom. 1:11). Here *stērizō* is in the first aorist passive infinitive: *stērichthēnai.*

The magnificent theological manifesto he went on to write was the substance of this stability he wanted to impart. Having completed his task, he ended with the crescendo of a triumphant doxology. "Now to Him who is able to *establish* you according to my gospel and the preaching of Jesus Christ, according to the revelation of the mystery which was kept secret since the world began but now has been made manifest, and by the Scriptures of the prophets has been made known to all nations, according to the commandment of the everlasting God, for obedience to the faith—to God, alone wise, be glory through Jesus Christ forever" (Rom. 16:25–27). "Establish" here is *stērixai*, first aorist active infinitive of *stērizō*, to make stable.

The antidote to stress is stability. The Lord is able! He has the power to make us stable in the midst of the stresses of life. The gospel is a strategy for stress. It gives us equipoise, an equal distribution of inner strength for the composite impact of the pressure and tension of the stress around us. For Paul the gospel is Jesus Christ. What the Lord did and does gives us stability. His reconciling death on the cross provides the fortification against the stress of guilt and condemnation; his resurrection is the promise that nothing can ultimately defeat us; his victorious presence with us gives us courage to face anything. But the "revelation of the mystery" is the gospel for our daily, moment-by-moment stability. The secret for stress is "Christ in you, the hope of glory" (Col. 1:27). Christ came into the world to save us; he now comes within us to stabilize us.

On that basis we can thank the Lord for the stress of life. It can be the creative occasion for the release of his stabilizing strength within us. But note that Paul speaks of "my" gospel. We cannot survive in stress and turn it into a stepping stone until the essence of the "He is able" gospel becomes ours as it was Paul's. The truth of the gospel must become our own controlling disposition when stress strikes. How to do that is the quest of this chapter. We will consider the deeper nature and cause of stress and then capture exactly how Christ stabilizes us with strength in it.

The word for stress in Latin is *strictus*, "to be drawn tight." In French it is *estrece*, meaning narrowness or tightness. In English the word has three major uses. It is a technical term in physics for the measurement of weight strain on a material. Stress in this regard is the force exerted between contiguous portions of a body or bodies generally expressed in pounds per square inch. In mechanics the word stress is used for the internal strength of a metal to withstand extreme weight or pressure. It is interesting to note that stress on metals is measured by what is called the yield point and the failure point. The yield point is when the stress on the material actually makes it stronger, but the failure point is when the strain breaks the load-bearing capacity of the metal.

In the world of communication, there is what is called rhetorical stress. This is the emphasis placed on a word as a point of emphasis. We say, "The point I want to stress is. . . ." A speaker stresses an idea; a writer stresses a thought.

The third use of the word in English is particularly germane to our consideration here. Stress is the mental, emotional or physical impact of people, situations, and circumstances which produce strain, tension, and anxiety in our lives. In this usage, however, the metaphors of the two other uses of the word for stress have interesting application. There is a yield point when stress makes us stronger.

Stress can also bring an emphasis in our lives. It can force us to examine our resources of resistance and it does develop our character. The stresses of life can be a megaphone alarm calling us to deeper dependence on Christ. The challenge we all face is to discover how to take advantage of the yield point.

Borrowing a page from the metallurgists, my definition of yield point in the mental, spiritual, emotional realm is that point when the weight of life's pressures and problems determines the strength of our character fortified by the indwelling Lord. In testing the strength of a rod of metal for example, the yield point is that point at which the elasticity of the metal is tested and its internal capacity can be measured. In our relationship with Christ, he becomes the power to bear the load of life and keeps us from the failure point when we would collapse.

In other words, Christ becomes the internal equalizer of stress. He uses the stress to emphasize our reliance on him, and gives us superhuman capacity. He is able to stabilize. He gives us balance when life is uneven, equilibrium when pressures throw us off balance, and steadiness when people around us fluctuate.

Now let's see how this works out in the major causes of stress. There are five that I want to deal with, each beginning with a "c." Any one of them can engulf us in the stress mess. A combination of several or all of them at once can bring us either to the yield point or the failure point.

Change, either positive or negative, causes stress. The impact of a change in the settled security of our relationships, ways of doing things, familiar surroundings, and habit routines causes stress. The now famous studies of stress by Drs. Holmes and Rahe of the University of Washington list 43 life events which cause major stress in the American people. The key word in all of these, written or implied, is change. The word appears in 15 of the events and is implied in the other 28. Everything from the death of a spouse, to money reversals, to the move from one location to another, can cause the stress prompted by change. When a multiplicity of changes in our basic fabric of relationships and responsibilities hit us all at once, we feel the stress of being pushed and pulled.

Add to change the element of *conflict* and the stress mounts. Conflict can come between us and others; between people we care about; between our inner self and the demands, pressures and differing values in our outer world—all these cause stress in our minds and cause our bodies to compensate with added spurts of adrenaline. When we feel misinterpreted or misunderstood, we can have a stress reaction. There comes the quickening of the pulse, stiffening of the muscles of our bodies, and actual symptoms of sickness. The alternative choices, fight or flight, are both equally unsatisfactory. We want to be liked, agreed with, affirmed in our convictions and perceptions. When conflict is persistent, we go into an agitated state of stressful unrest.

Closely related to conflict is *criticism*. It unsettles our insecurities and makes us defensive. We are knocked off-balance or tripped in our race toward a goal. Negative criticism tears down our sense of self-worth. It helps us little to know that most often people are critical of things in others which are festering in themselves. Debilitating criticism can be caused by perfectionism, jealousy, competition, or lack of self-esteem in the critic. Because few of us have learned how to establish a loving relationship, in which our insights and suggestions would be taken as expressions of caring, our criticisms communicate rejection.

It takes time and affirmation to become a trusted friend in whom others confide. We ask only a real friend for evaluation of what we are and do. A blast of criticism without the context of mutual acceptance leaves a person bruised and troubled. The stress which results comes from our efforts to regain self-worth. This is done either by rejecting the criticism with rationalization or the counterattack of criticizing the critic. Few things alert us to the need for Christ's stability more than the unsettling stress of criticism.

Now add *concerns* to change, conflict, and criticism, and our mental and emotional mettle is tested further. Concerns are the worries and anxieties we carry about ourselves and others. Our health, our success or lack of it, unresolvable frustrations, anticipated troubles—all congeal into this major cause of stress. The subliminal drain on our energies during the day and peaceful rest at night becomes immense. Tiredness sets in, effectiveness is dulled, and our resiliency runs down. We feel boxed in. Once again our bodies try to absorb the stress, but often they express the overload in a breakdown of health. The result can be a minor illness which, if the stress is not stabilized, will become major in proportion.

Another cause of stress is what I call *compression*. Life becomes a pressure cooker that stews us in the juices of our overinvolvement. Too much to do with too little time. Too many voices demanding our attention with too little patience to listen. Too much responsibility for our limited resources of strength and wisdom. Too many needs around us with too few answers. The stress of compression comes with overloaded schedules, conflicting dates, imperious deadlines. Our own needs for recreation and rest are squeezed out. Our inner voice of self-preservation cries out, "Hey, what about me?" The problem of compression usually happens when we least expect it and when we are least prepared because the other causes of stress have already taken their toll upon our reserves. The pace of life has had its effect. When the "straw" of one more problem hits us, it breaks the back of our resistance.

But there's still another cause of stress—a final "c." *Conscience*. Huck Finn said, "My conscience is so big, there's no room for the rest of me." Stress is caused by anything which we've done, thought about doing, or fantasized which contradicts our values and convictions of what's right. Whenever we must cover our tracks or avoid exposure, we are under stress. When something we've said or done has not been resolved, or confessed, or restitution made, or forgiveness sought, we will be burdened by stress. All we have to do is consider anything which is sticking in the craw of memory and the stress spasm agitates within us.

Put any two of these causes of stress together at one time and we are at the danger point. But my observation is that many people live with a complex of all of these stresses in varying degrees most of the time. A fact of life is that when one source of stress hits us we become vulnerable to the others. We are like a wounded animal of prey. Stress tends to multiply itself. We become like a reeling boxer who has had a bad body blow and is unprepared for further punches. The next blow may be a knock-out punch to the chin.

Stress is a part of life. It goes with the territory. The challenge is to turn it into what Dr. Hans Selye, Founder of the Institute of Stress, calls "eustress." The "eu" comes from the Greek for good. Dr. Selye suggests that there can be a constructive or healthy stress which not only tests the fiber of our character, it also teaches us to know and depend on inner resources. The question is how to find equalizing strength from within for the stress which bombards us from without.

Only Christ can give us that. What stabilizers are to a ship in a strong sea, his indwelling presence is to the Christian in the gales of life. He uses the stress that hits us to show us his ability in our disability.

Let's take the causes of stress we have enumerated and see how this works. Changes are the stuff of life. They expose our dependence on people, places, positions, presuppositions. The essential cause of stress in change is our fear of loss—loss of security, loved ones, the support system of the familiar, health, and the capacity to control our future. Heraclitus was right: "There is nothing permanent except change." We can accept that and live with it only if we are standing on the solid rock of a relationship with One who does not change. We need to hear what the Lord said through Malachi. "I am the Lord, I change not" (Mal. 3:6, KJV). Then we can say, "O Thou who changest not, abide with me."

The same is true of conflict. When Christ lives in us and we depend on his indwelling wisdom and guidance, his character begins to dominate our attitudes. We can search for truth in the midst of differing opinions; we are free from always having to be right; we can outgrow childish defensiveness, and can live with the ambiguity of the unresolved. Our relationship with the Lord becomes the most important thing in our lives. Dependent on his stabilizing strength, we can battle for what's right without paranoid personalizing of every issue. The emphasis of the stress not only catches our attention, but the Lord catches our attention through it.

But let's neither be simplistic or insensitive. Attacks on us personally hurt and fester. Criticism can cause a deep wound of self-doubt. "Do thy friends despise, forsake thee?" asks the old hymn. Often we shout a hurting, "Yes!" The advice of the hymn is, "Take it to the Lord in prayer." Talking it over with the Lord gives us perspective.

Recently some sharp criticism from an esteemed friend forced me to ask the Lord, "Show me anything about what has been said that is something I need to hear. With ruthless self-honesty help me to grow through any insight you may want me to hear from this. And give me your forgiving love for this person for any remarks that came out of jealousy, competitiveness, or malice."

It was amazing what the Lord said to me in the thoughts which flowed through my mind in the silence. He exposed my need to trust him and not the opinions and approbation of people. Then he alerted me by a reminder of his plan for my life. What had been criticized was a part of what he had clearly guided me to do. The stress of the criticism reaffirmed my determination to get on with the Lord's agenda.

From this point on I was free to learn from aspects of the criticism, whatever the motives were that had prompted it. I had been lumped in with a general criticism of "electronic preachers" whose methods and devices I had studiously avoided. The blast was untrue and uncalled for, and yet, the final word of the Lord was, "All right, the association was unfair. Now let's use it to redouble our efforts together to do a distinctly different quality of television ministry."

The stress oozed from my being like pus from a festering sore. The need to defend myself was gone; I was liberated to get on with obedience to the Lord instead of building my life on the opinions of people.

In the concerns which cause stress, we desperately need a gospel which is passionately our own. When the stress of worry wilts our confidence, we have a blessed opportunity to turn it into *eustress.* Surrender is the key. The yield point in the stress comes when we are refortified by the knowledge that nothing can separate us from the Lord and that he will use everything. Relinquishment of a concern is the point when we receive our actual infusion of the Lord's power. Mahalia Jackson found that secret in the stress of mounting concerns: "God can make you anything you want to be, but you have to put everything in His hands."

My experience goes even further. God can make you all that *he's planned* for you to be when you trust everything to his loving care. To take all that we are and have and hand it over to God may not be easy, but when it is done, the world has one less candidate for misery. Luther said, "I have held many things in my hands, and I have lost them all, but whatever I have placed in God's hands, that I still possess." The stress of our worries finally opens our hearts to hear the Lord's command: "Seek first the kingdom of God."

Next, consider how the stress of the compress of life's demands can be liberated by the stability of the gospel. We need a decisive reordering of our lives around its priorities. Stress as a result of an overpressured involvement in a multiplicity of things is a danger signal that some of what we are doing may not be guided by our Lord. Also, it may be a warning that with all we are doing we are not accomplishing his purpose for our lives. To be stabilized by the gospel means planning our time to accomplish its purpose in us and our use of time.

The commitment of our schedules to the Lord with the receptive prayer for help is the key. I am forced to do that repeatedly. The result is a rededication to essentials which enables me to grow in the stability of the gospel. For me that covers the spectrum from the sublime to the specific. Here are five things I must do to experience a stable life with a minimum of stress:

1. *Time alone with the Lord for Bible study, prayer, and quiet reflection on what the good news of the gospel means to me.* Each day I must recapture the salient truth that I am loved unreservedly and forgiven unqualifiedly; I have been called to be a Christ-filled channel of grace; I have a mission to be a servant to others in Christ's name that by all means I might introduce them to him; and I will be given enough strength and wisdom to do in each day what he wants me to do.

2. *A surrender of my involvements with an incisive inventory of the Lord's priorities.* This is a time to reaffirm what he reconfirms, delete what is getting in the way of his priorities, and say "yes" or "no" to new challenges which may be what he wants me to do. These could be a distraction from faithfulness and obedience.

3. *A reconsecration to people.* The gospel stabilizes me on the rock of refocused purpose. As I realize what Christ has done for me I am determined to rearrange my life to have time for people: my family, people with whom I work, and those whom the Lord places on my agenda.

4. *Setting of long-range and short-range goals.* In the light of ten-year goals, set specific and *realistic* goals for each year. That makes possible the precise planning of each week, being honest with myself about what needs to be, and can be, accomplished. Schedule engagements, appointments, and meetings ahead to move toward the goals. Refuse to overschedule so that there is time for interruptions, unanticipated crises or opportunities.

5. *Eliminate as many of the daily causes of minor stress.* Arrive early for appointments. Whenever possible, eliminate the tension of tardiness. Delay decisions until there is time for prayer to seek the Lord's perspective. Avoid living beyond income. Make as few financial decisions as possible which

will create a stress-provoking bind later. Get adequate rest so that the physical stress of tiredness does not rob me of effectiveness. Take time for adequate preparation so that I have the mind of Christ for each sermon, speech, or presentation.

That's a picture of stability for me. What would it be for you?

Finally, the inner stress of the unconfessed and unforgiven also is dissipated when the gospel becomes ours and we accept Christ's grace for ourselves. So often I find that stress in people is blamed on the pressures of life, when the real cause is something which is gnawing at their vitals.

I visited with a man the other day who complained about the stress caused by overwhelming schedules and responsibilities. The more we talked, the more the man realized that he was running from the person inside him. A few years ago he did something which has remained in his memory as a source of self-condemnation. Because he did not deal with it at the time, he has tried to atone for an inner feeling of guilt by busyness. It astonished him to realize that he was running off in all directions away from the conscience-stricken person in his own skin.

That day he stopped running, faced himself, and met the Savior. He accepted the forgiveness offered him and decided to stop hiding from himself and others behind an impossible schedule which gave him a false sense of worth.

Imagine yourself stabilized by the gospel. How would you look and act? What would your schedule, involvements, and priorities be? Get in touch with yourself. Are you under uncreative stress? What is it doing to your peace of mind and health of body? What are the causes of stress in your life? What is bending you out of shape, boxing you in, stretching you beyond what Christ has ordained? Most of all, what is Christ stressing in the stress?

What I've tried to say in this chapter is that Christ will give us stability and strength to accomplish his work by his power. We will be given superabundant resiliency to follow through on the seemingly impossible tasks he guides. His indwelling presence will equalize the pressure. But he will not give us more to do or allow more crises than we can take. If we dare to trust him with the stresses which come to us from any of the causes we've talked about, he will be able to make us stable. And he will help us reorder our lives around him and the gospel so that the self-induced causes of stress can be eliminated.

John Greenleaf Whittier gives us a prayer which can be a moment-by-moment reopening of ourselves to the inflow of his stress-dispersing power:

> Drop thy still dews of quietness
>   Till all our stirrings cease;
> Take from our souls the strain and stress
>   And let our ordered lives confess
> The beauty of Thy peace.

18

How Can I
Succeed at My Job
without Losing My Faith?

THE AVERAGE AMERICAN spends at least 150,000 hours working during his or her lifetime. Others who start working early in life, take little time off, and retire later in years, may log is as much as 200,000 hours. If we take even the most conservative calculation, most of us expend at least a third of our lives working.

For some, work is a delight; for others, a drag. It can be a way of accomplishing our goals or an end in itself. Success on the job can be an expression of our faith or it can be the object of our faith. Work in our society can become a diminutive god, or it can be a way to glorify God.

The purpose of this chapter is to discover how to glorify God in our work. Two biblical texts will pervade our response to the many people who have asked how to live out their faith on the job. The psalmist offers us a perspective on God as the Lord of all life. "The earth is the Lord's, and all it contains, the world, and those who dwell in it" (Ps. 24:1). Paul tops that with a cumulative conviction of our reason for being: "Whatever you do, do all to the glory of God" (1 Cor. 10:31). In response to the multitude of questions about how to be a Christian on the job, I want to look at the implications of these verses. We will be considering the perspective, priorities, and purpose of our work as a means of glorifying the Lord of all life during all the years of our life. The impact of our two texts, when applied to our work, is really something like this: "The earth is the Lord's, the realm of my responsibility at work and all with whom I work. Therefore, whatever I do and am in my work, I will do it to the glory of God." How to do that is the concern of most of us.

Here are some of the questions people have asked about being a Christian on the job: Why is it so difficult to incorporate my Christian belief into my secular professional life? How can I succeed in the business world without denying my faith? How can I live in my secular surroundings in the way the Lord wants me to? Can a Christian survive in the day-by-day mentality of the competitive system? If my job does not give me fulfillment, have I missed God's purpose for putting me on earth? How do you reconcile relating to people in a Christian way with being successful in a competitive business environment?

The question which capsulates all these and brings our thinking into sharp focus from the outset is this: How can I succeed at my job without losing my faith?

We are suddenly plunged into the crucial issue. Work is such a vital expression of our person that success or failure, recognition or relegation, advancement or disenchantment can determine our self-esteem and image, our sense of worth and value, and our overall status and security with others.

I want to introduce you to four people who have struggled with the issue of glorifying the Lord in their work. Each has given me permission to tell his or her story. Their experiences point up the difficulty of being God's person in the competitive, status-oriented, title-worshiping world of work.

Tom's voice was filled with hurt and anguish when he called me to ask if he and his wife could come over to see Mary Jane and me that evening. He sounded so urgent we cancelled other plans and were waiting for this successful executive and his charming wife, June. When they arrived it was obvious that something terrible had happened. Tom looked like a beaten animal. His whole demeanor was crestfallen. June's eyes were red, tears cutting rivulets in her otherwise impeccable make-up.

They sat down on our living room couch, a picture of deflation and disappointment. Tom's voice cracked as he tried to speak. June put her arm around him trying to give assurance and comfort.

"Out with it, Tom," I said. "What's happened?"

"Everything I've ever wanted is lost!" he said. "All I've worked for years to accomplish is down the drain. All the hard work, the late nights on the job, the missed days off, the skipped vacations, the sacrifices I've made to get ahead didn't work. You know I was up for promotion to head of my division. Everyone thought I was a shoo-in. Today, the president of the company announced that a man from one of the branches was being brought in to take the job. Everyone at work was shocked. They can't believe it. Nor can I. Ever since I joined the company after college, I have been working my way up to that job. I've earned it and deserve it. I've given them my life and they bypassed me! How could God let this happen?"

June and Tom were active church members. They had recently come alive in their faith. Both had made a deep commitment to Christ during a renewal conference at church. It had changed their lives completely—almost. They had become part of a prayer group, found new love in their marriage, and were seeking God's guidance in being parents to their two lovely children.

As an executive, Tom was admired, successful, and very ambitious. His devotion to his work had moved him ahead quickly. Everything, even his new faith, was marshalled to assure his goal of being vice-president of his division of the company. He had purchased a new home befitting the dignity of his anticipated position. The high monthly

mortgage payments were dependent on the salary he expected to earn when his life-goal was achieved.

Now on this day his world had fallen apart. His self-
worth had been tied to success on the job. The Lord, he
thought, had let him down. He felt so certain the influence
and power of that position were what the Lord wanted for
him. And of course, he had dedicated himself to becoming
the best Christian vice-president the company ever had.
The trouble was, he hadn't been given the job!

Tom spent hours in self-pity, incriminating the values
and motives of the company president. He searched his
soul concerning what he might have done or left undone.
Why was he bypassed? Then Tom and June were open
to pray to ask for the Lord's help to endure the disappointment. Just before we went down on our knees, Tom
said something that made our prayers real: "I guess that
job had become my real god. I expected the Lord to pull it
off for me."

It took more than that time of prayer for Tom's profound insight to take hold and give him freedom and
release. Months, and dozens of conversations later, the
realization became the fiber of real conviction. Work, and
not the Lord, had been the drummer that beat the driving
cadences of his life. To begin to march to a different
Drummer was the most painful transition in Tom's life.
Though he was an active Christian, officer in the church,
and a paragon of a community leader, the passion of his
life had been success on the job and his prize that vice-
presidency.

Al's story has a different twist. He was driven not just by
the need for success, but by fear of failure. He had been
raised in a Christian home where hard work, not just
cleanliness, was next to godliness. His parents had risen
out of the mire of poverty. Industriousness and faith in
Christ were syncretized in them both. They had imbued in
Al and his four brothers a belief that work and worth were

inseparable. Even though his father had suffered a stroke from the strain of overwork, and abhorrence of idleness had made his mother a fretful, anxious person, Al could not shake the impact of their personalities on him.

At work, he was a model of conscientiousness. He took on his own and others' work with gusto. Praise became a narcotic upper to keep him going. Over the years, he slipped into a deadly assumption: what he did on the job made him invaluable. Like Tom, he was a committed Christian. The heady mixture of confusing his production with his worth, and his fear of failing, dominated the attitudes of his life on the job, however. He became more tense as the years rolled by. The more insecure he felt, the more work he took on. Then one day, the creativity and drive burned out. He had become addicted to work. No one worked as hard as he did, he thought. The pity he had gained from his wife and children for how hard he worked didn't satisfy him any longer.

I wish I could give you an "all's well that ends well" conclusion to Al's story. I can't. The most hopeful thing I can report is that Al has accepted the fact of his work addiction and admits that much of the delight of being a father and husband has passed him by. But he's still in the bind. A group of Christian businessmen with whom he meets periodically keep asking him what it would mean for him to glorify the Lord in getting his work into perspective. One thing has become clear to him and the group: until Christ heals his inner insecurity and sets him free to love himself, he will kill himself trying to justify himself by overwork.

Now I want you to meet Ann. She has risen from her secretarial position to being head of the staff of clerks in her office. Ann is efficient, capable, attractive. She has worked hard over the years to attain high recognition and compensation. Now there is no further advancement open to her. She can do her job with little thought or effort.

Boredom has set in. The excitement is gone. When she awakes in the morning, the thought of going to work is a drag.

For Ann the real action of life is at church and in her circle of Christian friends. She'd love to resign her job and become a missionary or go to work for the church. There she falsely imagines that every moment would be as adventuresome as the events of the Book of Acts. But the doors seem closed. The most difficult place for her to be a Christian is on the job. "What does running that office have to do with the kingdom of God?" she keeps asking. She works now simply to pay her bills and keep life together. Though she is an effective visitor of potential new members as a part of the evangelism program of her church, she has never shared her faith with the people for whom she works or who work for her.

Sam's story is very different. He loves his work. He can't wait to get to the job and is always the last one to leave at night. As a research scientist he's doing exactly what he's dreamed of all his life and prepared for with extensive education, culminating in a Ph.D. with honors. His job is on his mind during every waking moment. And yet, for different reasons, he's ended up in the same condition as both Tom and Al. His problem is that no one is as dedicated to the job as he is. He can't find people to work for him or around him who will give the time and effort to the job he does.

Recently, exhaustion and fatigue have been creeping in. His love of work has become a compulsion. Overburdened, he has become irritable, defensive, cynical, paranoid and depressed. He's angry at the people whose work he has to assume because of pressures to get the job done on his timing and standards. Stress is evident on his face. His family is showing less excitement and admiration for his hard work. They would like to talk about other things than what he's doing at work. Sam also is a Christian, but he has never thought of his laboratory as a part of his stewardship of all life.

You may have found yourself in the skin of any one of these four people. Perhaps your circumstances are slightly different. But all four press us to ask some crucial questions regardless of where we work.

Here is an inventory which helps to determine whether we are in danger of losing our faith to succeed on the job. I have asked the following questions at conferences and meetings with businessmen and women.

Does work ever compete with the Lord for first place in your life? Do you think about your work a good deal of the time when you're not on the job? Has worry over your work robbed you of peace of mind or interrupted your sleep? Have you ever neglected or misused the essential relationships of life in the family to succeed? Are you ever tempted to compromise what you believe to gain or keep a position?

Is your job one that you can do to the Lord's glory? Has your job and your worth as a person become intertwined? Do you ever overwork as an escape from greater responsibilities? Would you say that you live a balanced, wholesome life of work, recreation, enrichment, and personal growth? Do the people with whom you work know that you are a Christian and sense the influence of your faith in your attitudes, decisions and values? Have you claimed the place where you work for the Lord and are you a winsome witness and servant to the people with whom you work?

Our answers to these questions directly affect the answer to the basic question with which we began. How can we succeed at our jobs without losing our faith? The four people we talked about were in danger of losing their faith. For Tom, the job had become his faith; for Al, the job was a justification by work rather than faith; for Ann, her job was a distraction; and for Sam, it was a storm center of conflict. If we really wanted to glorify our Lord in the third of our lives we spend working, what would we do? Allow me to suggest five things which are ingredients of a totally different attitude toward our work. Each is stated in a way to catch our attention and alert us to a new way to live on the job.

1. *Get a new job!* I mean it. Not a different job, but a new one. The great need is to do the same old job differently. That depends on how we look at work. God created work as a part of his plan for mankind. He entrusted us with the cultivation and preservation of the earth. We were programmed to be co-creators with him in the utilization of the resources which he has put at our disposal.

Jesus gives us a dignifying disposition toward our work. "My Father is working still, and I am working" (John 5:17). God worked in creation, he works constantly in providential care of his creation, he works all things together for good for those who love him and he works to accomplish his purpose through all we do. We were given the sublime responsibility to work, earn, and use the proceeds of our labor to care for ourselves and others. Individual initiative, industrious productivity, and enjoyment of the proceeds of our labor are all part of the biblical meaning of work.

We take a new job, even in the context of our old one, when we thank God for the privilege of being able to work. There's no joy in a life of idleness. Leisure is a blessing only if it is a hiatus between days of hard work. Our minds, bodies, and wills were given us for joyous investment.

This attitude of gratitude is a sure cure for the drudgery of work. Mark Twain said that he had not done "a lick of work" for over fifty years. And yet he lived a very productive life speaking, writing, and helping the rest of us to laugh at ourselves. His attitude toward his full and demanding life was to enjoy working. "I have always been able to gain my living without doing any work; for the writing of books and magazine material was always play, not work. I enjoyed it; it was merely billiards to me."

That may sound absurd to some of you who groan inwardly when you think about your work. But I think of the writers and speakers I know who approach their opportunities with a grimness, rather than the zest Twain showed. Deadlines are enemies; each line written is a taxing drudgery. A famous author said to me recently, "Well, I've got to get back to work. My publisher is pressing me for my new manuscript. Like it or not, I have to get it in!" "Why do you do it?" I asked. "Why not quit? Do something else. Throw it all over and become a waiter in a restaurant!" He was shocked. He really enjoyed writing bestsellers and yet he had become negative, losing the adventure. We talked at length about how we all twist the most exciting opportunities into obligations. Work becomes a means of self-punishment and negation.

Becoming a new person in an old job is the issue. Can you thank God for your work? Changing jobs will not help if we bring the same attitudes of drudgery to the new one.

The crucial thing is to discover our central calling. Anyone who believes in Jesus Christ is called into ministry. A minister is a servant. We are to serve Christ in all that we do, including our jobs. John Calvin said, "This, too, will provide consolation, that following your proper calling, no work will be so mean and sordid as not to have a splendor and value in the eyes of God."

And yet, we must honestly acknowledge that many people find themselves in jobs which do not express their capabilities or interests. We need to get to know the real person inside and find work that challenges our aptitudes, experience and desires. Life is too short to spend it on the wrong job.

Take a good aptitude test. Be honest in evaluating your intellectual capacities, education, training, and experience. Believe in yourself as much as God does. Ask yourself—if I could throw caution to the wind, what kind of a job would I like? It's never too late! If you cannot live out your calling to glorify God in all that you do on the job in which you're now involved, ask him to help you find one where you can.

But, be sure of this, even a perfect job will require a new
you to go to work each day. And that's dependent on the
second ingredient of succeeding at your job without losing
your faith.

2. *Go to work for a new boss!* For the Christian success on
the job is making the Lord the boss of our lives. We report
to the Lord; we serve our employer. Everyone works for
some human overseer. Some person is humanly in charge
of every realm. Every team must have a captain. Someone
bears the lonely task of stopping the buck. The laborer has
the job supervisor, the supervisor has the department
head, the president has the chairman of the board, and the
board members have the investors. Even the self-
employed person is dependent on others to utilize his services or assure his investments. We are all intertwined in
the fabric of interdependence.

I met an old friend recently. Years ago I'd been with him
when he accepted Christ as Lord of his life. As a part of
getting reacquainted, I asked a foolish question: "Whom
are you working for these days?" I asked this knowing that
his work in the television industry often brought frequent
changes of employers. "The Lord!" he responded with a
smile. He went on to tell me that the most difficult challenge for him in becoming a vital Christian was to work for
the Lord and express that allegiance by doing his best for
his employer.

Paul would have been pleased by that. In Ephesians
6:6,7, he gives us the servant's secret of going to work for a
new boss. "Don't work hard only when your master is
watching and then shirk when he isn't looking; work hard
with gladness all the time, *as though working for Christ,*
doing the will of God with all your hearts" (TLB). There it
is: work for a boss as if working for Christ. That changes
both our attitudes and productivity. Our task is to work
industriously and energetically as a part of our witness. We
are called to excellence in honor of Christ.

A man said a remarkable thing about one of my members. "He's the most faithful, loyal, energetic assistant I've ever had. He makes me look great! His life and attitudes have made me think about what I believe."

The only way to progress to greater responsibility is to give our maximum to the responsibilities we have presently. Loyalty to a boss, following orders joyously, lifting as much of the load of our employer as possible—this is the finest preparation for becoming a leader of others. If we can't follow, the chances are slim that we will ever be able to lead.

When we work for a boss as if working for Christ, criticism and undercutting are unaffordable luxuries. Our calling as a Christ-centered worker is to find creative ways to communicate our ideas or concerns to the person we serve and not to others in a critical attitude. That often means minding our own business and doing our own job with impeccable diligence. No one appreciates an omnipresent critic at work who writes into his or her job description the responsibility of analyzing everyone else.

We are deployed by Christ in our jobs. We have a ministry of intercession to the people for whom we work, who work around us, or work for us. The reason we are where we are is to share Christ's love and hope. Earning that right with a boss will mean a quality of work and faithfulness. An opportunity to talk about what we believe will be preceded by the affirmation and esteem we give an employer.

Paul gives the same advice to employers. In Ephesians 6 he goes on to give some stern admonitions to slave owners. His insight packs a wallop for those of us who employ others to work for us today. Insert the words employer and employee for slave owners and slaves in verse 9: "And you slave owners must treat your slaves right, just as I have told them to treat you. Don't keep threatening them; remember, you yourselves are slaves to Christ; you have the same Master as they do, and he has no favorites" (TLB).

The Christian employer has a major task. It is the success, in the deeper sense we've been talking about, of his or her employees. When Christ is the employer's boss, he or she will do everything possible to clarify goals and expectations, create a healthy working environment, provide affirmation and encouragement, and offer sensitive evaluation and accountability. Caring for employees as if caring for Christ also means concern for personal needs. Praying consistently for the people who work for us changes our perspective from just getting a job done to enabling great people. Under Christ, we are responsible for clear communications and the maximum creativity for each person.

Most of the problems we have on the job are related to people. At the center of every complexity is a complex person. We all have unmet needs. Personal problems can sap accuracy and effectiveness. With both the people who work for us and those for whom we work, listening to what is meant by what is said can make relationships at work a ministry. That leads to the third ingredient for success on the job.

3. *Stop working for a living.* Often the question is asked, "What do you do for a living?" The intention is to find out what kind of work a person does to earn a wage. The question, "What is your livelihood?" is equally ambiguous. For a Christian, Christ is our living. To be independent to preach Christ, Paul earned income by tent-making. His purpose in living was Christ. He did not say, "For me to live is tent-making," but, "For me to live is Christ."

Our god is whatever we think about most of the time. A job can erroneously become a consuming passion. When our work is the essential source of our self-esteem and value system, Christ must take second place. As it was for Tom, the deification of work can be a subtle process. We may use Christ and prayer as a means of succeeding. The job becomes the fulcrum around which our faith, marriage, family, friends, recreation and enrichment must revolve. We become what Wayne Oates calls a workaholic.

Our work gives meaning to our lives. We live to work rather than working to be creative and provide for the necessities, pleasures, and responsibilities of life. Titles, positions, salaries, and recognition become the lust of life. We end up owing our soul to the company store.

A friend of mine described a mutual friend who had drifted away from Christ in the pursuit of advancement. "He was born a man, reborn to be a Christian, but died an executive."

But how do we get out of the trenches long enough to find a perspective on our priorities? Years of working with people has convinced me that no one kicks the work habit alone. Like an alcoholic we need other people to help us admit that we are powerless over the narcotic of overwork. That presses us on to the fourth ingredient.

4. *Start a new company!* Not a new corporation, or a new organization, but a new company of believers with whom you can meet consistently to talk about what it means to live for Christ first and then work with freedom and joy. We all need a "company of the committed," to use Elton Trueblood's phrase, a band of trusted friends with whom we can talk about being faithful and obedient to Christ on our jobs.

I am part of a group that meets for breakfast frequently to talk about the problems of stress on the job. The men in the group come from all walks of life. Many of us are workaholics and need each other to gain and keep perspective. In an unstructured time each person can be accountable to the group and expose ways we drift into making our work our living. We keep tabs on each other's schedules, confess times when our work denies us a full and abundant life. We also talk over mutual problems of pressure we have in common.

I am gratified that the members of my church are clustered in prayer and support groups like this all over the city. Some of the groups are made up of people who work together in the same company or office. Their "church in miniature" enables them to claim their realm of the world for Christ.

The final ingredient of succeeding on the job without losing our faith summarizes all the rest.

5. *Bring ultimate meaning to your work rather than seeking to find it in your work.* This has become a motto for many who are trying to find the Christian purpose, perspectives, and priorities for work. A job can give us many things. The one thing it cannot provide is life's meaning. When it becomes our ultimate meaning, it competes with our loyalty to Christ.

A job should be an expression of the meaning of life we have found in Christ and never a substitute for it. Then we can work with excellence and integrity. We can seek first the kingdom of God and know that he will guide and empower us to bring our responsibilities under his Lordship. Each task or assignment can be done to glorify him. Problems and pressures can be faced and solved to honor him as Chairman of the Board of life. The result will be that we can become people-oriented, seeking to share our faith with fellow workers. We have been given our place of employment not only to do the work involved but also for the sake of the people with whom we labor. It is no accident that we are where we are. When we pray for the people around us the Lord will open up opportunities to talk with them about him and what he means to us and can do in their lives.

In "L'Envoi" Rudyard Kipling describes the future hope of the artist. It envisions what heaven will be for a painter, and yet it contains the essence of what I've tried to say we can live right now on our jobs:

> When earth's last picture is painted and the tubes are twisted and dried,
> When the oldest colours have faded, and the youngest critic has died.

We shall rest, and faith, we shall need it—lie down for an aeon or two,
Till the Master of all good workmen shall put us to work anew . . .
And only the Master shall praise us, and only the Master shall blame;
And no one shall work for money, and no one shall work for fame.
But each for the joy of working, and each, in his separate star,
Shall draw the thing as he sees it for the God of Things as they are![1]

Don't wait till heaven for that—start today. Go to work on an old job as a new person. Make the Lord your boss. Work for him as your true living. Claim where you work for him. Make your work meaningful by bringing meaning to your work. Your job is the Lord's and all the people who work around you. Whatever you do at work—do to the glory of God!

19

What Can You Do
When You've Failed and
Denied What You Believe?

THIS QUESTION AND others like it came out of the heart of a person who had stumbled badly. He felt he had no right to pray, and when he tried, he felt self-incrimination and condemnation. We all deny our Lord in so many little ways, but what do you do when the denial contradicts everything you've stood for and believed? Is there a way back? How does the Lord deal with failures?

The answer is vividly portrayed in the way Jesus Christ dealt with Simon Peter's denial. Some time ago I spent my annual study leave by the Sea of Galilee. One day I lingered for hours at the place where the resurrected Lord appeared to the disciples. In my mind's eye, I relived the encounter. In so doing I experienced the way the Lord heals the failures which deny our faith. Allow the scene to unfold in your imagination. . . .

Simon Peter tried desperately to get in touch with his feelings. As he sat before the breakfast fire on the shores of the Sea of Galilee, he realized that he was not part of the joyous reunion celebration with the resurrected Lord that swirled about him. An excited delight surged within the other disciples as they circled the fire—talking, laughing and eating in sublime companionship. Jesus was back with them! Hope leaped in their hearts once again. But not Peter. He could not even look the Lord in the eye!

No one seemed to notice that Peter was strangely aloof and had withdrawn into his own thoughts and feelings. "What's the matter with me?" he mused to himself as he raked the red-hot coals of the fire, staring at the burning embers, afraid to look up for fear that his eyes might meet the penetrating gaze of the Master. A dull ache pervaded Peter's feelings. Something was wrong inside him. A depression had been growing in him for weeks; now it was about to engulf him. He had first become aware of a gnawing inner disturbance during the long wait for Jesus' appearance again in the Upper Room in Jerusalem.

Was it sheer exhaustion from the excruciating experience of the crucifixion or the exhilarating excitement of the resurrection? Fear of arrest? Uncertainty of the future without the Lord? Or was it the dreadful memory of his denial on the night before Jesus was crucified? Peter could not handle the anguish of his cowardly denial. He had to block it out, try to forget; but his efforts were futile. Was that why he now could not bear to look Jesus in the eye?

Peter remembered the loving, commanding look in those eyes when, on that same spot beside the sea, Jesus had said, "Come, follow Me, and I will make you a fisher of men." The exciting events of the past three years flooded before him.

What adventure Peter had known following the Master! He remembered with self-affirmation how on the road to Caesarea Philippi he felt the Spirit rush within him. He had blurted out the conviction, "Thou art the Christ!" He would never forget the tone of the Lord's voice when he told him that the church would be built on the rock of his faith. A rock? The recollection reverberated with shock waves within him. "A rock that cracked!" he said to himself. With that, his mind irresistibly returned to the Last Supper and his arrogant protestation that he would never deny his Lord. Others surely would, but not Peter!

The whirlpool of spiralling memories irrevocably sucked up his conscious thought. His threefold denial, "I never knew him!" and the mocking sound of the cock crowing, thundered in his soul. Would he ever forget? Was that what had driven him back to Galilee—to the sea, the fishing nets, the old life? Had he decided in the deepest, occluded recesses of his mind that though Jesus was alive, he was not worthy to follow him in his postresurrection strategy? Peter had gone to Galilee to hide. And the Lord had found him!

It was at dawn, after a long night of unsuccessful fishing, that the Lord had appeared on the seashore. When John shouted triumphantly, "It is the Lord!" Peter had leaped recklessly into the sea to swim ashore to meet him. As the impetuous disciple waded out of the water he suddenly realized that, standing before the Lord, he could not lift his eyes to look him in the face. The Lord had been warm in his greeting, but Peter suddenly found he could not respond. There was a distance between them and the distance was in Peter's unforgiven heart. That's why all through the breakfast he had withdrawn into the disturbed chambers of his own mind.

Suddenly it was quiet around the fire. The other disciples had drifted a few paces away. Only the Lord remained. Still Peter could not lift his eyes. Jesus broke the silence. "Simon, son of John, do you love Me more than these?" The words cut like a sharp knife. Peter had said that he loved the Lord and would never deny him. Now he used Peter's own words. They cut into the wall of remorse that blocked his relationship with the Lord. Nothing could have touched the raw nerve any more than that question. But Peter hurt too much to respond with easy words. He would not speak beyond what he could be. He knew himself to be unworthy of loving the Lord. A friend? He could be sure of that. "Yes," Peter replied, "You know I am your friend." "Then feed My lambs." A fresh call to leadership? Peter was too stunned to hear.

Silence again. The anguish in Peter's heart was beyond control. He sobbed within as he sat motionless, his head laconically bowed, still unable to look up.

Again Jesus asked, "Simon, son of John, do you really love Me?" A further blow to Peter's bruised and battered ego. What was the Lord trying to do to him? This time the question stirred quenched emotions. Peter felt a surge of warmth and affection for Jesus. But he dared not say any more than he could back up with action. "Yes, Lord," he said, "You know I am your friend."

Peter's voice became stronger. It was good to say it again. Jesus responded with a repeated call to discipleship. "Then take care of My sheep." Peter caught the change. Lambs and now sheep. Jesus had used the metaphor of sheep and shepherds often during his ministry. The Lord was summoning him to a new picture of himself as a leader again. Simon pondered that. Would the Lord trust him again?

A third time Jesus asked, "Simon, son of John, are you even My friend?" Jesus' previous questions had used the word for love and Peter's response had carefully evaded the demanding sacredness of the word his previous denials had contradicted. Now Jesus descended to the best that Peter had been able to offer. "Are you sure about being My friend?"

That broke Peter wide open. Tears flowed from his eyes. He was trembling and sobbing uncontrollably. The Lord had broken the seal of self-condemnation from around his heart. Finally he could lift his eyes to meet the Savior face to face. Love and forgiveness flowed from the Lord to the broken disciple. Peter's beard was wet with tears. His lips quivered as he stuttered out the response of his contrite heart. "Lord, You know everything. You know what's in my heart. You know what I am. Forgive me for what I've done! I don't want to fail You again."

I imagine that Jesus embraced his forgiven disciple. While he held the massive frame of the fisherman, he gently repeated his restoring command. "Then feed My little sheep."

We have witnessed one of the most traumatic and yet tender encounters on the pages of Scripture. The drama of the restoration of Peter is our story. We cannot consider it long before we find ourselves in Peter's skin on that morning beside the sea. What happened to Simon is what needs to happen to most of us. It reveals the secret source of joy and power in the Christian life. Peter's dynamic, healing encounter with the Risen Lord gives us the gospel in miniature and show us how he wants to liberate us from guilt and frustration today.

The basic message of this passage, from which all others flow in progression, is this: the Lord's love does not fail however much we fail him. Peter had built his whole relationship with Jesus Christ on his assumed capacity to be adequate. That's why he took his denial of the Lord so hard. His strength, loyalty and faithfulness were his self-generated assets of discipleship. These natural endowments were recognized and affirmed by our Lord. He gave Peter a position of power and leadership because of them. The fallacy in Peter's mind was this: he believed his relationship was dependent on his consistency in producing the qualities he thought had earned him the Lord's approval. He constantly tripped over his own ego. The point is that he never allowed Jesus to love him profoundly. If adequacy is the basis of being loved, what do you do when you are inadequate?

Many of us face the same problem. We project onto the Lord our own measured standard of acceptance. Our whole understanding of him is based in a quid pro quo of bartered love. He will love us as if we are good, moral and diligent. But we have turned the tables: we try to live so that he will love us, rather than living because he has already loved us.

It is difficult to imagine that Peter could have missed the

central message of Christ. But he resisted it at every turn. Whenever Jesus spoke of his impending death for the sins of the world, Peter protested: "That will never happen to You!" At first blush, that sounds magnanimous. Further reflection exposes Peter's nature. He did not acknowledge that Christ would have to die for *his* sin!

The same reaction is revealed in his hesitation to allow Jesus to wash his feet at the Last Supper. He wanted to stabilize his relationship with the Master by what he did rather than what was done for him. The disciple's heart was fortified by the defensive device of serving rather than being served. The result was an inability to love deeply. We cannot give what we do not have. Simon was a stingy receiver. When he failed in the one thing that was his security, he fell apart.

What was the reason Jesus asked his disarming, disturbing question, "Do you love me?" It was not to expose once and for all to Peter that he had not loved and could not love him adequately. That was not the issue. The issue was allowing the Lord to love him. Peter lived through those painful days of depression inverted on himself because he could not tell the Lord how he felt and ask for forgiveness and a new beginning. Remember, he had three postresurrection chances: two in the Upper Room and one as he stumbled out of the sea that day in Galilee. He had totally missed the impact of the grace of God incarnate in the Lord.

It is amazing to contemplate that the major thrust of Jesus' message was not that we ought to love God on our own strength, but that God's love is freely given before we ask! When pressed by the Pharisees, Jesus repeated Deuteronomy 6:5 and Leviticus 19:18, "You shall love the Lord your God with all your heart, and with all your soul and with all your mind, and your neighbor as yourself." Jesus assumed the basic admonition, but knew that he had come to provide the motivation to live that command.

The people in Jesus' day knew the commandment but

could not live it. His message, life, death and resurrection
was God loving the world so that people could love in
return. Jesus was much more concerned about opening
people up to allow God to love them. Then they would be
able to love God as a response, not a qualification.

That leads to the second discovery which flows from the
first: the Lord wants to introduce us to our real selves
beneath our failure. That means that we are to allow him
to penetrate the depths of our personalities. Don't miss the
alarming and affirming thrust of this passage. Jesus appeared in Galilee for Peter. He had great plans for Peter in
the post-Pentecost birth and growth of the church. The
Lord had never wavered from his strategy of building his
church on Peter's gift of faith.

There is nothing we can do which will make the Lord
stop loving us. He comes to each of us right now. Listen to
him: "No matter what you've done or been; thought,
planned or fantasized; failed in or left undone; I love
you." That will never change.

Jesus Christ comes to each of us to do what he did for
Peter: to introduce the disciple to himself. The Lord
wanted Peter to know something more about Peter than
his failures and denials. Peter's heart was tightly closed to
love because he felt unworthy. He did not dare to love
again for fear of failure. Jesus would not leave him in that
condition. He wanted to get down to the bedrock in Peter.
That's why he persisted in his questions.

The Big Fisherman was more than his feelings of remorse. There was a genuine, authentic person inside of
that impetuous, blundering man. The Lord wanted to re-
build the man on the sure foundation of a realistic ap-
praisal of himself as one who was loved and accepted.
Jesus kept pressing him until he could say, "Lord, you
know everything! You know what I'm like." It was as if he
were saying, "Lord, you know all about me. It was foolish
of me to try to hide from you what you knew better than
I. Now, Lord, as long as you know, take all of me and make
me the person you meant me to be."

When we allow God to love us we can dare to open up all the recesses of our personalities to him. He knows all about us anyway. Real love can happen when aloof efforts of adequacy are replaced by intimacy. That means opening our innermost beings so that our intrinsic selves may be known in a profound, personal friendship.

The Lord has shown us his innermost nature in the incarnation. He has given us freedom of will to remain closed or open to him. Though he knows all about our innermost thoughts, he will not invade our privacy without our invitation. He wants to bring us all to the point where we acknowledge that he knows everything. He will persist, as he did with Peter, until we say, "Lord, you know all about me. I want to allow you to love me and make me the person you intended."

Now we are ready to consider the third way to let the Lord free us from our failures. Once we have allowed him to know us intimately, we are painfully aware of all that needs forgiveness and restitution. Then we must accept the forgiveness which is offered to us. There is great significance in Jesus' threefold question and Peter's response. The question, "Do you love me?" forced Peter to confess that he had not and probably could not love him in his own strength. Peter's persistent thrice-repeated response, "You know I'm your friend," was a confession of lack of love. Peter had denied his Lord three times because of lack of love. The Lord gave him an opportunity now to wash the dreadful memory from his mind. Twice Peter said, "I'm your friend," in response to the question about love. Then Jesus descended from the loftier word for love and asked if he was really his friend.

Peter had not been a very good friend either. But the Lord did not allow the equivocation of the issue. Peter had failed at both loving and friendship. He needed forgiveness.

That forgiveness was given and experienced is gloriously affirmed in the Book of Acts and in Peter's letter to the early church. After Pentecost, forgiveness through

Christ is the major thrust of the apostle's message. Listen to the liberated disciple: "Repent, and let every one of you be baptized in the name of Jesus Christ for the remission of sins; and you will receive the gift of the Holy Spirit" (Acts 2:38). Everywhere we meet Peter in the expansion of Christianity, he is preaching and modeling the message of forgiveness.

Because he allowed the Lord to forgive him, he became the most forgiving of all the leaders of the early church. Look at his relationship with John Mark. When this young failure defected from the mission with Paul, it was Peter who picked him up and helped him to let God love him. Or consider Cornelius the Gentile. Peter broke the exclusivism of the church and accepted Cornelius as a believer. The apostle led the way for Christianity to be the answer for all people regardless of race or religious heritage.

That leads naturally to the final aspect of what to do when you've failed. It is focused in this passage. To love the Lord is to allow him to give you a viable self-esteem. At a time when Peter had given up on himself, the Lord gave him a commission that restored his self-image. He called him to be a shepherd of the flock of God. Imagine how that watered the dry, parched wasteland of Peter's debilitated self-awareness. Peter expected to be drummed out of the Lord's legions. Instead, he was recalled to duty. Rather than telling Peter to stop thinking about himself, the Lord gave him a reorienting, liberating picture of himself. He was to feed the little lambs, the lambs and sheep of the people of God.

Jesus was profoundly concerned about the future of his mission. He had put a great deal of time and training into Simon, whom he called the Rock. I am convinced that Peter's denial and the Lord's Galilean appearance were the final stage of preparing Peter for Pentecost. It was crucial for Peter to know that his status with the Lord was not his infallibility. Broken by failure, he could accept the Lord's new picture of what he could become.

When we allow God to heal our remorse over failure, we are given the gift of a lively image of the person he intends us to be. We are all becoming the person we dare to envision.

The Lord's image of us always involves us in his strategy with people. He wants to make us creative lovers of others. Deep meditative prayer helps us imagine the person we were meant to be. As we are quiet in the Lord's presence, allowing his love to capture our minds and flood through our emotions, we feel new love for him and then for ourselves. Then we can relax and allow him to flash before the screen of our mind's eye the kind of person he wants to enable us to be in our relationships. As we hold the picture in our mind's eye and return to it each day, we will become new creatures in Christ.

Peter was given a new image of himself as a leader and sensitive enabler of people. He became what the Lord sparked in his imagination. Later, at Pentecost, he received power to live the new life Christ had pictured in his imagination. When the Living Christ returned in the power of the Holy Spirit and took up residence within the liberated apostle, Peter became a bold leader of the New Israel, the church.

Near the end of his life Peter wrote to the Christians scattered throughout the then known world. Listen to his confidence and conviction: "Blessed be the God and Father of our Lord Jesus Christ, who according to His abundant mercy has begotten us again to a living hope by the resurrection of Jesus Christ from the dead, to an inheritance incorruptible and undefiled and that does not fade away . . ." (1 Pet. 1:3,4). That's exactly what happened to Peter. The resurrected Lord infused the power of his death and resurrection into the disciple. Peter was set free from the past to become a lover of himself and other people. He was born anew, given a new beginning and a new life. "But you are a chosen generation, a royal priesthood, a holy nation, His own special people, that you may proclaim the praises of Him who has called you out of darkness into His marvelous light" (1 Pet. 2:9). Now feel the pathos of his own transformation: "Once (you) were not a people, but are now the people of God, who had not obtained mercy but now have obtained mercy" (1 Pet. 2:10).

Is that your picture of yourself? Loved and forgiven, enabled and empowered? It can be right now. And the most magnificent result will be in your relationships with people. The same secret of letting God love us is applicable to how we care for people. To love people is to let them love us. That means letting them know us by sharing the delights and difficulties of our lives. Vulnerability is the most dynamic means of communication.

Peter became an approachable, honest, open and contagious communicator of love because he no longer had to pretend he was stronger and more adequate than others. He never forgot his own fallibility. Arrogance was replaced by affirmation of the struggle in others. He had the joy and freedom of a person who knew who he was, whose he was, and for what he was intended.

The greatest gift we can give the people in our lives is to let the Lord forgive us. When we do we will be able to love ourselves in spite of our failures. That will liberate us to allow people into the inner recesses of our hearts. They will see and feel what Christ has been able to do with the raw material of our humanity. This is the key to helping others. It's more than telling people what they ought to believe, do, and be. Rather, it's the impelling, irresistible sharing of what we've been through and what we've discovered Christ can do with a forgiven failure.

We are all like Peter as he sat enveloped in his feelings of discouragement and self-condemnation. The Lord comes to each of us. He lifts our dejected faces and looks into our eyes and deep into our hearts. "Let me love you!" he says. "I know all about you. I know your memories and your hopes. I'm for you. You are very special to me. You don't have to pretend any more. Stop trying to be good enough to earn my love. I already love you more than you can imagine. All you can do is allow me to live my life in you. I'll make you the unique, cherished, irreplaceable person you were meant to be."

And our only response will be, "Lord, you know what I've done with the gift of life. I know I've failed you. But more than that, Lord, I now know I love you. And that's all I need to know!"

Now we too are ready for Pentecost. The basic purpose for which Jesus came, taught, died, was resurrected, and ascended was to begin a new creation with new creatures who are sure of his love for them and their love for him. Everything is fulfilled when Christ takes up residence in His reconciled, forgiven, released people like you and me. The incarnation was to prepare for the infilling of ready, receptive disciples. The purpose of Jesus' total passion is Pentecost and the empowering of his people with his Spirit. He will not settle for less nor can we!

20

How Do I
Get Out of the
Holding Pattern?

WE CIRCLED OVER Chicago in a holding pattern. My flight from New York connecting with a flight to Los Angeles was now dangerously late. When we finally landed, I darted off the plane and ran through the crowded terminal with O. J. Simpson agility. I reached the Los Angeles flight just in time, the door closing behind me as I boarded. I flopped down in my seat breathlessly, thankful that I would now be able to make a crucial appointment in Los Angeles on time.

The plane revved up its engines and taxied to the runway. And there we sat. After what seemed to be forever, the pilot announced, "Ladies and gentlemen, we are twenty-third in line for take-off. The traffic congestion is heavy this evening. We probably won't be in the air for an hour. Just sit back and enjoy the waiting time!"

My heart sank. I checked my watch. If we got off when the pilot predicted, I could still make it. When we finally took off, we flew at breakneck speed that must now be some kind of record in aeronautical history. But when we reached the Los Angeles area, my hopes were dashed again. Los Angeles was fogged in! We were put in a holding pattern, stacked up with dozens of other planes. After we had circled for half an hour, the pilot again made a bleak but apologetic announcement. "Sorry, friends, we've been rerouted over to Ontario airport where we'll land and wait until Los Angeles opens up." All hope of making my appointment was gone. There was nothing to do but accept the inevitable.

I looked around me at the other passengers. Some of them were as distressed as I was. Others didn't seem to be concerned at all. One woman said, "Just like life—holding patterns that keep you from getting where you want to go." A man seated near me seemed much too content. "What are you so happy about?" the man next to him asked. "So who cares?" he responded. "I didn't really want to go to Los Angeles anyway. I've got some things waiting for me there I don't want to do. I'm in no hurry!"

We arrived in Los Angeles at 3 in the morning. I crawled into bed at 4:30 A.M. A night full of holding patterns had left me exhausted and frustrated.

I was amazed a week later as I reviewed a packet of questions people had sent in. I found this one: "How do I get out of *life's* holding patterns?" What I had been through that night prepared me to answer with fresh, personal experience. The man who submitted the question must have been on my flight! Or one like it. It is a condition of life we all face at times. Life does have its holding patterns when there is nothing to do but wait. We seem to be blocked from making progress, placed on a shelf of immobility, stifled from realizing our potential.

Some of life's holding patterns are caused by other people. Their resistance or reserve keeps us locked on dead center. They hold us back, fearful of change or the call of adventure. But also, there are holding patterns we inflict on ourselves. We resist growth and development. Like the man on the plane, our destination is not exciting and we welcome the hiatus of a holding pattern.

For some, life is one continuous holding pattern. We hold life at bay panicked by its challenges and pressures. We keep circling, never landing. The ruts of routine are a

welcome relief. Sometimes we actually create the routine
to keep control of the status quo. It happens in our personalities, relationships, responsibilities, and opportunities. We become gray, dull people.

There are also other holding patterns which are forced
on us by the seemingly inexplicable mystery of life. They
come when we least expect them, feel we least deserve
them, and are the least prepared to endure them. An illness sets us behind in our agenda. Or our timing is thrown
off by difficulties in someone we love and we are denied
the fulfillment of what we've planned. Disappointments
strike and dreams for the future must be put in the "sus-
pense" file.

Waiting, holding patterns also impede our development
in the Christian life. One person asked, "Why does it take
so long to become mature in Christ? Why do I so often
battle the same old problems? If I'm a Christian, why do I
still struggle?" The struggles of life are the holding patterns. Whether they are caused by us, others, or life
around us, we all cry out, "Dear God—what is the meaning
of this?"

We dare not blame God for our struggles, but also we
dare not suggest that he will not use them. My years of
walking with the Lord have taught me that he alone can get
us out of the holding patterns of life. He uses them to help
us grow. In each of them we discover a deeper experience
of his love and providence. As nature abhors a vacuum, he
abhors our plateaus. We are programmed to grow through
all that happens. The Lord loves us as we are, but he never
leaves us there.

That's the seasoned, tempered message of Moses at the
end of his life. His last will and testament to the people of
Israel before he died contains an image which shifts the
metaphor. It gives us a biblical answer for our questions
about our struggles with life's holding patterns, particularly the ones we inflict on ourselves and the ones imposed
on us by others.

Looking back on the forty years in the wilderness, Moses selected the eagle and its training of the eaglets to fly as an impelling illustration of God's providential government and how he trains and protects us. The Lord had given him the metaphor nearly forty years before when Moses first climbed Mount Sinai. "You yourselves," he said, "have seen what I did to the Egyptians and how I bore you on eagles' wings and brought you to Myself" (Exod. 19:4). Now at the end of his life Moses compares how God had been like an eagle in training his people. Here's a way to get out of holding patterns.

> Like an eagle that stirs up its nest,
> That hovers over its young,
> He spread His wings and caught them,
> He carried them on his pinions.
> The Lord alone guided him (Deut. 32:11–12a).

This passage tells us three crucial things about God. He is a disturber, a developer, and a deliverer. The destiny of an eaglet is to fly. The eagle must do everything it can to force the eaglet to leave the nest and learn to fly. God does nothing less to us in our holding patterns.

Consider first the Lord's loving disturbance. "Like an eagle stirs up its nest." After the time of hatching and the birth of the eaglet, it is dependent on the parent eagle for food. Feeding time is kept with precise regularity as the eagle brings food to the comfortable nest. But there comes a time when the eaglets must learn to fly. Now feeding time is not to be followed by comfortable sleep. Instead, the eagle stirs up the nest. It purposely makes it uncomfortable. The bedded straw is withdrawn, and the nest is no longer the soft, comfortable place it has been. The purpose of the discomforting disturbance is to get the eaglets out of the nest.

The Lord's disturbance of our nests of contentment is much the same. He removes the comforts of accommodation to life as it is. He creates a dissatisfaction with our present level of growth and creates in us new daring. There is a sure sign that the Lord is working in our lives. It is that we become more excited about the future than the past. Wherever we are in our faith, our personality development, our life goals, and our realization of the immense potential of God's plan for us, there is always a next step. And to get us ready, the Lord stirs up a creative discomfort.

Sometimes this preparation to get us out of the holding pattern comes with crises, and often with difficulties which force us to get in touch with where we are. These are times when God must close some doors to get us to notice the ones he has standing open for us.

There's a false idea which debilitates getting out of our holding pattern. It's that we can finally get things sorted out and settled down. We strive to solve all the problems we face, work through all the challenges, and resolve all the conflicts in our relationships. Our energies are invested to finish up projects and meet deadlines in the vain hope that then we can sit back comfortably. There is a great emphasis in our culture to get the right job, save enough money, accumulate the security of a home and comfortable furnishings, establish the right friends, and travel to see the places we've always wanted to visit.

Also we are pressed on by the illusion that if we can just get through the pressures we are presently facing, then we can relax. The problem is that our preconceived ideas of what settled security is going to be are in themselves holding patterns which may be keeping us from God's best for our lives. The question I am forced to ask myself is, "Lloyd, where will you be when you arrive at where you are going? What will you have accomplished when you think you have accomplished your goals?" When I begin to review those destinations with the Lord, I am usually discomfited by the realization that he has plans which are way beyond my own. He stirs up my nest—makes me impatient with my self-created holding pattern.

My experience is that the Lord constantly allows those disturbances which will wake us out of somnolent satisfaction. He will use problems and conflicts to get us moving again. Whenever life falls apart in some area, he is giving us a chance to grow. Life really becomes exciting when we accept, rather than resist, the rough, tight places that wake us up to new ways of being our best for him. Every event which befalls us has a meaning beyond itself. Our task is to ask the Lord what he's trying to say to us.

The prelude to a new step of growth is the stirring of the Holy Spirit in us. It happened to Samson in preparation for the task the Lord had for him. "And the Spirit of the Lord began to stir him" (Judg. 13:25). Ezra was pressed to discover what was ahead. Note how "the Lord stirred up the spirit of Cyrus"(Ezra 1:1). The same Lord challenged through Joel a word for all of us in all times. "Stir up the mighty men!" (Joel 3:9 RSV). The American Standard Bible renders "stir" as "rouse." The Lord stirs and rouses us; the nest becomes uncomfortable; it's time to fly!

After the eagle in Moses' metaphor stirs up the nest, it "hovers over its young." The Hebrew word for "hover" is also translated as "broods." It is the same word used in the creation story—the Spirit brooded over the waters. It is an active verb of creation, not just protective care. The eagle's brooding over the eaglets implies more than watching out for their safety and provision. It is an exciting, impelling brooding, including whatever is necessary to get the eaglet out of the nest.

A study of how eagles do this is fascinating. First the mother presses the eaglets to the edge of the now uncomfortable nest. Often she will swoop down from behind, actually pushing the eaglet to the precipice. Then she will fly around in front of the eaglets who are fearfully tottering on the edge. Flapping her wings, she gives the eaglet both example and inspiration of the possibility of flying. If this does not entice the eaglet to try its wings, the mother eagle will fly around once again and actually push the eaglet off the edge. Now the hovering and brooding be comes even more active. The eaglet falls through the air discovering its previously unflexed wings.

This, too, is an example of how the Lord deals with us. If our uncomfortable nest does not rouse us, he will command the circumstances of our life to push us to the precipice. We are all wavering on some edge of a previously comfortable nest. What is it for you? What leap of faith has the Lord shown you that you need to make? If you were sure you would succeed, what would you dare to try? G. Campbell Morgan put it this way: "What is life for? To teach us to fly, to teach us to exercise our half-fledged wings in short flight that may prepare us for and make possible for us to take longer flights until we are able to graduate to being mature eagles."

Our task is not to look for some spectacular flight but to trust the Lord and dare what is at hand. The immediate opportunities prepare us for greater ones. None of us knows all that the Lord has ahead. But we can be sure that we cannot take the longer flight of a momentous challenge if we are afraid to fly off the edge of the nest to try our wings today.

This forces me to ask, "Am I—are you—settled in the nest, being stirred, on the edge, ready to leap, or in flight training?"

But press on. Our eagle Lord is not only disturber and developer, he is also our deliverer! We could not dare to take a fledgling flight of faith if we were not sure of that. Moses' image splendidly includes that. Note how the impersonal "it" referring to the eagle changes to the personal "He." "He spread His wings and caught them, He carried them on His pinions." This is the vivid picture of the fledgling flight of the eaglet, falling in space, trying its wings, and at just the right moment, the eagle swoops down, spreads its gigantic wings, to catch the eaglet. The process is repeated until the eaglet becomes fully capable of flying by itself.

What a lovely, powerful image. It is the moving picture

of how God delivers us. He will not allow us to stay in the nest or even on the precipice of the nest in indecision; but as we do leap and try our half-fledged wings, he catches us when we have fallen too far.

Moses expands on this image further on in his benedictory message to his people. "There is none like the God of Israel, who rides the heavens to your help, and through the skies in His majesty. The eternal God is a dwelling place, and underneath are the everlasting arms" (Deut. 33:26, 27). Here is the sublime assurance of God's intervention when we need him. He did that for all creation in the incarnation. At the fullness of time, the right time, he came to rescue us. The everlasting arms were stretched out on a cross. Paul caught the image. "Now to Him who is able to keep you from stumbling . . ." (Jude 24). Christ is with us in calling us out of the nest and he keeps us from falling into anything which would ultimately harm us, now or for eternity.

How can I get out of the holding pattern? That's not really the question, after all. The person who asked it has indicated by so asking that the Lord is stirring up his nest. The real questions are: What are the fears and reservations which keep us in our holding pattern? What do we have to lose? What is that in comparison to discovering our destiny to fly in obedience to the Lord's guidance? What would life be like out of the holding pattern (or the nest, to combine our metaphors)? Have we asked the Lord what are the next steps of his strategy for us in the adventure of growing in our relationship with him? Am I becoming the person he meant me to be, and doing the particular thing I was born to accomplish? If that is clear, what is the first step to be taken today?

Each day we stay in the nest is a diminutive death. Every time we say "no!" to the Lord's stirring, the more uncomfortable he will make us. We have this choice: fly or die!

Sir James Barrie said, "To have faith is to have wings." And I would add—to soar. The eaglet is fully an eagle not only when it develops its wings, but when it learns that there is a jet stream which catches and propels its flight. No longer is it the strength of its wings, but the mysterious power of the wind. When we dare to leap from the edge of the nest, we discover that the everlasting arms do more than catch us; they are like the wind lifting us.

We have been called to live a supernatural life in which what we are enabled to say and do is infused with the Spirit of God. To soar, we need the Spirit's lifting, engendering power. What we thought impossible will begin to happen—not by our striving, but through his strength. The psalmist's affirmation will be ours: "And He sped you upon the wings of the wind." The people around us will be astonished and we'll be a wonder to ourselves.

Can you accept these great truths about God and his dealings with us? Our growth as persons is dependent on his disturbance, deployment, and deliverance. To stay in the comfortable nest involves a lethargy which means spiritual death. We were programmed to fly! By the process of disturbance, by his brooding love, by the inspiration of his outspread wings as he lures us into flight, by the great strength with which he swoops beneath us and catches us on his pinions, He is perfecting our strength and leading us to heights as he develops within us the person we were meant to be—now and forever!

The quest for answers to our deepest and most urgent questions is a sign that we want to get out of the nest and learn to fly. Our questions can be a holding pattern—or the next step in our flight plan.

We'll always have questions. There are so many more I wish I had space to deal with. I hope I've shown that there is no question too big for our Lord. The Scriptures are a limitless resource of his answers. It is a comfort and a source of courage that we can ask him anything!

Notes

Chapter One

1. Sidney Lanier, "The Marshes of Glynn."

Chapter Three

1. "Be Still My Soul," by Katharina von Schlegel, translated by Jane L. Borthwick. *The New Church Hymnal,* Lexicon Music, Inc. 1976, p. 370.

Chapter Four

1. This account of Howard Everett, a veteran missionary to the Cape Verde Islands is told by Dr. James Dobson in *Emotions: Can You Trust Them?* (Glendale, CA: Regal Books, 1980).

Chapter Seven

1. A. T. Robertson, *Word Pictures in the New Testament,* vol.

4, *The Epistles of Paul* (Nashville, TN: Broadman Press, n.d.).
2. Siegfried Grossmann, *Charisma: The Gifts of the Spirit,* (Wheaton, IL: Key Publishers Inc., 1971), p. 84.
3. Leslie B. Flynn, *Nineteen Gifts of the Spirit,* (Wheaton, IL: Victor Books, S. P. Publication, 1975), p. 141.
4. William Barclay, *Daily Study Bible: The Letters to the Corinthians* (Philadelphia: Westminster Press, 1956), p. 122.

Chapter Sixteen

1. Alexander Maclaren, *Expositions of Holy Scripture: Hebrews 7 to End of James,* (Grand Rapids: Baker Book House, 1974), p. 11.
2. From "The Eagle and the Hawk" by John Denver, © 1971 Cherry Lane Music Company.

Chapter Eighteen

1. From Rudyard Kipling, "L'Envoi," in *Kipling—A Selection of His Stories and Poems,* vol. 2, ed. John Beecroft (Garden City, NY: Doubleday & Co., 1956).

How to Use This Book

The questions and exercises in this study guide are designed for individual study which will in turn lead to group interaction. Thus, they may be used either as a guide for individual meditation or group discussion. During your first group meeting we suggest that you set aside a few minutes at the outset in which individual group members introduce themselves and share a little about their personal pilgrimage of faith.

If possible, it is a good idea to rotate leadership responsibility among the group members. However, if one individual is particularly gifted as a discussion leader, elect or appoint that person to guide the discussions each week. Remember, the leader's responsibility is simply to guide the discussion and stimulate interaction. He or she should never dominate the proceedings. Rather, the leader should encourage all members of the group to participate, expressing their individual views. He or she should seek to keep the discussion on track, but encourage lively discussion.

If one of the purposes of your group meeting is to create a caring community, it is a good idea to set aside some time for sharing individual concerns and prayer for one another. This can take the form of both silent and spoken petitions and praise.

Study Guide

Chapter 1: What Is God Like?

1. Dr. Ogilvie says that he believes "agnosticism is the silent agony of our age." What does he mean by that statement? What is an agnostic?

2. If you were asked to state two of the most disturbing unanswered questions you have about God, what would those two questions be? Share them with your discussion group.
   If you have not already done so, read aloud Isaiah 40:25–31 before going on to the next question.

3. According to Dr. Ogilvie, what does it mean to say that God is holy?

4. Dr. Ogilvie suggests that when the perplexing questions of life trouble us and pull us apart, contemplation on the greatness of God can pull us together. Have you tried any kind of disciplined meditation focusing on the greatness of God when things get rough in your life? If so, how do you pray or meditate? If you don't do this, how could you begin? What Scripture passages would be most helpful to use as the focus of your meditations? Discuss this in your group.

5. How does the life and ministry of Jesus help you to "think magnificently of God"? Choose your favorite or best known story of Jesus in the Gospels, and tell how you think the story answers the question, "What is God

like?" (If you are in a group, ask each member of the group to choose a different Gospel story.)

6. What would your answer be to Dr. Ogilvie's question: "How would you live the rest of your life if you really believed all that we've said about God thus far?"

Chapter 2: Is God Really in Control?

1. Compare the soft, pampered man-boy of Dr. Ogilvie's opening story with the character of Joseph in the biblical story. What important differences between the two strike you as significant? How did God use the events of Joseph's life to produce a mature man?

2. Have you ever found yourself in a situation where you were asking, "If God is all-powerful, all-knowing, and all-loving, why doesn't he do something?" Briefly relate the circumstances and tell how you felt in that situation. What was the ultimate outcome?

3. Examine the three presuppositions Dr. Ogilvie makes on pages 25–26:

   a. God is supremely in control when he limits his control.
   b. He is sensitively in control as he grants us the gift of free will.
   c. He is sublimely in control as he intervenes and brings good out of evil that happens to and around us.

   What do each of these statements mean? Do you accept them?

4. Would you have said that God was really in control during Jesus' agony in the garden of Gethsemane, during his trial, and during his suffering and death on the cross? In what sense do you feel God was ultimately in control and/or limiting his control during these events in Jesus' life?

5. How does the resurrection of Jesus answer the question, "Is God really in control?" What would you say to someone asking that question?

6. Reflect back upon the most difficult time in your life—the time when you experienced the most acute sense of sin, pain, tragedy, or failure. Can you identify ways in which you now believe God was ultimately in control of that situation?

7. Suppose that you heard Dr. Ogilvie preach this sermon during a Sunday morning worship service. How would you summarize the message for a friend who was not present at the service? What ideas would you choose to share? Write a brief paragraph to help you remember what is most significant to you about the message.

Chapter 3: Where Is God When I Suffer?

1. If you have not done so already, take the time to read Psalm 42 before beginning your discussion. Read the psalm aloud.

2. Do you ever experience sleeplessness due to worry or wrestling with personal fears and problems? What kinds

of thoughts most frequently occupy your mind during such periods of insomnia? How do you usually cope with such sleeplessness?

3. Dr. Ogilvie suggests that "the night" in Psalm 42 is a symbol of human suffering. In terms of this psalm, what does Dr. Ogilvie see as the purpose of the night, that is, what is one of the purposes of human suffering?

4. In what ways do you think we sometimes set an agenda for God, but then are are angry or disillusioned when God does not follow our agenda? Try to think of a specific example to illustrate this.

5. In light of Dr. Ogilvie's comments, how would you describe in your own words what the psalmist's phrase, "I will sing the Lord's song in the night," can mean for the modern Christian?

6. What impact do you feel the suffering, death, and resurrection of Jesus Christ has upon the question, "Where is God when I suffer?" How is it that suffering can ultimately lead a person to yield to God's sovereign lordship over his/her life?
   Do you know of someone now who is seriously suffering physically, mentally, or emotionally? What might your own private prayer be for them right now? How can you pray that they will experience God?

7. Without being simplistic, how might you share with that individual some of the insights you have studied here? Think about this, and if helpful, write down some notes to help you remember some of the ideas you have studied.

Chapter 4: How Can I Know God's Perfect Will?

1. Why do you think so many people seem to have real concerns and difficulties over the matter of coming to know the will of God for their lives? How do you deal with the question of knowing God's will for your life?

2. Do you or other Christians you know speak of God's "perfect will" and his "permissive will"? What do these expressions mean to you?

3. How does Dr. Ogilvie define and distinguish between the "perfect will" and the "permissive will" of God? In Dr. Ogilvie's opinion, why does God exercise a permissive will with human beings?

4. Can you think back over your life and identify a situation or series of events in which you think you failed to follow God's perfect will, but were acting under God's permissive will? Share your experience with the group. How do you think you could have learned or better known God's perfect will during that experience?

5. Dr. Ogilvie offers some strategies for knowing God's will: daily Scripture reading, daily prayer, and sound advice from other people who know us and love us. Do you have difficulty disciplining yourself to read Scripture and pray daily? Most people do. Discuss how you can improve your self-discipline in these areas.

6. What kind of experience have you had with seeking the advice of other people on matters concerning God's will for your life? What are some of the pitfalls and the possible benefits of seeking such advice?

7. Take a moment of silent meditation to think about the final questions posed by Dr. Ogilvie in this chapter. How would you answer these questions to God: Have I fulfilled the reason for which I was born? If not, why not? If not now, when and how?

Chapter 5: How Can God Know and Care about Me?

1. According to Dr. Ogilvie, what does the Apostle Paul mean in Romans 8:29 when he says that God has "predestined us to be conformed to the image of his Son"? What does this tell us about the purpose of God for our lives?

2. Dr. Ogilvie believes that the proper translation of Romans 8:28 is: "God works all things together for good for those who love him." How do you think this statement then relates to Romans 8:29, which speaks of God's purpose for our lives?

3. State in your own words how Dr. Ogilvie has defined the words "foreknew" and "predestined" in Romans 8:29.

4. According to Dr. Ogilvie, what role does an individual's "free will" (the freedom to respond or not respond to God) play in relationship to Paul's statement that God calls us? Discuss.

5. Recall the story Dr. Ogilvie told about the man who on his deathbed refused to accept God. Dr. Ogilvie said this was an example of the exercise of free will, and that the dying man "chose not to accept his election" (calling). What did Dr. Ogilvie mean by this last statement?

6. In Dr. Ogilvie's view, what does it mean to say that a Christian is justified and glorified, according to Romans 8:20? How do these terms then relate to the previous expressions, namely that people are foreknown, predestined, and called?

7. State in your own words how Romans 8:28–30 answers the question, "How can God know and care about me?"

Chapter 6: Why Are My Prayers Unanswered?

1. Why do you think the Scriptures counsel us to "wait on the Lord"? What does that phrase mean to you?

2. What does Dr. Ogilvie identify as the primary purpose of unanswered prayer?

3. In general what do you believe is the meaning and purpose of prayer? Is it primarily asking God to meet our needs by giving us certain things and changing our circumstances? Is it trying to change God's will? Is prayer primarily opening oneself to God and listening to him in silence? Is it communing with him in a deepening relationship? Now try to agree upon a brief definition of prayer!

4. Dr. Ogilvie says that, according to Paul, unanswered prayers are God's way of bringing us into a closer, deeper relationship with him. Can you recognize a time in your life when unanswered prayer brought you into a deeper union with God? If so, reflect upon or describe some of the feelings you had while undergoing that experience. Did you doubt God or get angry at him? When

and how did you finally realize that the unanswered prayer was for a positive purpose?

5. What do the words, "My grace is sufficient for you," mean to you? Have you experienced this kind of grace amid unanswered prayer, the grace about which Paul spoke? If so, give an illustration from your own experience, and explain what you learned about grace from that experience.

6. Discuss this statement: "After we have prayed, during the waiting for an answer, something happens to us. Prayer doesn't change things, it changes us in the way that we relate to things."

7. As a means of summarizing what you have read and discussed in this session, how would you now answer the question: "Why are my prayers unanswered?" Suppose a skeptic, agnostic, or atheist heard your answer and responded by saying that you were just rationalizing. How would you reply to that skeptic?

Chapter 7: How Do I Get More Faith?

1. Dr. Ogilvie distinguishes between "the primary gift of faith" and "advanced faith." What is the distinction he makes? How does Dr. Ogilvie relate this distinction to the phrase, "from faith to faith" (Romans 1:17)?

2. George Muller's breakfast blessing is an illustration of faith's audacity. When was the last time you could say that your faith took on the quality of audacity?

3. Pertinacity means "resolutely adhering," "persisting," or "endurance with a vision that enables a dream to

come true by God's power." Have you ever been persistent about something and felt that your faith was rewarded because you endured and held to your dream or
vision? If so, share this with the group.

4. Advanced faith contains at least four qualities: imagination, audacity, pertinacity, and risk. Which of these
qualities do you feel you need more of?

5. What is the most important idea you gained from studying this message?

Chapter 8: Is It a Sin to Doubt?

1. Dr. Ogilvie has suggested that everyone has certain
doubts about the availability, the interest in, and the
power of God for his or her life. We all ask questions
like: "Does God know about my situation or problem?
Does he care? Can he, and will he act? If God does act,
will it make any difference?"

2. According to Dr. Ogilvie, what does the writer of James
1:2–8 identify as the "antidote" to doubt?

3. In 1 Corinthians 12:8 the Apostle Paul identifies wisdom
as one of the gifts of the Holy Spirit. What do you think
the New Testament means when it speaks of the "gift of
wisdom"? Share with the group a recent example or
situation in your life in which you feel you have experienced wisdom as a gift of the Holy Spirit.

4. Read and discuss the following statement by Dr. Ogilvie:
"Faith makes possible the trust which enables God to
bless us with wisdom. He takes our doubts as our gift to

him and turns it around and gives us the specific gift of
wisdom that we need for it" (see James 1:6).

5. Discuss: How is doubt related to growth in the Christian
   faith? Why do you think James 1:2 counsels us, "My
   brethren, count it all joy when you face various trials"?

6. On the basis of your study of this chapter, how would
   you answer this question: "Is it a sin to doubt?" Explain
   your answer.

Chapter 9: What Is a Born-Again Christian?

1. When you hear the phrase, "born again," what is the
   first reaction which comes to your mind? What public
   figures or religious groups do you associate with the
   expression "born again"? Do you think the phrase has
   more than one meaning? If so, discuss them.

2. Dr. Ogilvie points out that many people who were baptized, confirmed, and participated in the traditional,
   formal practice of the church for years, only later re-
   ported an experience of being born again. Can you identify with this phenomenon? If you or someone you know
   has had such an experience, share it with the group.
   Why do you feel this frequently occurs in many
   churches?

3. Dr. Ogilvie says there are two kinds of crises: the "crisis
   of trouble" and the "crisis of potential." What does he
   mean by this? Which kind of crisis seems to have
   brought Nicodemus to Jesus?
   Have you ever experienced a "crisis of potential" which
   brought you to an encounter with Jesus Christ? If so, tell
   about it.

4. In your understanding, what is the bottom line truth to be learned from the story of Nicodemus? If you were faced with the task of leading a Bible study or Sunday school lesson dealing with Nicodemus, what is the main idea you would emphasize?

5. React to this statement in the context of Nicodemus' conversation with Jesus: People seldom change. Church members who are set in their ways from years of hearing the same words and following the same routines are among the most resistant when it comes to change.

6. How would you respond to Dr. Ogilvie's questions: "Would you like to be born again? Are you willing?"

Chapter 10: Why All This Talk About Commitment?

1. Dr. Ogilvie speaks of three aspects of the human personality: the intellect, the emotions, and the will. Which one of these do you feel is most involved in the process of commitment? In what ways are the mind, emotions, and will inseparably related when it comes to commitment? Why does Dr. Ogilvie place so much emphasis on the will and its relationship to commitment?

2. What does it mean to you to be truly committed to another human being such as a husband, wife, parent, child, or friend?

3. Dr. Ogilvie notes that the Greek word for commitment in 2 Timothy is a banking term. Do you recall the meaning of that term? What does that word suggest about the meaning of commitment?

4. In committing ourselves to Christ we also commit our concerns to him—or do we? Does it seem to you that people often separate their faith from the practical concerns of their lives? How do they do this? Give an example.

5. How did Jesus' commitment enable him to endure the cross? What were some of the final words of Jesus on the cross that revealed the totality of his commitment?

6. Dr. Ogilvie speaks of three commitments: a commitment to Christ, a commitment of our concerns, and a commitment of the challenge for which we were born. What does he mean by this last kind of commitment?

7. Ask yourself this question: "Why was I born?" Have you arrived at a satisfactory understanding of what God wants of your life? Share with your group.

Chapter 11: How Can Christ Help Me When I'm Tempted?

1. If you have not already done so, read the account of Jesus' temptation experience in Matthew 4:1–11. Read also Hebrews 2:14–18.
   Temptation is an experience common to all men and women (1 Cor. 10:13), but people are often reluctant to discuss openly their struggles with temptation. Why do you think this is true? Do you think it would be helpful if people were better able to discuss the temptation they feel?

2. According to Hebrews 2:18, the reason Jesus is able to help those who are tempted is because he himself suf-

fered and was tempted. Does it help you to realize that
Jesus underwent temptation also? In what way does it
help you? How can the knowledge that he is with you
during your temptations help you in the future?

3. In the temptation to turn stones into bread, Dr. Ogilvie
   asserts that Jesus was tempted to accomplish his own
   purpose, that is, to meet a legitimate need by using God's
   power. Have you ever seen people who seemed to use
   God to accomplish their own self-centered purposes—
   perhaps even in the life of the church? Can you give an
   example?

4. How do you react to this idea: "Only people change the
   world, and the key to changing any situation is to change
   the people in the situation." Do you agree with this completely? Agree, with some reservations? Or do you dis-
   agree? If you agree with the above statement, what
   implications does this have for solving social problems
   such as crime, the nuclear arms race, world hunger, etc.?
   Discuss.

5. According to Dr. Ogilvie, what is the symbolic, spiritual
   meaning of the second temptation? Of the third temptation? How did Jesus reply to all of Satan's temptations?
   Discuss this statement by Dr. Ogilvie: "The purpose of
   Satan in our lives is constantly to unsettle our status of
   grace, to make us feel that we have to do something to
   prove ourselves to God and to other people. . . . to be
   more, to achieve more, so that God will say, 'You've
   finally measured up.'" Can you think of some ways in
   which you and people you know experience temptation
   and give in to it? How do church people sometimes try to
   do things to prove themselves to God? How does this
   contradict your understanding of grace as a New Testament principle?

6. Can you think of any ways in which you feel the Christian church today may be trying to accomplish God's purpose by using Satan's power? Discuss.

7. Now that you have studied this chapter, how would you answer the question: "How can Christ help me when I'm tempted?"

Chapter 12: Why Are Some Christians So Dull?

1. Dr. Ogilvie has suggested that the antidote to our dullness as Christians is allowing Jesus Christ to get inside us and touch our real thoughts, emotions, and will. What are the real concerns and issues that trouble you the most and occupy your thoughts and emotions? Do you think these concerns ever worry or depress you to the point of making you a dull person?

2. Respond to this statement by Dr. Ogilvie: "I think that the reason for dull pulpits is that pastors preach sermons that don't really reach the needs of people. We skim right over the heads and hearts of people, talking about irrelevancies when people are aching inside." Have you encountered this as a problem in your experience in the church? How do you think pastors can make their preaching more relevant in the church today? How can lay people help their pastors in this matter?

3. What is the significance of the fact that Jesus helped the two disciples on the Emmaus road understand who he was by explaining the Scriptures to them? What role do you think a person's intellect should play in his/her religious faith? What role should emotion play? In Dr.

Ogilvie's view, what interrelated roles should a Christian's mind, emotions, and will assume in responding to God in a wholistic, lively way?

4. In what sense can Christian fellowship be an antidote to dullness?

5. Another cure for dullness is found simply in sharing your faith. When did you last share your faith verbally with another person?
To conclude your study of this chapter, ask yourself the following questions: Have I been willing to care and share? Have I asked the Lord for opportunities? Am I open to listen and be the kind of friend others can trust implicitly? Have I been vulnerable to share what Christ has done in my own life? Have I been loving enough to be incisive when the time is right?

Chapter 13: Is It Possible to Change Human Nature?

1. Dr. Ogilvie suggests that human nature is one of the few things in all creation that can be changed. Can you think of a personal habit you've tried to change in your own life? Were you successful in changing the habit? Do you think it is possible to change human nature in spiritual matters?

2. What do you think Dr. Ogilvie means when he says, "The only way human nature is changed is to make us more human"? How does God make us more human?

3. Discuss this statement by Dr. Ogilvie: "God is more concerned about the person we will be than the person

we've been." In this context, what is the meaning and significance of 1 Corinthians 13? What role does love play in the process of transforming people?

4. Try to imagine what your relationships would be like if you behaved as one who truly knew that you were loved, accepted, and forgiven. Do you think your relationships with others would be significantly different if you were consistently forgiving, affirming, tolerant, and hopeful?

5. What do you think Paul means by each of the following statements? Discuss what each means to you and try to illustrate your explanations:

   a. "Love does not insist on its own way" (1 Cor. 13:5).
   b. "Love is not easily provoked" (1 Cor. 13:5).
   c. "Love does not rejoice at wrong" (1 Cor. 13:6).
   d. "Love bears all things, believes all things, hopes all things, endures all things" (1 Cor. 13:7).

6. In what situations of your life do you feel you need to learn how to be more loving? How can you begin to do this?

Chapter 14: How Can I Forgive and Forget?

1. Dr. Ogilvie states that "our mental health, as well as our relationship to Christ, is dependent on being forgetfully forgiving." What is mentally harmful in harboring grudges and holding on to painful memories? Name the negative feelings a person usually has when he or she is unforgiving.

2. Dr. Ogilvie says that the cross is the secret of victorious living, but that the concept of bearing our cross has been widely misinterpreted through the years. What does he

see as the erroneous interpretation of Luke 9:23? What meaning does Dr. Ogilvie give to this verse?

3. What is the connection between forgiving oneself and forgiving others? Would you say that people who seem to be critical (unforgiving) of others are probably very critical (unforgiving) of themselves? Why is it necessary to be able to forgive oneself in order to be able to love others?

4. How can one go about acquiring "the gift of a bad memory"?

5. Dr. Ogilvie asked the man who was dealing with a painful divorce to write out all that needed to be forgiven and to sign the list "Forgetfully Forgiving" with his name. In private, make your own list of hurts and allow Christ to lift the weight of those hurts by the power of his cross.

Chapter 15: What Can I Do with My Moods?

1. Are you a joyful Christian? Or, do moods seem to control your attitudes and reactions to others? What do you think Dr. Ogilvie means by the statement, "Joy is no option"? Do you think he means a Christian should just ignore negative emotions? Why or why not?

2. Comment on this statement: "A moody Christian is a contradiction of terms."

3. Dr. Ogilvie says: "Bad moods are playing God." What does he mean by this? Share any reactions you have about this comment.

4. Recall the last time you were in a bad mood. What caused it? Was the primary cause of your bad mood the conditions around you, condemnation, or conditional love?

5. How do you handle disappointment in yourself when you fail to do something you should have done?

6. What is the first essential step to becoming a joyful Christian?

Chapter 16: What's the Secret of Being a Confident Person?

1. Think back to your childhood and adolescent years. What were the main insecurities you felt while growing up? Are any of those insecurities still a part of your life? In what areas of your life and your personality, if any, do you feel the most insecure today?

2. Do you recall the story Dr. Ogilvie told about the woman with a low self-esteem whose insecurities were rooted in hurts experienced during her childhood and teen years? If you are a parent, what can you do to help build confidence and self-esteem in your child? What kinds of things are harmful to a child's self-esteem? If you are in a group with other parents discuss this and exchange ideas.

3. Dr. Ogilvie points out that we build up confidence (or the lack of it) layer by layer throughout the stages of our lives. We store up our experiences like a computer. Confidence is fashioned out of consistent, constant experi-

ences over a period of time. Identify an area in your life in which you feel a strong degree of self-confidence. How did you arrive at that self-confidence? Discuss.

4. Earlier in this presentation Dr. Ogilvie alluded to a distinction between "self-confidence" and what he called "Christ-confidence." What does he mean by that? How does Hebrews 7:25 relate to the idea of "Christ-confidence"?

5. Having concluded listening to this presentation, from a Christian perspective how would you now answer the question found in the title of this chapter, "What's the secret of being a confident person?"

6. Recall question 1 above. What insecurities did you identify as a part of your life? What have you learned from this message that may help you cope with these insecurities?

Chapter 17: How Can I Find a Strategy for Stress?

1. Dr. Ogilvie says that everyone is "either under stress, is a cause of stress, or is deeply concerned about . . . a loved one or friend because of stress." Do you agree? If so, relate how you find this observation to be true in your life. What evidences of stress are there in your life and in the lives of people around you?

2. Is it difficult sometimes for you to realize that you are under stress? What actually happens when you feel stress? How do you feel? What happens to you physically and emotionally? How do you try to deal with stress?

3. Dr. Ogilvie says that change, conflict, criticism, life concerns, complexities of demand, and conscience pangs are all causes of stress. Which of these factors do you feel is the most frequent contributor to your stress and to that of your friends or loved ones?

4. When was the last time that change, conflict, or criticism caused stress in your life? Describe the circumstances. How did you handle the situation?

5. What is it about knowing God as your Father and Jesus Christ as your Lord that can help you personally in coping with stress?

6. As a group, see if you can formulate your own strategy for getting a handle on stress. You may want to relate other passages in the Bible to this topic (see Philippians 4:6–7, 11–13; 1 John 1:9, etc.).

Chapter 18: How Can I Succeed at My Job without Losing My Faith?

1. How do you perceive the relationship between your job and your personal faith commitment? What, if anything, troubles you the most about the relationship between your work and the fact that you are a Christian?

2. What does it mean to you when you hear someone referred to as a "workaholic"? What do you feel are some of the dangers inherent in becoming a workaholic? Why may such a lifestyle be unhealthy for one's Christian faith and witness?

3. On page 213, Dr. Ogilvie offers a brief written exercise dealing with the relationships between faith and work.

Think (or read) back over the questions asked by Dr. Ogilvie. Which question disturbs you the most? That is, which one raises the most difficult personal issues or stirs up feelings of guilt for you? Why? Discuss.

4. Dr. Ogilvie offers the following five essentials on how to glorify God where you work. Discuss what Dr. Ogilvie means by each of these, and how you can apply them in your life:

   a. "Get a new job."
   b. "Go to work for a new boss."
   c. "Stop working for a living."
   d. "Start a new company."
   e. "Bring ultimate meaning to your work rather than seeking to find it in your work."

5. How would you summarize in a few sentences the message Dr. Ogilvie was conveying in this chapter? What practical things can you do beginning now to apply these principles to your work life? Discuss.

Chapter 19: What Can You Do When You've Failed and Denied What You Believe?

1. In Dr. Ogilvie's view, what was Jesus' purpose in asking Simon Peter the three questions recorded in John 21:15–17?

2. If you were to identify three specific ways in which you most frequently "fail God," what would they be? Think carefully about your answer. Do your answers seem to focus more on formal, external rituals, rules, and commandments, or do you think of your failures more in

terms of a personal relationship with God, as if he is a close friend?

3. What can you do to turn your guilt and failures over to God and realize the resurrection? Does your church observe a time for confession of sin during the regular weekly worship service? How can this time be valuable for worshipers in dealing with their failures and rediscovering the meaning of the resurrection?

4. Dr. Ogilvie has said that the Lord comes to us so that we cannot only realize the resurrection but also be regenerated by it, recalled into active duty, and given resilience for living. What evidence is there that Simon Peter was regenerated, recalled, and given resilience in this sense after his conversation with Jesus by the Sea of Galilee? Have you felt what it's like to experience a new beginning after a major failure in life? If you wish to do so, describe the circumstances and events comprising that experience. In what sense did God regenerate you, recall you, and give you resilience?

5. What is the most encouraging truth you found in this chapter about Christ using our failures? How has this address changed or added to your understanding of God's attitude toward our failures?

Chapter 20: How Do I Get Out of the Holding Pattern?

1. How does one recognize that one's life has entered a holding pattern? What does Dr. Ogilvie mean when he speaks of holding patterns in our lives? Are there any

telltale signs that would suggest that a person is in the midst of a holding pattern? When, for example, was the last time you think you were in such a situation? How did you come to realize it?

2. According to Dr. Ogilvie, how does God often break the holding patterns in lives? If forcing us to struggle is the means by which we grow and by which character is developed, what implications does this have for the way parents often try to insulate their children from the struggles of life?

3. Can you think of some specific ways in which we encourage ourselves and other people to settle into holding patterns?

4. How has God been a "disturber" in your life? Can you relate a specific example? How long afterward was it before you realized that the "disturbance" was actually a beneficial gift of God?

5. Dr. Ogilvie mentions that God is not only one who disturbs us from our holding patterns, but he is one who deploys us for growth and helps us to develop. Think about the past five years of your life. How has God caused you to grow and helped you in that growth process? In what ways was that growth painful? In what areas do you feel you still need to grow the most?

6. Deuteronomy 32:11–12a is a beautiful passage. Why not memorize it and share its meaning this week with someone you know. Relate what these verses mean in your life.